SOME OF THE OUTSTANDING FEATURES OF THIS EXTRAORDINARILY VALUABLE BOOK:

—How weather, coaching, playing at home, winning and losing streaks, injuries, and other factors can influence results.
(Note: There are big surprises here!)

—Common betting fallacies that can cost you money.

—How point spreads are calculated and what they can tell you.

—Tempting sucker bets to be avoided.

—How to find a bookmaker and how to assess him.

—The differences between pro and college sports.

—Ways to profit from seeming disasters befalling the team you want to bet on.

—Clear charts and convincing statistics demonstrating the secrets of successful betting.

—The latest government policy on taking your winnings.

All this is just a sampling of the rich lode of essential information and expert advice in this encyclopedic guide for everyone who likes to have money riding on the sport of his choice.

"The most comprehensive and enlightening book of its kind!" —FORT WORTH PRESS

"Thoroughly researched. . . . No matter how sophisticated the bettor, there is something here for everyone." —KIRKUS REVIEWS

Other Sports Books from SIGNET

☐ **INSTANT REPLAY: The Green Bay Diary of Jerry Kramer edited by Dick Schaap.** From the locker room to the goal line, from the training field to the Super Bowl, this is the inside story of a great pro-football team . . . "The best behind the scenes glimpse of pro football ever produced."—*The New York Times*   (#E9657—$2.50)

☐ **PAPER LION by George Plimpton.** When a first-string writer suits-up to take his lumps as a last-string quarterback for the Detroit Lions, the result is "the best book ever about pro football!"—*Red Smith.* "A great book that makes football absolutely fascinating to fan and non-fan alike . . . a tale to gladden the envious heart of every weekend athlete."—*The New York Times*   (#J7668—$1.95)

☐ **PLAYING PRO FOOTBALL TO WIN by John Unitas, with Harold Rosenthal.** A bruising inside look at the pro game by the greatest quarterback of them all. Revised and updated.   (#W7209—$1.50)

☐ **SCREWBALL by Tug McGraw and Joseph Durso.** "You gotta believe!" when baseball's star reliever and super flake rips the cover off the game he plays and life he's led . . . "It's the best!"—Roger Kahn, author of *The Boys of Summer* in *The New York Times* Includes an action-packed photo insert.   (#Y6421—$1.25)

☐ **THE PERFECT JUMP by Dick Schaap.** What happens to a world-record-breaking athlete when he's reached that once-in-a-lifetime perfection he can never achieve again? The glory and heartbreak of an athlete who reached the top and had nowhere left to go. With an exciting sports photo insert!   (#E7248—$1.75)

Guide to Sports Betting

by Kelso Sturgeon
and the Editors of *Sports Action*

CONTRIBUTING EDITORS:
Lou Boeri • Phil Glick •
Jack Hyland • Jack Lewis •
Lou Ronan • Wellington K. Sumner •
Kelly Troutman

A SIGNET BOOK
NEW AMERICAN LIBRARY
TIMES MIRROR

Contents

Chapter 1

What Sports Betting Is All About

There is no point recorded in history at which man began to take chances—to gamble. Anthropologists and psychologists tell us that prehistoric men in barbarian cultures began to gamble as soon as their mental processes developed to a point at which they realized there existed an elusive element called luck. Some contend that Adam took the first gamble when he went against God's warning and ate the forbidden fruit from the tree of the knowledge of good and evil in the Garden of Eden. We do not care to debate the philosophical implications of the fact that Adam lost, but, if this, indeed, was the beginning of it all, it sent mankind off into a life built around taking chances.

For instance, in 1973 the American public wagered $7,-173,573,823 on legalized horse racing. However, as stunning as is this figure, it is but a small amount when compared to the volume of money wagered in the United States on sports such as football, basketball, and hockey. The late Robert F. Kennedy, then Attorney General of the United States, stated that in 1962, while no one knows for sure the amount of money wagered on sports, it was somewhere between $7 billion, which he said was probably a low estimate, and $50 billion, which he said was likely too high. Regardless of the figure, it has multiplied many times since then. Both the federal government and gambling authorities estimate the total money bet legally in this country at the nation's racetracks represents from 5 to 10 percent of the money bet on sporting events. If one projects this figure, it would put the total money wagered on football, basketball, baseball, and other sports at approximately $60 billion in 1973. This figure doesn't include money wagered legally at the casino tables of Nevada.

Mortimer Caplin, who was Commissioner of the Internal Revenue Service in the early 1960s, testified before Congress that a total of $25 billion was bet in the country each year, most of it through illegal means. In the days before gambling became socially accepted, the IRS produced sobering figures on the amount of money bookmaking operations handled during a year. The figures were arrived at by examining, where possible, the actual books of bookmakers who had been raided by the government. A routine check of bookmakers who were busted in the late 1950s and early 1960s reveals that a former Los Angeles "sports accountant" reported an income of $4,511,000 one year. In Miami, a bookie took in $1,594,000, and a Tennessee bookmaker who handled little more than football took bets totaling over $1,600,000 during a routine year. A bookmaker operating from the Virginia side of the Potomac, but within sight of the mall in Washington, D.C., booked bets totaling $1,221,000 during one year.

From these figures it is obvious that gambling is big business, and the biggest of all, by far, is sports betting, which, except for horse racing, is illegal in almost every state in the country. If you want to bet on a sporting event legally, you presently must journey to Nevada. The state legislature in Massachusetts recently passed a bill to legalize sports betting and can implement it shortly. New York has laid the legislative groundwork for making it legal to bet on sports, and the states of New Jersey, Pennsylvania, Maryland, California, Connecticut, Louisiana, and others are expected soon to follow suit.

Most states are no longer concerned about the morality of sports betting, but want only to tap the tax revenues coming from it if it were legalized. Conservative estimates by the federal government indicate that legalized gambling on sports would raise over $10 billion annually for local, state, and federal governments.

The biggest single betting event in the country each year is the Super Bowl, professional football's championship game. The biggest betting event, overall, however, is the World Series. It is bigger than the Super Bowl only because more than one game is required to complete it. Ranked in third place behind these are the college football bowl games, while fourth place goes to the National Collegiate Athletic Association (NCAA) annual basketball playoffs. Rounding out the top five are the National Basketball Association (NBA) playoffs.

Sports betting is one of this country's biggest industries, although it is illegal in most places. Because it is against the law, most bookmakers operate in the very gray area of the law and it is almost impossible to know the actual number of them in the United States. All one can do is make projections. The federal government, through the Internal Revenue Service, places itself in the hypocritical position of licensing bookmakers throughout the land. In the early 1950s, the Kefauver Commission was instrumental in getting passed federal legislation which it felt would put the bookmaker out of business. It reasoned that if a bookmaker had to come forth, identify himself and his place of business, purchase a federal gambling stamp, and then collect a 10 percent tax on each dollar bet with him that he would go out of business. Nothing could have been further from the truth. In 1972, the Internal Revenue Service reported that it had issued 32,284 Federal Gambling Stamps at $50 each.

The FBI and the IRS both conclude that fewer than 10 percent of the bookmakers in the land buy the stamp, which means we must have well over 300,000 people from the Atlantic to the Pacific and from the Gulf Coast to the Northwest taking bets illegally.

One must ask a basic question: how is it that these 300,-000 individuals are allowed to operate if gambling is illegal? And how can the 32,284 people who purchased the $50 gambling stamp remain in business once their names and addresses of business are a matter of public record? Simply put, it is all a matter of the enthusiasm of the masses. From the steelworker in Pittsburgh to the housewife in Seattle to the aircraft worker in Van Nuys to the auto company executive in Detroit, hundreds of thousands of people gamble every day on the outcome of a horse race, a sporting event, a number, a lottery, or dozens of various other games of chance. The mother gambles; the service station attendant gambles; the college professor gambles; the maid gambles; the corporation president gambles.,

Law enforcement officials have little time, or desire, to police an illegal business which the public demands and will have in one form or another, regardless of how difficult it is made for them to get a bet down. The moralist might contend that gambling chips away at the moral fiber of the nation, laying the groundwork for its collapse hundreds of years from now. None of us will be around to know whether he was right or wrong, but most would bet he's wrong. The United States is the only major country in the world which treats gambling as a moral issue and keeps it underground. The moralist insists on policing the conscience of his neighbor. The moralist might not even know your name, but he does know that it is bad for you to gamble. His mind is so narrow that he cannot see that gambling has many healthy, redeeming values. It is a recreation that is filled with excitement and pleasure. It is an escape from the tough, rugged realities of life. Some people like to sail, some like to play golf, some like to fish, some like to hunt, and then there is that man or woman whose greatest joy and most relaxing moment comes when he or she bets $20 on a football game and relaxes in front of the television set to watch it, with all the troubles of life oh so far away.

From a psychological standpoint, gambling can be a healthy outlet for the frustrations and tensions that turn men and women into mental disasters. Dr. Felicia Campbell, a professor at the Univeristy of Nevada, has just completed a book on the psychology of gambling for use in social science courses. A little gambling now and then can act as a deterrent to some of the frustrations that boil within the souls of people, Dr. Campbell says. She notes that when a man or woman makes a bet on the outcome of a sporting event, he finds himself on a plane of equality he's never known before, nor will he ever know in the realism of life. When the individual makes the bet, he has the same chance to win as does a John D. Rockefeller or an Alfred G. Vanderbilt. They are equal in all respects for the moment, and Dr. Campbell says if that were the only redeeming grace of wagering, it would all be worthwhile. True equality is something for which the id of man struggles all of its days and gambling is one of the few places where everyone has the same chance.

Public acceptance of gambling is clearly before our eyes every day, particularly during the football season. During the fall and winter months, almost every major newspaper in the country carries a betting line on football games. Because football is the biggest of all betting sports, it receives the most gambling coverage in the press. Betting lines are offered also during the baseball and basketball seasons, but not in the same volume nor on the same scale as with football.

While wagering on horses is legal in twenty-eight states, bookmakers in those states and in those that have no legalized horse betting declare, to the man, that horses represent only about 5 percent of their business. The average bettor does not identify with horses, knows nothing about them, and doesn't care to find out anything about them. Any interest the average bettor has in horses was learned, and never came to him through natural exposure. By the same token, most men are exposed to sports such as football, basketball, and baseball during their growing-up years, identify with them, and love to bet a dollar or two on the outcomes of games involving their favorite teams. Not all of this betting is done with bookmakers. Most of it is done at the corner pub where Joe and Fred express their opinions on the Green Bay–Chicago football game and then back them up with money. Green Bay is a three-point favorite and Joe thinks the Packers will win by more than that. Fred, on the other hand, likes Chicago. Thus they enter into a verbal agreement, with Fred taking Chicago and three points. For Fred to win, Chicago must either win the game outright or, at worst, get beaten by two points or less. The role is reversed for Joe. For him to win, Green Bay must win outright, and by more than three points. If the final margin is just three points in Green Bay's favor, the bet is declared a tie and no money changes hands. The amount of the wager could be anything from a cigar to hundreds of dollars. However, the average bettor probably would bet $5 to $10 on such a game. There is something psychologically satisfying to Joe and Fred in this situation. Both know they have an equal chance to be right and both satisfy a natural desire to compete.

The biggest drawback to sports betting is the lack of helpful information available to the bettor. The individual going to a racetrack can purchase the *Daily Racing Form* and examine for himself the past performances of a horse. He can see, in black and white, just what a horse has done in the past and then attempt to relate it to his chances to do well today. He studies the horse's won-lost record, how he performed previously at the distance of today's race, his jockey, his trainer, his breeding, his opponents, his times, and dozens of other details which enlighten the complete handicapper. However, when one begins to handicap a sporting event he operates at a complete disadvantage because very little has ever been published on the subject, despite its popularity. The average sports bettor knows little more than he reads in the newspaper, if he even understands that. Unfortunately, in the process of reading his newspaper, he becomes even more misguided because the individual who wrote the story concerning his team probably didn't know his subject either. Thus, the sports bettor operates as a blind individual, hoping Lady Luck will keep him in front of his bookmaker and in action. This within itself is the greatest indication of man's determination and desire to gamble. He is willing to risk his money betting on a game which he really doesn't understand, although he probably thinks he does.

Even though sports betting is a $50-billion-plus business in the United States right now, it is a young business with little informative data available to help the sports bettor. The sports betting boom, as big as it is, is just starting to bloom. It began in the late 1950s when television became a part of most Americans' lives and it has grown as television coverage of sports events expanded. Maybe the time will come in which we will have a *Daily Racing Form* for sports bettors. However, at the present time, the bettor is very limited in the number of publications designed to give him insight into betting on sports. The only two that do a reasonably complete job are *Sports Action* and *Sports Eye*, two Now York-based racing/sports tabloids. Both of these publications do a tremendous amount of research and statistical work which they try to relate to what goes on in the athletic field and try to help the bettor take an edge. For instance, the *Sports Action* statistical department made a detailed study of the point-spreads in college football games over five seasons. The betting public had long ago accepted that favorites beat the pointspread half the time, while underdogs beat it the other 50 percent of the time. Until *Sports Action* did its study, no one knew any better. On all games in which the pointspread was from ½ to 5½ points, the underdog won 57 percent of the games over the past five years. Of all games in which the pointspread was from 6 to 12 points, the underdog won 54 percent. On games in which the underdog was from 12½ to 14 points, the underdog won 53 percent of the time. The only category in which the favorite came out on top in the percentages was in the 14-or-more-points contest. In those games, the favorite won 56 percent of the time. The one thing the study clearly indicated was that it was strictly a myth that the favorite and the underdog split the games evenly. This is the kind of information that helps a bettor take the edge that means the difference between winning and losing, but it just isn't that available to him.

The whole of sports betting is an extremely difficult, but

not impossible, puzzle of many pieces, just as is the handicapping of a horse race. The more one understands the importance of various factors and how they relate to one another, the greater are his chances for success as a sports bettor. However, regardless of how much one knows, or how much he understands and relates, he still will never be able to guarantee himself a winning bet. A risk is involved every time one makes a wager.

The purpose of this book is to explore every single piece of this great puzzle as it relates to football, baseball, basketball, hockey, horse racing, and other sports upon which people bet. After examining the pieces, we will then try to put them together properly, bringing into clear focus the picture of successful sports betting. For example, when we approach a football game, there are at least fifty different elements that are important to the bettor, including knowing when to take the points and when to give them, the coach, the importance of every position on the team and what happens when injury takes out one or more players, the factor of offense as it relates to defense, what age and experience mean, how the game plan affects the bettor, and the schedule factor. Only when one correlates these and many other factors can he take the edge that separates the winners from the losers.

In this book we have included most of the basic statistics and records that should be kept by or at least be available to the sports bettor. It is our suggestion, if you are serious about sports wagering, that you keep these records up to date. The information to do this is readily available in your local sports pages and in such publications as *Sporting News*, *Sports Illustrated*, and *Sports Eye*.

Even though betting an athletic contest sounds so complicated and challenging that only an IBM computer would dare tackle it, it's not. A successful sports bettor must be equipped with only two things: a little common sense and the ability to think ever so slightly. Armed with these two things, the individual is on his way.

How Do You Place a Sports Bet?

If you are in the market for a new car or want to take your best girl to a fine French restaurant, you know exactly what to do. New car agencies are visible by the dozens. You know where they are, what they sell, and how to buy from them. You also know if they are reputable and if they stand behind their products. As for the French restaurant, let us say you know of it and its excellent reputation, but you do not know where it is located. All you need to do is to pick up the telephone directory and get its number. However, life might not be so simple when it comes to finding someone with whom to bet sports.

If you are in Nevada, where sports betting is legal, you have no problem; you just go to the nearest handbook and bet. Or, if you wager with a fellow steelworker, a business acquaintance, the guy across the hall, the boys at the pub, or a friend, you can easily get into action. But, if you want to bet with a bookmaker, and many gamblers do, the situation presents special challenges.

Bookmakers are not readily visible. They don't walk the streets with sandwich boards on their backs, advertising their business. Nor do they parade beautiful girls across the television screen telling you you can get the best price with them. You won't find any advertisements in newspapers, nor will you find a special listing for them in the Yellow Pages. But you can find a bookmaker. There is an excellent chance someone in your office or shop already is doing business with one and will put you in touch with him. If not, ask your local bartender, or a friend, where you can find a sports accountant. A bookmaker can be found only by word of mouth and you will have to take the initiative to find him. The nature of the game prevents the bookmaker from coming to you. But a bookmaker is not hard to find once people know you are looking for one.

It is an unfortunate state of affairs that we in the United States must hustle the back alleys and bars to find a bookmaker. This multi-billion-dollar-a-year business, even though licensed by the federal government, still operates in a foggy area of the law. Maybe the day will soon come when it will be unnecessary for us to sneak into dimly lit doorways to place a bet on our favorite team.

The bettor must be extremely careful with which bookmaker he does business. Because *Good Housekeeping* does not give bookmakers its seal of approval, and since Dun and Bradstreet does not run a credit rating on them, it is sometimes difficult to determine if our man is financially sound. By that we mean, will he have enough money to pay off if we ever really hit him?

Never forget that most bookmakers want a business relationship with their customers. They want you to pay when you lose, and they intend to pay you when you win. Bookmakers are a proud lot, and the only thing with which they are concerned is their reputation with their players. And this reputation is based solely on one thing: does the bookmaker pay off, and on time? A bookmaker who wants to pay off does so, and on schedule. The better ones even do it with a smile, although they might be dying a bit inside.

If you are a small bettor, a $25-a-game, or less, man, you need not be overly concerned with your bookmaker's ability to pay off when you beat him. However, if you are a big bettor and wager in such fashion that you could beat your man for hundreds, or even thousands, each week, you must take the time to determine if he has the money to pay you, and, in fact, if he will pay. It is difficult to check a man's credit rating. For this reason, it is important that someone recommend a bookmaker to you. If a friend or business associate has done business with an accountant over a long period of time and has never had trouble collecting, the chances are heavily in your favor that you won't either. It is extremely dangerous from a financial point of view to do business cold with a bookmaker, without knowing anything about him. This is doubly dangerous if he demands the money from you in advance.

The sports bettor should never forget that he must do business with a reputable man if he wants to get paid. There is no worse feeling than to beat a man for several hundred dollars and then find he has left town. One has no recourse. A reputable bookmaker stands behind his business 100 percent. We have known of cases in which accountants were hit for thousands of dollars in sports betting coups and were forced to sell all their assets, personal and corporate, in order to pay off. But they did it. They wanted to protect their reputations and stay in business and the only thing important to them was to pay off.

After you have found a bookmaker, you should meet him in some quiet place and have a frank discussion with him. Explain to him that you want to conduct your business in complete confidence and tell him, even though your good friend Angus recommended you to him, you do not wish Angus or anyone else to know your business. Most bookmakers never discuss a client with anyone, but never take that for granted. Declare yourself up front, in a nice way of course, and let it be known that your man is never to speak of you to anyone. You then should explain to him exactly how you want to bet and the approximate amounts you will wager on games. You should determine from him if he accepts anything other than straight bets (a straight bet is a single bet on a single team to win) and if he does, at what odds he pays off on a parlay or other exotic bets. (A parlay is a bet in which you couple two teams to win and both must win for you to collect. While the usual straight bet pays even money, parlays usually are paid off at odds of 12 to 5.)

On the matter of financial stability, your bookmaker will expect the question, so don't be reluctant to tell him you intend to pay when you lose, and you expect the same businesslike treatment when you win. You can shoot as straight with your bookmaker as you can with your psychiatrist. There is no reason for you to play games with him, nor he with you. Do not be surprised if he already knows more about your finances than your wife. He's like you. He wants to be paid and he isn't going to give you unlimited entree to his bankroll unless you have the financial ability to pay off those big bets you intend to win—but might lose.

While your original relationship with your bookmaker might start off on what appears to be a bit of mutual mistrust, this is not the case. He looks at you in the same manner a banker might. If you have the references and the ability to pay, the sky is the limit for your action.

If you have been highly recommended to this bookmaker by a client of his, he might give you a telephone number right from the start at which you can reach him during certain hours to make your bets. If he is a little nervous about you—or doesn't want to use a telephone—he will tell you where to meet him, and when, in order to place your bets. And he most likely will ask you to put up the money in advance. However, after mutual trust has been established, you can become a credit customer of almost any bookmaker in the country.

If you go on a credit basis, your bookmaker most likely will want to settle with you once a week, regardless of who owes whom. You may call him or meet him seven days a week and place your bets, but there will be only one day on which he will want to settle up. Most bookmakers on the East Coast, for instance, settle up on Monday if you owe them and on Tuesday if they owe you. The reason for this is simple. They collect from the losers on Monday and use the money to pay the winners on Tuesday. If you are working on a day-to-day, cash basis with a bookmaker, and many operate only like this, you will get paid daily when you win. All accounts will be settled within twenty-four hours.

The Mechanics of Betting

Now that you have made arrangements to bet, your bookmaker will become your authority on pointspreads and odds. It will make no difference to him that the New York *Post* has Kansas listed as a 6½-point favorite over Iowa State in one of the week's college football games. His price is Kansas minus 7½ and that is the price with which you will have to live. Your bookmaker will be your first and last word on this matter. If you don't like his line or set of odds, you can take your business elsewhere or not bet at all. As we will discuss in great detail throughout this book, it is much better to have two or three betting outlets. Just as you can buy chickens at one supermarket for 79 cents a pound, at another for 77 cents, and at yet another for 75 cents, bookmakers will sometimes have different price lines on games, particularly those involving college basketball teams. It pays to shop around for the best price, for sports betting is a game of points and odds. You must take every edge you can.

While we go into great detail on price lines, pointspreads, and odds later in this book, it is important for you to understand the three or four "lines" to which you will be exposed during the course of the day. The "line" is the focal point of all sports betting, for the line determines whether you win or lose. First of all, a sports betting line is published in almost every major newspaper in the country during the football, basketball, and baseball seasons. The line is published as a service to the readers of sports pages who also happen to be bettors. However, this line, while close to the actual price at which teams are offered, is by no means official. It is simply a "newspaper line" and probably originates with a bookmaker from whom someone in the sports department has made arrangements to get it each day.

The Las Vegas line is the only *official* football line in the country and is the line your bookmaker will use to determine the pointspreads and odds on both college and professional contests on which you will bet. The football line originates in Miami, Florida, while the basketball line comes from about a dozen sources. The baseball line comes from about twenty different individuals who are spread throughout the country. The opening line, which is the first Las Vegas line your man will have, is made by a group of analysts. After it is made, it is sent to Las Vegas, where a group of selected big, big bettors are permitted to bet into it, spotting all its weaknesses within seconds. After these people bet into the line, it is adjusted and posted on the boards and sent throughout the country. This is the actual "opening line."

As the money is bet, the line is adjusted in an attempt to keep an equal amount of money bet on each team, thus insuring the bookmakers a profit. (As we will discuss later, most bets are made on a 6 to 5 or 5½ to 5 basis, which means you have to pay off either $6 or $5.50 when you lose a $5 bet, but collect only $5 when you win. This edge is the bookmaker's profit for handling the action.) The linemaker's job is to make the favorite and the underdog equally attractive to the public, and he tries to make his price line appear attractive to bettors. If he is off, and too much money comes in on one team, he will adjust the odds to make the other team just as attractive.

We will go into detail in later chapters on the subject of betting particular sports and how you can know when to take the points and when to give them, and when to take the odds and when to give them.

As a gambler, either novice or veteran, you must likely have been confronted with advertising literature on sports services, which, for a fee, will advise you as your stockbroker might. However, instead of telling you they think Ramada Inn is a good buy at 9, they will tell you Alabama minus 14 is a steal against Tennessee. As is your stockbroker, sometimes they are right and sometimes they are wrong. There are a great number of football handicapping services because of the interest in that sport. However, there probably are only twenty-five legitimate basketball services (if that many) in the country and only about a dozen individuals or companies which handicap baseball.

The services offered by these sports brokers run a broad range, beginning with weekly publications in which games are analyzed to very refined telephone services which offer last-minute information which hopefully will give the bettor that slight edge he needs for winning. Many of these services try hard, know their business, and operate with some degree of success but seldom at any better percentage than you could have by doing your own selecting. Some services are worthless. There are very few sports-handicapping services in the country, regardless of their operations, which, overall, end up picking more than 50 percent winners, which means they also pick 50 percent losers.

We will speak of three sports services later (see pages 89–90) which, through the years, pick a better than average percentage of winners. All three services have one thing in common: they are in the sports-handicapping business on a full-time basis. It is their only source of income. They live and die with their abilities to pick winners.

The best football-basketball service in the country is the Nevada Hotline, which is the only sports brokerage house in the land which operates completely on a money-back basis. Matt Nevada, who operates the service out of New York, is generally accepted as the finest sports analyst in the United States. During the football season, he offers a weekly best bet in the colleges and a best bet in the pros. His basketball service is operated on the same basis, although he works strictly with college basketball teams. The Nevada Hotline might be the highest-priced service in the country, but Nevada will tell you that, as with most other purchases, you get what you pay for. His games sell for $50 each, or at a lesser rate if you subscribe for the season. During the 1972–73 football and basketball season, Nevada picked over 80 percent winners with his best bets. Midway through the 1973 football season, he had hit seven out of eight college selections and six out of eight pro selections.

There is no way for us to tell you which services know their stuff. And claims they make about their past successes mean little. Many of them are made up. If you plan to do business with a sports-handicapping service, try to find one that has been in business for a few years and then go slowly with its selections until you find out for yourself whether those running it know what they are doing.

You the Sports Bettor

In case you are wondering how you stack up to the average bettor, we can only say that you and he, or she, demographically look pretty much alike. Bettors come in all sizes and shapes and from every level of the country's social structure. If one were to do a survey of the average bettor, he or she would be just like the guy or gal next door. The average American bettor is the average American.

What Is a Bookmaker Like?

What does the average American bookmaker look like? If we accept the Hollywood image of a bookmaker, we visualize him as a greasy little man with a potbelly and a smelly cigar jammed between his teeth. He talks with an ever-present Brooklyn accent, even though he might be making book in Augusta, Georgie. In the movies, he slobbers a lot, sips bourbon from a half-pint bottle, and talks about "hoiting" people who don't pay.

The bookmaking industry needs a good public relations man. The average bookmaker is just as normal as the average American. He puts his pants on one leg at a time, worries about his children, and gripes about high taxes.

We would like to introduce you to an average bookmaker, whom we will refer to as Charles. Charles operates a big handbook in Maryland. He is thirty-eight years old, resides with his family in a two-story brick house in suburban Towson, Maryland. Charles also owns a liquor store, which he acquired recently because he didn't want to expose his children to possible embarrassment when they explained to their school chums and friends what he did for a living. He admits he needed a legitimate front. "I don't have any moral qualms about being a bookmaker, but kids can be cruel and I don't want my children to start getting hangups before their time."

Charles graduated from college in the mid-1950s with a degree in history. He wanted to teach high school students, but was called up to help keep the peace in Korea. Upon his discharge from the United States Army, Charles met Amy, whom he married six months later.

It was at college that Charles, now a graduate student, began to consider becoming a bookmaker. He was hurting for money, his wife was expecting their first child, and he was extremely nervous about his financial future. "I started distributing football cards and taking numbers on campus for a friend of mine who had been booking for years," Charles said. "He gave me a percentage of the money I took in and I made a good living at it. College kids love football cards. Most of the male students like to gamble and they could lay out a dollar, pick six of seven teams, and have a chance to win $50. In those days we were all in the same boat—broke—and I pulled hard for all of them to win. I got my share, win or lose.

"By hustling a little, I was making over $300 a week just distributing the cards and taking numbers," Charles said. "It took me a while to realize that I could do this without any partners—and keep all the money. I didn't say anything about it to Amy at the time. I was putting out the other guy's cards all along and she really didn't know when I went into business for myself.

"Then, one week I showed a profit of $1,400. I was so excited I had to tell someone, and I told Amy. We had a long talk about it—my becoming a bookmaker—and she said it made no difference to her what I was so long as we were together.

"From my business with the students, I put together enough of a bankroll to start taking all kinds of action on sports and horses. I never have been in business with anyone else, and I have never paid a nickel to police to operate. This doesn't, of course, mean that some bookies don't pay off police and politicians, but I have never. In addition, I have not had a year since 1960 in which I didn't show an after-tax profit of over $40,000. I have a federal gambling stamp and have an arrangement with the Internal Revenue Service through which I pay a flat tax fee each year."

Charles says he has all the problems of any other business, including that of finding good, reliable help.

"If General Motors had trouble finding good people, what kind of problems do you think I have?" he asked. "Every business needs good people who will treat its customers like ladies and gentlemen. They're almost impossible to find, regardless of how much you pay."

Charles says he also worries about people "past-posting" him (getting in a bet after an event or race is over) and has an elaborate security system to see that it doesn't happen. He says the system works for him and that even his employees are unaware of just how it functions. "It keeps everybody honest."

If you were to meet Charles on the street, we would lay 10

cents to $1,000 that you would never known his occupation. He stands 6-feet-1, weighs 195 pounds, has a few gray hairs mixed with his black locks, dresses casually, and looks exactly like a high school history teacher.

When you deal with a bookmaker, you are not dealing with a freak, you're dealing with an average Joe like yourself. He just happens to be in the business of booking bets. He could be your neighbor, your best friend, your golfing partner, or a member of your church. In fact, he probably is.

Chapter 2

Football: The Number One
Betting Sport

Baseball may be "the great national pastime," but as far as fan interest and gambling activity are concerned, football has gained tremendously in popularity during the last ten to fifteen years, so that it now vies with baseball for the top spot in both categories. Several reasons can be offered for this interest recently shown by the fans and bettors in the game played with "the crooked ball." As has baseball, both professional and college football have gone through several scandals involving not only the fixing of the outcome of games, but also such things as "unscrupulous practices" in recruiting, and the association of players with gambling and "underworld" characters. Because of these boo-boos, football is now policed to the nth degree and the faintest hint of misconduct on a team's or player's part results in thorough investigation and prompt discipline. Furthermore, with the superinflated salaries that the pro stars are now commanding, and with the fringe benefits that are thrown in for good measure, it is hard to think of a lure that could tempt any successful ballplayer unless he happened to be crazy or stupid or both.

Thus, with the "purity" of football now certified and practically insured, both bettor and bookie alike are not reluctant to enter into a friendly wager. This fact and the increase in the number of games played each season (brought about by the expansion of the pro leagues) combine to make betting on football games through bookmakers a better than $3 billion per season industry. This figure represents an increase of close to $1 billion over the past decade. To this total you can add at least another $10 billion bet on football cards (pools). Obviously this is not nickel and dime action. It is big business and is conducted as such.

Since wagering on the outcome of a football game is illegal in all but one state—Nevada (the reason for this, of course, being the fact that bookmaking is illegal in all but one state—Nevada), 99 percent of all nonpersonal wagers on football games are made illegally (through bookmakers outside Nevada). In fact, even if a bookmaker wanted to make his home base in Las Vegas or Reno, so that he could operate within the law, it would be impossible for him to do so since the state levies a 10 percent tax on all gambling activities. This would, of course, not only negate his edge but would, in fact, put him into the red. The fact that this enormous industry not only exists but has been escalating at a rapid pace— all outside the law—doesn't seem to bother bettor, bookie, or bureaucrat (whose state loses many millions of dollars each year in potential tax revenue by not legalizing gambling). And to make the matter even more ridiculous, the articles and headlines printed on the sports pages of every newspaper in America are an integral part of this nationwide system of wagering on football contests (as well as other sports). The lifeblood of football betting—the pointspread—which once cost the book from $50 to $100 per week to obtain—is now his for the price of the daily newspaper. Every daily journal not only prints the early line, but most of them keep their readers informed up until game time of any change in the spread on any given game. The point of all this is that it is ridiculously easy for anyone to bet a football game, and, as the already quoted statistics show, more and more Americans are obviously taking advantage of this opportunity.

College football in the United States was popular long before the start of the professional version. In fact, the game that was played for money by former college players was "semiprofessional" at its best. The appearance of the immortal Red Grange—the "Galloping Ghost" from the University of Illinois—changed that, however. The supergreat Grange—ol' number 77—along with his manager, C. C. "Cash and Carry" Pyle, drew the first substantial gates that made pro football a business. A professional football league was formed, and ownership of most of the franchises turned out to be a source of income beyond the wildest dreams of the pioneers who got in on the ground floor.

There had always been gambling on college football, mostly friendly, personal wages between supporters of rival teams, and collegiate associations had tried—with negative results—to discourage it. As the pro game's popularity grew, so did gambling on the sport. Bookmakers found a new and substantial source of revenue, and the point-handicapping of games became an important business.

Professional gamblers—aware of the enormous "take" of soccer pools in many European and Latin American countries—began football pools in this country, at first only in the cities where professional teams operated. These parlay tickets became so popular that they soon spread across the country and could be purchased almost anywhere—illegally, of course. (See pages 91–95 for more details on football cards or pools.)

Several "upstart" leagues attempted to challenge the supremacy of the National Football League from its very inception. All met with dismal failure. When the American Football League went into business in the fifties, it was a different story. A population explosion in the United States had created new and prosperous markets. Television rights in some of them insured a profitable operation. Owners of the franchises in the "other league" had been carefully chosen on their ability and inclination to compete with the NFL, and they refused to be frightened off. With just one league, the football draft had put players in a poor bargaining position. As soon as the AFL started bidding for their services, the National League became indignant, then, conciliatory. Perhaps the single most important incident which ensured the future of the AFL was the signing of Joe Namath by the New York Jets. Namath, like Dizzy Dean and Cassius Clay (Muhammad Ali), was a "pop-off" artist who delivered. He was a highly desirable commodity sought after by both leagues, and the prestige of the AFL went up enormously when he chose to play with its New York franchise. The rest is history. Adhering to the old adage "if you can't beat 'em, join 'em," the NFL went one better and invited the lucrative AFL franchises to join with it. This soon came about, and professional football became the wealthy monster that it is today. As interest in the game increased, the desire to bet on it did likewise and continues to grow each year so that, in spite of the fact that the number of baseball games played each year far exceeds the number of football contests, bookmakers now handle just about as much action on football bets as on baseball. While there is no way of knowing the total take of the football pools, it is obvious that they have grown in proportion at least as much as bookmaker-placed, individual bets.

Betting on Football

As far as the mechanics of betting a football game are concerned, there is no difference between the colleges and the pros. Each week during the season (usually late on the Monday night preceding the upcoming weekend's games) the early line is released to the press, which conveys it to the public at large through its Tuesday editions. To understand fully how wagering on football is conducted, it is an absolute necessity to understand what is meant by the line or pointspread (the terms are synonymous) on any given game, and how it is arrived at. Considering the latter question first, it should be obvious that, as in any betting situation, odds must be established. For example, in horse racing, the odds on any given horse in any race are established by the amount of money wagered on him in relation to the total amount wagered on the race. If $10,000 is bet in a particular race, and half of this total amount is wagered on horse X, that particular animal goes off at odds of 1 to 1 (even money). Similarly, if one-third of the total pool is bet on a certain animal, his odds would be 2 to 1, and so on. The odds in racing are determined by the betting public and are variable. In other games of chance, the odds are fixed—they never change. One example of this is the game of roulette. No matter where you play this game, if you place a "unit" wager on any given number and that number hits on the next spin of the wheel, you receive 35 times your wager in return; if you place a unit on black, and the ball stops in a black hole, you get even money on your bet. This is what is meant by fixed (never-varying) odds. In football wagering, however (as in other sports betting such as baseball, basketball, ice hockey, etc.), although the odds are fixed (11 to 10 in individual games; 12 to 5 on a parlay) there is a tremendous variable introduced so that, theoretically at least, every game is an even match no matter how much better one team may be than its opponent. This variable is the line or pointspread, and it is determined by a few knowledgeable individuals—none of whom is known to more than a handful of people within the gambling industry. The original line is known as the Las Vegas line and originates in Miami, Florida. This Las Vegas line is not to be confused with a popular line made by Jimmy (The Greek) Snyder. The Greek's line receives a tremendous amount of publicity and is sold to various newspapers around the country, usually appearing in Tuesday's editions. Many people believe that Snyder makes the Las Vegas line, while in fact he has nothing to do with it.

The Las Vegas line is determined by a small staff of people who know football as no one else in the country knows it. It is almost impossible to crack this select group of people to pick their minds. They feel, because gambling is illegal in most parts of the country, that they have nothing to gain and everything to lose by identifying themselves. However, for the sake of discussion let us say there are eight individuals involved in making the Las Vegas line. These eight individuals, who are the most knowledgeable people in the business, each make a college line and a pro line on games. They then get together and compare notes, usually making the spread on a game the average of the sum total of each man's feelings as to what a team should be. For instance, let's say that all eight felt that Washington should be a 10-point favorite over Philadelphia. The points would total 80 (8 × 10) which, when divided by eight, would be 10 points. After these individuals make the line, it goes to Las Vegas, where minor adjustments are made in it by another group of smart football people many of them big bettors. Then, on Tuesday, the Las Vegas line is posted and distributed throughout the country as the opening Las Vegas line. The line is then adjusted as money is bet into it, and it is money that will determine the final pointspread on any game.

It is these pointspreads that are vital to the football bettor, for they will be used to determine whether he won or lost. The points will be added to the final score of the team which the linemaker has made the underdog (or looking at it the other way, subtracted from the favorite's total points actually scored). By way of an example, let's consider a hypothetical situation.

Let's assume that Notre Dame is playing Michigan State this coming Saturday afternoon and that the spread (as determined by Mr. Snyder or perhaps some other linemaker) has Michigan a 10-point underdog. What this means, in essence, is that the "consensus" says Notre Dame is 10 points better (on paper) than Michigan State and should beat them by that exact margin—or, at least, very close to it. We'll further assume that we desire to place a wager on this game. We get on the phone to our local book and tell him that we want to "get down" on Notre Dame for $100. He verifies the bet and we're in action. Obviously, we bet the favorite, and in so doing, we gave up 10 points to Michigan State. In order for us to win our bet, Notre Dame must beat Michigan State by more than 10 points (actual score of the game). If they fail to win by 11 points or more—even though they may win the game—we lose our bet. If the bet winds up a tie (the actual score of the game is Notre Dame by 20–10, or 17–7, or any combination where 10 points added to Michigan State's actual final score or subtracted from Notre Dame's leaves the two teams deadlocked) the bet is "off." This, then, is an illustration of how the line or the spread, adhered to by bookmakers all over the country, affects the bettor.

Some bookies, to eliminate the possibility of deadlock or tie, which requires the returning of the bettors' money, add an extra half-point to the pointspread quoted by the professional linemaker for the favorite team. Thus, our hypothetical line could be quoted as "Notre Dame 10½ points over State."

This half-point is also employed as a means of price-changing and as a come-on to induce bettors to wage on a certain underdog. If, for example, the price line reads, "Texas 6-point favorite over Arkansas," and the bookmaker receives a flood of Texas money, he may try to balance his book and lure his customers into betting on Arkansas by changing his bet line to "Texas 6½ points over Arkansas." Both ways, Texas still needs a 7-point victory in order to pay off its backers.

Not all games played, however, lend themselves to a pointspread. One team may be so much better that in order to attempt to make the final outcome even, as many as 30 or more points would have to be given the underdog. Bookmakers are hesitant to do this, for in any football game—but especially in certain college match-ups—anything can happen, although logic (and past performance) dictates that the favorite is so overpowering that it should easily win "by the spread." As a result, they ordinarily don't like to take action on these games either way. What they do in this case is take the game "off the board"—meaning they will not accept any bets on this game. This happens very often, and a prime example is the Nebraska teams of the past few seasons. These teams were so great, so overpowering, that no matter whom they played, they were usually favored by three touchdowns

(21 points) or better. As a result, it was a rare occasion when a bookmaker would take action on a Nebraska game, regardless of its opponent.

How does one pay off or get paid off on a football wager? As previously stated, the odds are fixed, and you can shop from here to eternity among books and all will quote you the same odds (you may find a variation in the spread among bookmakers, but never in the odds). Naturally, as in every other betting situation, the bookmaker has an edge, but in football wagering, this edge is important only when you lose. The basic odds on an individual game are 11 to 10 (and, of course, its divisibles and multiples such as 5½ to 5, and 22 to 20). Some small bookies deal what is called a "6–5 pick 'em line," which means that you must lay him odds of 6 to 5 no matter on which team you wager. The bookie dealing 6 to 5 has a favorable edge of 8⅓ percent. On the other hand, the 11 to 10 line gives a bookie an advantage of only 4⁶⁄₁₁ percent. So, if you don't want to get "two-timed," either insist on 11 to 10 odds with your favorite bookie, or go elsewhere if he won't oblige.

The hypothetical bet which we made on the Notre Dame–Michigan State game was for $100. If Notre Dame had won by the spread, we would have gotten back $200— the $100 we bet and $100 we won. If Notre Dame had lost by the spread, however, we would have been required to pay our friendly book $110—the $10 being "juice" or "vigorish" he earned for handling the wager. If we had won a $50 bet, our profit would have been $50, but had we lost, our loss would have been $55. It can then be stated that we are paid off at even money odds on a winning bet, but when we lose, we are required to pay 10 percent of the amount of our bet (in addition, of course, to the amount we bet). If we feel extra lucky (or if we're extraordinarily stupid) and feel that we want to parlay two games, the odds are a straight 12 to 5, meaning if both the teams we select win, we are paid $12 for every $5 bet. If one of the two teams loses (even though the other wins), we pay off the actual amount that we bet (if it was a $50 parlay bet, we pay $50 flat; if the bet was for $100, we lose an even $100, etc.). That really is all there is to betting football. You either bet one team (at 11 to 10) or parlay two (at 12 to 5). Some bookmakers will take "oddball" bets such as three-game parlays, and "ifs and reverses" but these bets are so illogical that we won't even go into them in this book.

Behind the Making of the Line

The man who bets football each week knows that the professional bookmaker is getting the best information available anywhere in the land. If he makes the Dallas Cowboys a 6-point favorite over the Chicago Bears, you can bet that he'll come close to hitting the spread right on the head.

Bookmakers and linemakers working college and professional football do not shoot in the dark and come up with a line by accident. They have a pipeline of information that is so good it makes the smooth operators of the Central Intelligence Agency look like a group of Boy Scouts.

A bookmaker handling football action must be much more careful with his line and his system of operation than anyone else in the gambling business. A slight mistake can spell disaster—the end of the line. It is much easier to pick the winner of a college football game by studying past performance than it is to pick the winner of a baseball game or a horse race.

The bookmaker who is careless will be broke in quick order. For this reason, he must have the best and most up-to-date information possible. He has no margin for error. Almost without exception, there is nothing that goes on behind the scenes in either college or professional football of which bookmakers are not aware.

There have been hundreds of incidents during the past year or two in which teams—both college and professional—reported phony injuries to key personnel in hopes of throwing off the game plans of their opponents (see page 32). They may have convinced the opponents that something was wrong, but the point line on those games never wavered. By the same token, sudden, from-out-of-nowhere changes are made in a line, and people begin asking why.

It becomes obvious twenty-four hours or so later, if even then, when it is announced that Fran Tarkenton, or someone of like stature, is not going to be in the starting lineup for a big game because of an injury. The gamblers' pipeline had this information fifteen minutes after it was decided—maybe even before the owner of the team knew.

There is no reason for us to betray the sources of this information, but it should be obvious to anyone that the information must come from someone close to the team. It could be a team physician, a coach, a locker-room attendant, a player, a member of the front-office staff, a secretary, or even newspapermen covering a team. There is absolutely no way to hide this information from the pipeline. It has been tried before, and failed.

As we said, the professional bookmakers' line is not made by accident. When it fluctuates, there is a reason. It could be simply a change of a point or two as he balances his books to account for a heavy bet on a particular team, or it could be late information that could alter the outcome of the game.

The professional bookmaker and linemaker takes many things into consideration in making his original line and then altering it. His prime concern is in the area of injuries to key players, the sum total of all injuries to all personnel, team morale, who the team plays next week, and what it means to a team to win or lose. Of course, the professional linemakers have the information, patience, understanding, and means of evaluating every factor that might affect the outcome of a game. They leave nothing to chance or to someone else's opinion. They know what is going on, and they make their line accordingly.

At the present time, as previously stated, the original bookmakers' line (not be be confused with Jimmy [The Greek] Snyder's line or with the newspaper line) comes out of Miami, Florida. Until a few years ago, the line originated in Cincinnati and Minneapolis. Bookmakers around the country buy a line from those who make it, and that is the line upon which you bet. The official bookmakers' line is known as the Las Vegas line.

The more study one does on how sports betting lines are made—and changed—the more fascinating the subject becomes. We have been informed that the linemakers in places such as Reno put the pointspreads on the board and then let five or six select, big, big players bet into the lines. The Reno linemakers say these particular individuals are so sharp that they spot weaknesses in seconds. After letting these people place their action, the books alter the line accordingly and then open the doors to all customers.

They lose a little money letting the pros have a go at the line first, but it is mere peanuts compared to what it would be if they held open house and let the general public bet into the weaknesses. Recently, we had an interesting call from a traveling salesman concerning the betting line. He explained it was not unusual for him to be in New York on Monday, Cleveland on Tuesday, Chicago on Wednesday, and Dallas on Thursday, and that he had found great discrepancies in the line—particularly as related to college football—in each area of the country. For instance, his travel plans one week took him to Boston, Oklahoma City, and Phoenix. In Boston, Georgia Tech was a 7-point favorite over South Carolina; in Oklahoma City they were an 8-point favorite; and in Phoenix they were 9 points.

"Someone woke me up to this about three years ago," he said. "And today a group of us take advantage of it. All of us bet football big and want to take every edge we can.

"Five friends, including myself, all live in different areas of the country. Every Friday night we get on the telephone and compare notes and betting lines. If I like Penn State over Stanford and I get a better line in Indianapolis than I do in New York, I let my friend bet the game in Indianapolis. If he wanted Stanford and the points, I'd bet for him in New York. There have been occasions where the spread differences were so great that both of us won, but only because we shopped around for a price.

"I know it's hard to do, but the man who wants to shop around for a price can usually get it. All of us have friends who bet football throughout the country. This has worked for me, and I think it can work for other people. Money won in Chicago is just as good as money won in Denver, and vice versa."

The man has some good thoughts. Do with them what you will.

Betting on Professional Football

The successful football bettor cannot arm himself with too much statistical data. The overall past performance of a professional football team and its ability to beat the spread can sometimes be determined by a careful analysis of the statistics. Of course, there is no magic formula for selecting potential winners in the grid game due to such unpredictable factors as injuries to key players, vagaries of the weather, condition of the playing surface, team psychological reaction to certain happenings, and the home field advantage, among other things. But statistics and trends do remain fairly consistent from year to year and the wise bettor relies upon them to cash in many husky wagers.

Let's take a look at some of the factors that, if considered when making a bet on a professional football team, just *might* increase your chances of winning.

Defensive and Offensive Averages

As you already know, the football bettor seldom cares who wins or loses—it's the points in which he is interested. If he lays 10 points, he wants to win by 11. If he takes 10 points, he doesn't care how badly his team gets beaten so long as it doesn't exceed 9 points. His life is a game of points.

In the early weeks of the National Football League schedule there exist many good opportunities for pro football bettors to make some big money wagering on key contests which, for one reason or another, are improperly figured by the linemakers. In other words, you must know when to spot points and when to take them.

Utilizing the 1972 NFL schedule, for example, if one analyzes the game results, he may come up with some very enlightening facts in the form of scoring—defense statistics. Actually, the statistics which usually draw the most interest are those concerning team scoring for, after all, scoring is the name of the game these days and the teams that are able to rack up at least three TDs a game are usually the teams that collect the playoff and championship loot at the end of the year.

In the scoring-power category, teams that have a scoring potential of three TDs a game are Miami, New York Jets, and Oakland, garnering 28, 26, and 26 points respectively, in a typical 1972 game. San Francisco and Pittsburgh are good for 25 points a contest; Detroit, Washington, and New York Giants, for 24; Denver and Dallas, for 23; Green Bay and Minnesota, for 22; and Cincinnati and Los Angeles, 21 apiece. Kansas City gets 20 in a typical contest.

The teams with the weakest scoring punch are Philadelphia and Houston. These two squads scored an average of 10 and 12 points each. New England and St. Louis are good for only 14 points each; New Orleans gets 15; Chicago collects 16; while Baltimore can be figured at approximately 17 average game points in the early part of the 1973 season. These teams generally have a very tough time getting points up on the board and a hard time staying within the pointspread against almost any of their rivals. Any team which can't average over two TDs a game is usually a pretty risky bet in the pro ranks when one considers that the average game comes out to something like 52 points total.

Turning to the defense category, the defending Super Bowl champs, Miami, are rugged as ever, yielding only about 12 points per game. Pittsburgh, AFC Central Division winner, gave up only 1 point more. These two teams stand as far and away the best defensive elevens in the NFL. Next in line come Washington and Green Bay, who hold their opposition to 16 points a tilt. Dallas and Cincinnati are much better than average defensive teams, too, yielding only 17 points a game each. The New York Giants and Cleveland can be had for 18 points a game.

The most porous defense belongs to New England. The Pats give up an incredible 32 points a game. Houston yields 27 points a tilt, while New Orleans, Buffalo, Philadelphia, Denver, and San Diego can be hit for 25 each. The New York Jets are the next most generous in giving points to their opposition—23.

Although average winning or losing margins can be deceptive at times, they are usually good clues to solid wagering propositions. In this category we found that Miami whips its average victim by about 16 points a game, while Pittsburgh is next in ilne at 12 points a tilt. Washington and Oakland usually win by 8 points, San Francisco by 7, and Dallas, Green Bay, and the New York Giants score by 6 each.

New England can usually be expected to lose by the biggest average margin: 18 points. Philadelphia and Houston go down by 15 points each, while New Orleans drops an average game by 10 points. Buffalo (9), St. Louis (8), and San Diego (6) are also rather consistent losers.

Study the information presented here very carefully and decide for yourself whether you want to concentrate your action on teams that can score or teams that win or lose their typical game by a certain number of points. After you decide which type of team you're going to wager on, obtain the pointspread for the weekend's games and seek out the game or games that afford you the biggest edge for potential profit. Some weekends the points are cut so fine that you'll come up with no action at all, and if such is the case, then you'd better develop patience enough to sit it out until a favorable spot comes along. And it will. But, remember, if you're going to have any success in pro football betting, you must let the action "come to you" instead of trying to bend and stretch solid statistical advantages a bit here and there just to have action on all fourteen games every weekend. More on the defensive and offensive averages aspects on the outcome of betting can be found on pages 53–54.

The Home Field Factor

The home field edge in pro football, in general, is the slimmest of just about any professional team sport. An average grid squad wins about 57 percent at home (excellent teams win 80 percent or more), while average baseball teams win 60 percent, basketball teams 64 percent, and hockey clubs 67 percent. A study of the home team won-lost standings covering the seasons from 1969 through 1972 reveals some very interesting facts, many of which are probably unknown to most casual gridiron fans.

In 1973, as in most other years, the average home team in the National Football League enjoyed a distinct edge over its visiting rival, although the advantage slipped a few percentage points from the previous year. Overall, the average is down 26 points over the last two years, which means the home field may be lessening even more. The survey revealed that altogether the 26 home teams won 484 games, lost 370, and tied 35, for a winning percentage of .567. In 1971 the figure was .593 and in 1972 it was .574.

Several things can be learned by the football bettor by compiling and studying won-lost statistics such as these. For instance, give any of the poorest home teams a wide berth when it comes time to put your hard-earned cash on the line, or, better still, bet against them if the spot is not too big. But, perhaps, the most important factor of all is that in a "pick 'em" (even) game with neither team favored, the home team would have the slight edge, especially in a game between two of the loop's perennial losers.

Many experts feel that the apparent drop in the home field advantage in the 1970s may be attributed to the installation of artificial turf. They feel this surface makes for generally more uniform field playing conditions, thereby eliminating mushy and muddy spots which good broken-field runners and pass receivers have utilized to their advantage in seasons past.

NFL Home Field Advantage: NFL Home Team Records
(1969 through 1973)

	Won	Lost	Ties	Pct.
Strongest Home Teams				
Miami	30	5	2	.857
Oakland	30	6	2	.833
Dallas	30	6	1	.833
Minnesota	32	7	0	.820
Washington	27	8	2	.771
Kansas City	24	8	3	.750
Los Angeles	23	10	2	.696
Detroit	23	11	0	.676
Pittsburgh	24	12	0	.666
Above-Average Home Teams				
Cincinnati	22	13	0	.628
Baltimore	22	13	2	.628
Cleveland	21	13	2	.617
Average Home Teams				
San Francisco	20	14	3	.588
Green Bay	19	14	3	.575
Atlanta	18	16	0	.529
San Diego	17	16	2	.515
Denver	16	16	3	.500
Below-Average Home Teams				
New York Jets	17	18	0	.485
New York Giants	16	17	1	.484
New England	15	20	0	.428
St. Louis	14	19	1	.424
New Orleans	14	20	1	.411
Poorest Home Teams				
Buffalo	13	21	1	.382
Philadelphia	12	21	2	.363
Chicago	11	23	1	.323
Houston	9	23	2	.281
Average of All Home Teams:	484	370	35	.567

In an offshoot to our home team survey, we found that many final scores are very close, with about 45 percent of the regular season tilts being decided by 8 points or less. This statistic alone points out the reason why underdogs, as a whole, are performing well of late. Combining this statistic with the known abilities of each and every team on its own field, one can surmise that it may be highly profitable to concentrate your early-season wagering action on the best home teams which are held as slim favorites or which are actually the recipients of points on the day of a game.

Road Victories Key to NFL Superiority

Since the football season is relatively short (in the number of games played), the elevens which are going to make it to the playoffs and the Super Bowl, as well as those which are going to fare quite well in the "Pointspread League," are the teams which play winning ball away from home. Eighteen of the twenty-six NFL teams have had winning marks at home over the course of the past five seasons, but only a bit more than half that number win on the road.

Over the five-year period, ten clubs have compiled winning road marks, but one club—Dallas—has been simply murder away from the friendly confines of Texas Stadium. Tom Landry's crew has a record of 26–9–0, for a winning percentage of .742—the only eleven to play .700 ball on the road.

NFL 5-Year Road Leader Records

Team	Won	Lost	Tie	Pct.
Dallas	26	9	0	.742
Los Angeles	23	10	2	.696
Minnesota	24	11	0	.685
Baltimore	24	11	0	.685
Cleveland	24	11	0	.685
Oakland	21	10	4	.677
Kansas City	22	12	1	.647
Detroit	18	14	3	.562
Miami	19	15	1	.558
San Francisco	19	15	1	.558

NFL 5-Year Road Loser Records

Team	Won	Lost	Tie	Pct.
Buffalo	4	29	2	.121
New Orleans	5	26	4	.161
Pittsburgh	6	28	1	.176
New England	7	28	0	.200
Cincinnati	8	26	1	.235
Philadelphia	8	25	2	.242
Denver	9	26	0	.257
Houston	9	24	2	.272
Atlanta	9	23	3	.281

On the other side of the coin, the Buffalo Bills are definitely the most pitiful team of all on the road. The New York State-based eleven has won only 4 of 35 tilts over the surveyed span. This comes out to an average of .121. New Orleans is next in line with a 5–26–4 slate for a not-much-better .161 percentage. Even the highly respected Pittsburgh Steelers also always seem to encounter a great deal of trouble on the road. They've won only a half-dozen of 35 games played away from the Smoky City since 1968. In 1972, for instance, when their regular season record was 11–3–0, all three losses occurred on the road.

It should be very clear by now that it's wise to watch the superior road teams (and also the weak ones) when the pointspreads are acceptable. You're sure to find an average of a couple of games a week where the spread is out of line, but you're also going to have to keep up to date on your homework if you want to show a steady profit over the course of the campaign.

Grid Injuries and the Bettor

The biggest winning edge a football bettor can take is that of understanding injuries, and what a coach does when they occur. In football betting everything is relative, and an injury may or may not be an important factor when trying to decide whether to give the points or take them. In order to get some insight into this matter, it is important to know the contribution of each player.

The football bettor faces a most difficult task in trying to determine which of the eleven men on the field is the most important (see page 36). It becomes immediately obvious that the greatest case can be made for the quarterback, but, in truth, it is not necessarily so in the pros. One basic rule to follow in trying to analyze a team, position-by-position, to determine how it will perform against another team is to accept as fact that the absence of any starter will make some difference in how a team performs. But maybe not much.

Most teams would miss a starting quarterback such as Joe Namath of the New York Jets or Bob Griese of the Miami Dolphins. But, wait, didn't Miami win 17 games in a row and the National Football League Super Bowl in 1973 with Griese on the bench with an injury most of the season?

Indeed they did, with the quarterbacking duties falling to a much-traveled journeyman named Earl Morrall, who has spent most of his life as a second-string signal caller in the NFL.

This brings into focus the great misunderstanding which seems to baffle bettors when trying to determine the importance of an injury. It would be simpler to comprehend if the bettor would but stop, think, and then give a coach some credit for thinking, too. A coach who knows he is going to go into a game with a key player out will make adjustments for it offensively and defensively.

Let's say that the New York Jets, a wide-open, ball-throwing offensive-minded team, find themselves without the services of Namath. That an adjustment in a game plan will have to be made is obvious, but what form it will take, and how the bettor can determine what it will be and take an edge, are major questions. With Namath out of the lineup, we know that the Jets have little chance to put a lot of points on the scoreboard. From the standpoint of the bettor, this should make little difference.

Think about it for a minute. With Namath out of the lineup, the oddsmakers are going to drop the points you will have to give if the Jets are favored to win or raise them if the Jets are an underdog. All of this theoretically will compensate for the absence of Namath, but it really won't, and all because of this hidden factor called adjustment.

If the Jets were going to be playing New England, they might be a 7-point favorite if the game were being played in Boston. With Namath out, the line would drop to 3 points in favor of the Jets as Namath is considered a 4-point quarterback which, in the language of those who make the Las Vegas line, means that his presence on the field is worth 4 offensive points to the Jets.

It will be up to the bettor to decide whether the Jets are a better bet at minus 7 points with Namath or a minus 3 without him. This is where the adjustment factor comes into consideration and where the ability to analyze a team position-by-position becomes of paramount importance. With its offense grounded, the Jets will most assuredly do two things: they will try to control the ball offensively, giving it to New England for as little time as possible, and will spend most of their time during the few days before the game beefing up the defense to stop New England from putting points on the board. On a position-by-position comparison, New York is far superior to New England and in theory should be able to make the adjustments which will bring about victory—maybe by even more than the 7 points one would have to give if Namath were in the game.

By controlling the ball most of the time and giving New England few offensive opportunities to score, New York has won half the battle already. Now, if its superior defense can play at an average efficiency level, trying never to give the Patriots any long runs or passes, victory should be there.

It goes without saying that the football bettor who jumps in blindly and bets against a team just because a key man is out for a game is inviting trouble. The adjustment factor will usually throw him for a loop.

While we have discussed here what an injury to *one* key player means or does not mean to a team, the factor of injuries to two or more players is extremely important, too. One of the classic adjustments of all time came in 1964 when Coach Paul (Bear) Bryant decided it was in the best interest of his Alabama football team to suspend superstar Joe Namath. His assistant coaches, who seldom second-guess him, did everything they could to convince Bryant that Namath should be reinstated for the pending Sugar Bowl battle with Mississippi.

One by one they came to him, advising him that there just wasn't any way Alabama could beat Mississippi without Namath. The young man from Beaver Falls, Pennsylvania, was the key to all of Alabama's offense, and the assistant coaches were speaking the truth. Without Namath, the Crimson Tide offense wouldn't scare a second-rate team, let alone Mississippi, which, under Johnny Vaught, had one of its most powerful teams.

The issue finally became so heated that Bryant advised one of his assistant coaches that he had made a decision: the coaches could go to the Sugar Bowl with either him as head coach or Namath at quarterback, but not both. Needless to say, everyone got the message and Namath stayed home.

Bryant, who is one of the master coaches of all time, decided he could beat Mississippi with his field goal kicking game. He felt he could stop Mississippi from scoring more than a touchdown. Thus, in the weeks leading up to the

Sugar Bowl, Bryant polished his defense and worked with his kicker. History tells us that Alabama's adjustment to Namath's absence was successful. It played an unspectacular defensive game before a sellout crowd of 80,997 and beat Mississippi 12–7 on the strength of four field goals.

In making adjustments for the absence of a good player like Namath, a team which has worked together for a season, or many seasons, can compensate for the loss, with each individual taking up whatever slack is caused. However, there are few teams in professional football which can stand the loss of two or three starters without becoming a risky betting proposition, regardless of the adjustment in the game plan or in the pointspread.

If a starting offensive right tackle is lost to a team, the adjustment factor sets in, with the right guard now teaming up with a second-string lineman who probably is an excellent player himself. The regular starting guard works with the new tackle, covering for him when he has to and neutralizing the effect of his regular blocking partner being on the bench. However, let us say that both the tackle and the guard are out, or the tackle and the center are out. No adjustment in the world is going to make up for the loss of two key men in this situation. The biggest adjustment will be made by the opposing team's defense, which will keep pressure on the lesser substitutes all day long, until they finally wilt.

We don't want to get involved in speculations about first teams and second teams, regulars and substitutes. On paper, the difference between a first-string player and a second-team player seems ever so small—such a fine line that if it should tip in either direction the two individuals reverse roles. That, my friend, is just so much armchair philosophy, for the average difference between a starter and a substitute on a professional football team is as great as the difference of play in the Ivy League and the Southeastern Conference.

The regular is a regular because he gets off the line 1/100 of a second faster than the second guy. He is a regular because he is 10 pounds stronger than the other guy. He is a regular because he thinks 100 percent of the time and the second-team guy has his brain in operation only 96 percent of the time. The differences may be small, but they are the differences that make a play go or not go.

As we have said, ten regulars can cover up these imperceptible deficiencies of a second-team player. They cannot, however, operate as efficiently with two second-stringers in the lineup. The overall quality of the team's operation must suffer. The situation could be likened to a racing team of eleven runners, all of which can cover a mile in less than four minutes. When one of these eleven is replaced with a miler who can run in 4:03, but no faster, there is still a good chance that the average time of the milers will be under four minutes. However, add another man who can do the mile in only 4:09, and the average begins to break down. The same can be said of a football team.

As we have stated in the case of Namath, the quarterback is worth points to the Las Vegas linemaker. His absense or presence will help determine the pointspread in a game. While the Las Vegas linemakers have never given points to other positions, they should exist. After the quarterback, the most important man on the field is any member of the defensive front four. He is a specialized individual who will be extremely difficult to replace.

Thus, the bettor should be wary of any situation in which any member of a team's defensive front four is going to be absent. These men have the job of containing the opposition's running game and keeping the passer under pressure all afternoon. If any breakdown occurs here, its results can be devastating. Give the worst quarterback in the league one extra second to throw the football and he'll make Otto Graham look like a sandlot player. Give the so-so running back an extra step to the outside and he'll operate with the quality, class, and virtues of Jimmy Brown and Gale Sayers.

The fine line separating starters and second-stringers is no wider among the defensive front four, but it is of greater significance. The front four operate as a unit, reading plays, telling one another what is happening, smoking over things such as the draw play. They know instinctively when these things are going to happen and, because football is a game of split seconds, they don't have time to write a letter to the second-stringer about it. It happens so fast that even our television cameras will miss it on occasion. Meantime, the finely oiled gears of the defensive front four mesh together in majestic perfection to stop a surprise play. They are closer together than the average husband and wife and the presence of an interloper can't help their operation.

There is little question in the mind of the average professional football coach that his defensive front four is more important to him than his best running back, with the only exception being when that particular running back is the only offense a team has.

The opposing offense has the edge when a defender is out of a game. It is the offense which will make the adjustments and exploit the weakness brought about by the second-stringer.

Without going into great detail, let it suffice to say that any coach in the NFL, or college ranks, is going to make adjustments in a game plan when a key player is missing. The pointspread will be adjusted up or down to compensate for the loss of the player. It goes back to what we have said before: maybe the New York Jets are a better bet at a minus 3 without Namath than they are at a minus 7 with him.

Before leaving the subject of injuries, we would like to say a word or two about the injury lists. When the National Football League stared releasing injury reports a few years back, it appeared the bettors had an inside track on a team's upcoming performance on Sunday. Knowing who's hurt, and what kind of injury might keep a player out of the starting lineup had previously been classified information, obtainable only by spies or runners, who, for a price, would relay the dope to big-time gamblers and bookies (see pages 24–25).

Now the betting public has access to this information through local newspapers and although this can sometimes be used to return profits, there are many instances when the small bettor gets taken. The league rule stipulates that each NFL team must submit two injury reports each week, the first two days following the game, and a second later in the week that includes the latest up-to-date revisions.

It's all based on an honor system with every team expected to list each and every injury that is reported by its players. But club officials who are responsible for the injury reports have been known to tell a little white lie now and then by playing up or toning down a specific injury or just leaving an injured player off the list entirely. This isn't a planned plot to bury the bettors but just a way to keep next week's opponents guessing as to who's going to start and who's not.

Using the injury report as a guideline to beating the pros usually ends in disaster. First off, the "injured" players are labeled as "doubtful," "questionable," "possible," or "probable" starters. This is all rather hazy terminology that can lead only to confusion. Only in extreme cases will a player be designated as "definitely out." Many times a player listed as "doubtful" will see as much or maybe even more action than a "probable" starter. The obvious question that arises here is: what determines a player being listed as "doubtful" rather than "questionable," or "possible" rather than "probable"? Actually, the severity of each injury is known only to the team physicians, and, of course, they consult with the coach before handing in their reports.

There have been several instances each season that would cast doubt on the credibility of the injury reports. For instance, a couple of seasons back, San Francisco's great receiver Gene Washington, a prime weapon in the 49ers explosive attack, was, with a hamstring pull, a "doubtful" starter to play against the Chicago Bears. But you would have had a hard time convincing the Bears' defensive backs that Washington was lame after he caught a John Brodie pass at midfield and outraced everyone to the end zone to complete a 79-yard touchdown play. Washington also caught another TD pass from Brodie as San Francisco won, 37–16.

Another example of how the betting public can be fooled occurred the same year in Los Angeles. The Rams were 17-point favorites against the disheveled New York Jets. Rookie quarterback Al Woodall was expected to be harassed all afternoon by the Rams' defensive front four, led by All-Pro end Deacon Jones. But Jones, who had not been listed on the Rams' injury report, did not start and was used sparingly late in the game after the surprising Jets were well on their way to a 31–20 victory. It was later revealed that Jones had a bad knee.

Experience and the Winning Team

There are many reasons why a professional football team turns in either a winning or losing campaign, ranging from individual players' abilities, injuries to the team, the severity of the schedule, and player morale and experience. Recent statistical studies of the teams in the National Football League seem to verify that of all the factors, *experience* is by far the most important.

If you should doubt this, just consider for a moment that fifteen of the sixteen clubs which qualified for the championship playoffs during the 1973 and 1972 seasons averaged more than five years' experience per player. Only Pittsburgh, with a 4.4 average, didn't meet the criterion of this angle. What's more, four of the teams, with average player experience of six years or more, turned in a combined won-lost mark of 73–36–3, a .670 winning percentage. These four clubs were the Dallas Cowboys (6.6) 21–7; Los Angeles Rams (6.0) 14–12–2; Minnesota Vikings (6.4) 18–10; and Washington Redskins (7.1) 20–7–1.

Conversely, the team with the lowest years-of-experience average, the Buffalo Bills (4.0), had the poorest 1971 record —a horrendous 1–13, while Houston (4.8) had a miserable 1–13–10 mark in 1971. It may be pointed out that O. J. Simpson's team is also the youngest club in the NFL, averaging just 24.6 years of age per man. The teams next in order above the Bills, New Orleans and Cincinnati (4.1), came up with 6–19–3 and 12–16 records, respectively.

It's interesting to note that the Miami average (5.1 years) was topped by the Redskins' 7.1—the NFL high. The experience statistics follow:

American Conférence

	Average Age	Average Years of Experience	1971–72 Won-Lost
Baltimore Colts	26.9	5.0	15–13
Buffalo Bills	24.6	4.0	5–22–1
Cincinnati Bengals	25.8	4.1	12–16
Cleveland Browns	27.1	5.7	19–9
Denver Broncos	26.8	4.9	9–18–1
Houston Oilers	26.6	4.8	5–22–1
Kansas City Chiefs	27.1	5.8	18–9–1
Miami Dolphins	26.4	5.1	24–3–1
New England Patriots	26.5	5.0	9–19
New York Jets	26.8	5.2	13–15
Oakland Raiders	27.2	5.7	18–7–3
Pittsburgh Steelers	25.9	4.4	17–11
San Diego Chargers	26.5	4.7	10–17–1
AFC Average	26.5	5.0	

National Conference

	Average Age	Average Years of Experience	1971–72 Won-Lost
Atlanta Falcons	25.9	4.3	14–13–1
Chicago Bears	26.4	5.3	10–17–1
Dallas Cowboys	28.0	6.6	21–7
Detroit Lions	26.3	5.3	15–11–2
Green Bay Packers	26.8	5.1	14–12–2
Los Angeles Rams	27.6	6.0	14–12–2
Minnesota Vikings	28.0	6.4	18–10
New Orleans Saints	25.6	4.1	6–19–3
New York Giants	26.8	5.3	12–16
Philadelphia Eagles	27.4	5.3	8–18–2
St. Louis Cardinals	27.3	5.4	8–18–2
San Francisco 49ers	27.6	5.9	17–10–1
Washington Redskins	28.5	7.1	20–7–1
NFC Average	27.1	5.5	

Watch the Weather

Have you ever considered the effect that weather has on pro football games? You'd better, if you want to win some vital bets during the colder portion of this year's NFL slate.

Some teams fall apart in cold or rainy weather, but others, like the mailmen, just keep pushing through the rain, snow, ice, and mud, carving out win after win. Consider the Minnesota Vikings, for instance. A few years ago, attesting to the Purple People Eaters' unconcern for the weather, the Vikes defeated:

Los Angeles, 13–3, on October 26 in a driving rain and 15-mph winds at home;

Green Bay, 10–3, on November 22 in 16-degree temperature and wind gusts to 40 mph at home;

Chicago, 16–13, on December 5 in 9 degrees and gusts to 40 mph at home;

Boston, 35–14, on December 13 on an ice-cragged field in Boston;

Atlanta, 37–7, on December 20 in the Georgia mud.

True, the Vikes dropped a playoff game that year to San Francisco in December at Bloomington, but that was the first home loss for Minnesota over the course of two years. Going into the '71 season, the weather hadn't much bothered coach

Bud Grant and his crew who won fourteen straight regular season games and two playoff games at Metropolitan Stadium. "You go outdoors to play football," said Grant. "You go in the house to get warm."

The Vikings don't use heaters, gloves, or other fancy cold-weather gear, other than long underwear, when they play in nasty weather. "We want our people thinking about the game when they're on the field," stated Grant, "not trying to get their backsides up to a heater."

And, as a general rule, as the season wears on into November and beyond, you'll find that "warm-weather" pro football clubs don't do well in late-season and post-season games in northern climes. Coach George Allen gave his thoughts on the subject. "In the days when I was an assistant coach with the Bears," he said, "I never realized what it meant to take a team from a warm climate into the ice-box area of the Midwest. To my sorrow, I found out twice in three years."

He was referring to two Western Conference championship games. In 1967, the Rams posted an 11–1–2 record during the regular season, but went into Green Bay and lost a 28–7 decision in the title contest. In 1969, they won eleven straight, lost three meaningless games after they clinched their division crown, and played the conference championship title in near-zero temperature in Minnesota. The Vikings won, 23–20.

Other post-season examples are Baltimore over Oakland, 27–17 in 1970, the Jets over Oakland in the '68 playoffs, and Green Bay a few years back when Bart Starr sneaked home for the winner in the final seconds for a 21–17 edge. Then there was 1969, when the Cowboys went to Cleveland as favorites to take home the Eastern Conference title, only to fall before the Browns, 31–20. Back on November 2 of that year, after a 42–10 beating by the Browns in the very cold and raw conditions prevailing at Municipal Stadium, coach Tom Landry of the Cowboys said, "It was just a mess." Bill Nelsen riddled the Dallas defense with five touchdown passes that November afternoon in Cleveland when Milt Morin caught seven aerials for 101 yards. But wise bettors took this one-sided loss as a real clue to the Texans' inability to perform up to par in cold weather and went heavily for the Browns with points in the playoff tilt.

Consider the cold-weather angle very carefully the next time you're tempted to bet against a "cold-weather" team. Especially remember that the average temperature for late December in a place such as Bloomington, Minnesota, is 16 degrees; the average snowfall about half an inch. The record low is minus 20, the record high 46 degrees. Actually, some professional gridiron bettors specialize in cashing big wagers on football on raw, rainy days when form gets knocked into a cocked hat and the big underdogs pull their "upsets." One of New York's biggest bettors revealed his approach. "I study the early lines on the college and pro games each week. Come Saturday and Sunday mornings I call the weather bureaus in the towns where the games are being played which involve the biggest pointspreads of the day. I particularly go for those 18-, 19-, 20-point (or more) spreads, and I tap out on the 'dogs. . . . I win many more bets than I drop, and I recommend this method of play very much to anyone who would care to try it."

Of all the major games featuring big pointspreads on Saturday's schedule, a few years ago, Mr. X learned that only the annual Notre Dame-Purdue bloodletting at Lafayette, Indiana, was to be played in a downpour. He immediately went for Purdue and the 20 points.

The then second-ranked Irish gambled for a 2-point conversion after turning a fumble into their only touchdown with 2:58 left in the game as they slipped by Purdue, 8–7, in a nearly steady rain, and Mr. X was a winner.

The following weekend he couldn't find a college game to fit the high-spread/rain pattern anywhere in the country, so he waited for the next day's pro action. Burning the phone wires all morning, he found out that the unbeaten Washington Redskins (+10) were tangling with Dallas in the Cotton Bowl and that the Texas city was being drenched with rain. He went for George Allen's crew in a big way. Despite the heavy downpour, the Redskins successfully rushed against the Cowboys, while stopping their running game. At game's end, the Skins had a 20–16 victory.

The *Sports Action* research department has studied the weather and its relationship to winning and losing and has drawn these conclusions:

—Favorites still win most of the games played in bad weather, but they seldom cover the spread.

—It is extremely difficult for a team to score more than three or four touchdowns under adverse weather conditions, particularly rain, or the combination of wind and snow.

—Because of the second factor, a bettor must take the underdog in most games in which he is getting 15 points or better. If the underdog scores one touchdown, which is likely, it would have 22 points going for it and statistics show this is a tough number to top.

—The professional teams play better in bad weather than do college teams, although not much.

—Teams from places such as Miami, Los Angeles, Houston, Dallas, Atlanta, New Orleans, and San Francisco are severely handicapped when playing November and December games in such places of extreme cold as Buffalo, Denver, Green Bay, Cleveland, and Detroit.

These are the only conclusions the research department at *Sports Action* said the facts justified. Weather is an important factor in the life of the bettor, but there is no system one can use to insure his success when the weather is a major factor. The statistical department said one should always give extra consideration to underdogs, whether college or pro teams, if the weather is bad and you can get enough points.

It goes without saying that every bettor should check for himself to determine the weather in various cities in which his betting games are played. It is impossible to list the telephone numbers for weather bureaus in all major college cities, but here is a list of the numbers of weather bureaus in twenty-five National Football League cities. We did not list Houston, because all pro games there are played in the indoor comfort of the Astrodome.

American Football Conference			**National Football Conference**		
City	Area Code	Number	City	Area Code	Number
Baltimore	301	936-1212	Atlanta	404	763-2541
Buffalo	716	643-1234	Chicago	312	936-1212
Cincinnati	606	936-4850	Dallas	214	357-1537
Cleveland	216	931-1212	Detroit	313	932-1212
Denver	303	630-1212	Green Bay	414	494-2363
Kansas City	816	471-4840	Los Angeles	213	554-1212
Miami	305	666-2044	Minnesota	612	725-6090
New England	617	936-1234	New Haven (Giants)	203	772-0410
New York	212	936-1212	New Orleans	504	525-8831
Oakland	415	562-8573	Philadelphia	215	936-1212
Pittsburgh	412	936-1212	St. Louis	314	731-3002
San Diego	714	289-1212	San Francisco	415	936-1212
			Washington	202	936-1212

Other Factors to Worry the Bettor

Winning is usually attributed to one of the following: (1) the team has better players or (2) the team has superior coaching. Of course, coming up with superstars and top-flight personnel these days is generally more a matter of luck than skill due to the common draft and the availability of common computerized scouting reports on key college players throughout the nation. However, the molding of the rookies into a veteran team calls for talent that is not so easy to come by. Coaches such as Don Shula, George Allen, "Bud" Grant, Tom Landry, and Hank Stram are "class" all the way and could probably show a winning record with any team over a reasonable period of time. Actually, Don Shula of the Miami Dolphins has the best won-lost record, percentagewise, of any coach in the National Football League. He is followed closely by John Madden of Oakland and George Allen of Washington. Tables on page 45 show the complete professional records of the NFL's twenty-six coaches.

One of the biggest keys to winning is an art that must be taught. That's the art of getting and holding onto the ball. In this regard, a survey was undertaken, comparing the top six teams in college ball with the top six teams in pro football. As the clock is stopped more often in school ball, the collegians average about 18 more plays a game than the professionals. The college teams averaged 81 plays to 63 for the pros.

The survey also pointed out that no pro team averages 70 plays, while in the last few years virtually every college team has surpassed that figure. However, the teams which are able to play a ball-control type of game win many more tilts than the clubs that handle the "duke" only an average number of plays.

While the won-lost records of both teams and coaches are not necessarily against the pointspread, they do offer insight into a team of which the bettor should be aware. The coach of a professional team is every bit as important as his collegiate counterpart. A good coach today must cope with the psychological condition of his team. This is often something that the bettor doesn't know. That is, a bettor doesn't know if a white northern quarterback and his black southern pass receiver are on speaking terms or if the coach and his top run-

American Football Conference

Coach	Team	Years	Won	Lost	Ties	Pct.
Don Shula	Miami	11	120	32	5	.789
John Madden	Oakland	5	48	7	7	.738
Paul Brown	Cincinnati	23	205	95	9	.683
Hank Stram	Kansas City	14	119	67	10	.639
Sid Gillman	Houston	10	115	87	8	.569
Nick Skorich	Cleveland	20	130	129	7	.501
Weeb Ewbank	New York	6	41	38	5	.519
Lou Sabin	Buffalo	13	80	89	7	.473
Chuck Noll	Pittsburgh	5	33	38	0	.464
John Ralston	Denver	2	12	14	3	.461
Chuck Fairbanks	New England	1	5	9	0	.359
Howard Schnellenberger	Baltimore	1	4	10	0	.283
Harland Svare	San Diego	6	20	51	4	.281

National Football Conference

Coach	Team	Years	Won	Lost	Ties	Pct.
Chuck Knox	Los Angeles	1	12	3	0	.800
George Allen	Washington	8	79	29	5	.731
Bud Grant	Minnesota	7	67	31	3	.683
Don McCafferty	Detroit	4	28	18	2	.609
Tom Landry	Dallas	14	109	81	6	.573
Dick Nolan	San Francisco	6	43	36	5	.544
Dan Devine	Green Bay	3	19	19	4	.500
*John North	New Orleans	1	5	6	0	.454
Alex Webster	New York	5	29	40	1	.420
Norm Van Brocklin	Atlanta	12	64	94	7	.405
Mike McCormack	Philadelphia	1	5	8	1	.384
Don Coryell	St. Louis	1	4	9	1	.307
Abe Gibron	Chicago	2	7	20	1	.222

* Took over after five games of 1973 season

ning back hate each other's guts. Old wounds do not heal easily and old feuds do not end easily.

Because of divisional play, now in use by the NFL, one team can face a murderous schedule, while a team in the same division can face a fairly easy one. For this reason, it's sometimes very difficult to get a true line on a given team from week to week. Each year, because of a changing schedule, there are some interesting holes interlaced in it, in which a smart bettor might slip through a winning ticket. But even when it appears the bettors have the edge in a lot of sports, the primary question is whether or not the bookmakers will let them get away with it. The prediction here is that the bookmakers are much too smart and much too wise to give away money. Incidentally, the caliber of play between the two conferences is now about equal.

Another consideration: what will a win or a loss mean to the team? For instance, if Dallas has already wrapped up its divisional title and is meeting a Washington Redskins team which needs a win to get into the playoffs, that factor becomes important in the way you bet. Of course, the team that is fighing for a championship or even a playoff berth has incentive, and incentive produces momentum. A team such as this playing one that's out of the running is always a good bet. In other words, it is usually a good idea to bet the team with momentum. You will find many more games of this type later in the season.

But, you must remember that in the pros the players are playing for money and, although each player is part of a cohesive unit, every one of them wants to shine individually whether it's scoring points or keeping his opponents from doing so. The reason for this, of course, is to arm themselves with all the ammunition they can so that they'll have more bargaining power when it comes time to talk next year's contract. There's seldom any gentlemanly "coasting" when a pro team is ahead.

One of the most successful pro football bettors we know of confided to us that he relies heavily on psychology (yes, we said psychology) and on expert (and we mean expert) scouting reports.

Without good information you're dead. And we don't mean the kind of tidbits you pick up in a bar; we mean good, solid, reliable info that can be had only from top reporters who cover the clubs. Read everything you can get your hands on; and then read between the lines. The latter part is especially significant as many writers covering pro teams can only hint at certain facts. In addition to the best scouting information you can get your hands on, you must also develop an ability to "feel" what's coming up. By this we mean that you should attempt to psychoanalyze each competing team before each game. For example, when two mediocre cellar teams meet, it is generally best to bet the underdog. The underdog in a situation like this has a lot going for it. Players do have pride, and nobody wants to be the very bottom.

Another instance is when a favorite loses a big game and is

then favored the next week—don't bet them. Such a club will be too anxious to reestablish itself and will probably make a lot of mistakes.

Still another instance is an underdog that the experts just won't believe. Teams like this love to go out and kill favorites, one after another, until they have finally earned their place. That is when it is time to stop betting them.

Definite Edges

Betting on professional football, like all other wagering, is an inexact science at best. In order to be successful, one must take every edge that is available and keep pushing his luck when he's winning and retrench when winners are few and far between. Actually, the edge in betting on pro football is the knowledge that the teams usually perform true to form. There may be an occasional variation from this, but seldom does a *good* team play two bad games in a row. For example, in 1973, New York Giants and Detroit were definite exceptions, but both the Chiefs and Lions were overrated and had a lot of injuries, over which the bettor had no control.

The line on a typical professional football game is much closer than on college games. You might occasionally catch a linemaker off base on a college tilt, but you'll seldom find him off too much on a pro game. This brings up the question of whether it is easier to find a favorable line on a college game than on a professional game. The answer is yes, but you have to know what you're doing and what to stop for.

The professional sports bettor who stuck with Miami, Denver, Buffalo, and Los Angeles in recent seasons made a lot of money. The teams consistently beat the spread and obviously were trying hard in all their games. Possibly it is because the coaches of each of these teams take nothing for granted—even games which are a breeze. In the cases of Miami's Don Shula and Denver's John Ralston, the teams spend just as much time getting ready for Houston as they do for Dallas, and they play every game with the same determination and effort.

Frequently, extra money can be picked up by the alert pro football speculators who do their homework. These smart money operators know which teams have been producing within the past year and will probably continue to produce up until the final whistle is blown on the current campaign. A team that produces is an eleven that can win, either at home or on the road, when the pointspread is either too small or too large, as the case may be. In this regard, we reviewed NFL results for several years to learn how the favorites and underdogs, as a whole and individually, did at home and away in the various pointspread categories. To make the survey as meaningful as possible, pointspreads were broken down into seven different areas, ranging all the way from 1-to-3 points up to 20½ points and up. Pick 'em contests were not considered. The results were very interesting, to say the least.

Not counting games which wound up as ties pointwise, the survey showed that favored home teams won only 47 percent of the time; favored visiting squads won at a clip of 42 percent. Obviously, no one can expect to make any money at all by playing strictly the supposedly superior team on each week's betting line. The survey did, however, point out a few very good categories to concentrate on. As far as favorites go, the games to watch are those in which the home team spots the opposition from 10½ to 14 points, and away contests in which the favored eleven is on the hook for only 1 to 3 markers. In the home contests in this category, the pick won about 67 percent of the games; the away contests saw the choice come out on top by an even stronger margin, 75 percent. The combined winning mark of these two categories is a splendid 70 percent.

On the other side of the coin, in the underdog department, the strongest plays were visiting underdogs getting anywhere from 5½ to 7 and 1½ up to 10 points, and homestanding underdogs getting 3½ to 5 points. The winning total in each of those columns was 60, 63, and 76 percent respectively. The overall mark was a very fine average of 66 percent. Even the most expert football analyst would be more than happy to settle for such a good mark almost any year. The home underdogs getting 3½ to 5 points are, apparently, an exceptionally sharp bet when you can find one.

Teams especially to watch when favored within the margins indicated above, whether at home or away, are Denver, Miami, Los Angeles, Cincinnati, Buffalo, and Cleveland. For some reason they always seem to put out just a little harder when they're carrying the mantle of the favorite.

Underdogs to keep an eye on in key situations when

they're on the road are Denver, Buffalo, Cincinnati, and Cleveland. When it comes to underdogs playing on the home turf and getting a bonus of from 10½ to 14 points, always give a bit of extra attention to New Orleans, Green Bay, Denver, Cincinnati, and Atlanta. Denver is an especially good home team bet with points due to the fact that the thin air usually plays havoc with teams that aren't in the best of physical condiion. And the crowd in Baltimore is particularly unnerving to the Colts' rivals. No collection of football customers in the land matches the noise generated on behalf of the Colts in their Memorial Stadium "Dirt Bowl." Some experts say the noise and home field automatically give the Colts a 7-point advantage before the opening kickoff.

If you intend to speculate on some of the NFL tussles, give careful consideration to the results hung up by the teams over the course of past campaigns. Once a pattern is established it seldom changes too much one way or the other, so the figures as shown can be expected to continue fairly much status quo during the present season.

Although pro football continues to be the most heavily wagered-on sport, betting on the play-for-play madness was once again a hazardous profession unless you developed the patience required to seek out the superior bets each weekend, as did the smart money boys. Have no doubts that weekly betting on the twenty-six National Football League teams is huge business. And bookies don't provide the gambler with anything resembling a betting edge, as they command a 6–5 "spot" on wagers of less than 10 units and a 5½–5 "spot" on huskier plays.

In order to aid the average gridiron fan who'd like to elevate himself to the professional wagering ranks, we've compiled three charts that should prove to be real eye-openers. The charts cover the standings of the teams in pro football's "Pointspread" League for the year 1973 and for the years 1969–1973, combined.

These highly informative charts reveal exactly which teams are the safest bets to be found, based on both recent and overall past performances, as well on which elevens came on strong or actually tailed off both pointwise and at home in the last campaign.

Over the five-year haul, the Miami Dolphins were the safest bet, winning 21 more times than they lost for a .662 average, while the Cincinnati Bengals were next at .600 per cent and the Detroit Lions third at .590. Going into the 1974 season, these teams, statistically, will once again be the safest bets when spotting points. Conversely, the trio of teams that dropped the most games pointwise over the five years were the Houston Oilers (22–44–1, .333), the St. Louis Cardinals (28–40–1, .418) and the Buffalo Bills (28–38–1, .420). This means, statistically, that these are the safest teams against which to wager.

Notice that about twenty teams have either won or lost only a few more games one way or the other over the five-year span, thereby graphically underlining the futility of trying to select every game on the week's schedule. Studying the results from the 1973 season alone, pro grid bettors who went with Denver, Buffalo, Los Angeles, Atlanta, Cleveland, Dallas, Miami, and Minnesota won some big cash. Denver beat

Pro Pointspread League Standings
1973 Season Final Standings
Against the Points

Team	Won -	Lost	Tied
Denver	10	3	1
Buffalo	10	4	0
Los Angeles	10	4	0
Atlanta	9	5	0
Cleveland	9	5	0
Dallas	9	5	0
Miami	9	5	0
Minnesota	9	5	0
Cincinnati	8	5	1
New Orleans	8	6	0
Pittsburgh	8	6	0
Washington	8	6	0
New England	7	7	0
St. Louis	7	7	0
New York Jets	6	7	1
Chicago	6	8	0
Detroit	6	8	0
Kansas City	6	8	0
San Diego	5	8	1
Baltimore	5	9	0
Philadelphia	5	9	0
Oakland	5	9	0
Green Bay	4	10	0
Houston	4	10	0
New York Giants	4	10	0
San Francisco	4	10	0

Pro Grid Pointspread Standings
Regular Season 1969–1973

	Won	Lost	Tied	Pct.
Miami	43	22	3	.662
Cincinnati	39	26	1	.600
Detroit	41	29	0	.590
Denver	38	27	2	.588
Cleveland	39	28	1	.587
Philadelphia	35	32	2	.585
Los Angeles	38	31	1	.557
Dallas	36	30	2	.550
Atlanta	37	31	0	.548
Pittsburgh	37	31	2	.548
Minnesota	35	32	1	.527
New Orleans	34	32	3	.524
Washington	35	33	1	.519
San Diego	33	34	1	.497
New England	33	34	2	.497
New York Giants	32	35	2	.489
Green Bay	33	37	0	.477
Chicago	30	34	2	.476
San Francisco	31	37	2	.468
Oakland	30	37	2	.455
Kansas City	29	37	2	.450
Baltimore	30	38	2	.443
New York Jets	29	37	2	.440
Buffalo	28	38	1	.420
St. Louis	28	40	1	.418
Houston	22	44	1	.333

the spread in 10 of its 13 games, while Buffalo and Los Angeles clicked 10 of 14 times. The other teams were right there in nine of their 14 regular season contests.

With pro football betting now reaching astronomical heights each succeeding year, the person who hopes to wind up the campaign in black ink needs every possible edge he can come up with. It is not impossible to beat the game of football betting, but you must pick your spots after careful consideration and take every edge that is available to you.

The Overlay in Pro Football

A season or so ago, the so-so Cincinnati Bengals took on the Pittsburgh Steelers, who were being touted by those in the know as an excellent bet to go all the way—not only in their division and conference, but in the entire NFL. Pittsburgh was favored to beat Cincinnati, but the Steelers lost 15–10.

Three weeks later, this same Cincinnati team took on the highly regarded and favored Kansas City Chiefs. The result was the same: another *upset* as the Bengals prevailed 23–16. The following weekend, October 22, a little farther west, the Denver Broncos were stampeding heavily favored Oakland by a 30–23 score. And one week later, Oakland did it to a favored Los Angeles team by a resounding 45–17.

It must be remembered that the favored team in any NFL contest wins approximately 75 percent of the time (outright, but disregarding the pointspread). Conversely, of course, the underdog then wins about one of every four games contested. One-hundred-eighty-two games are now played during the fourteen weeks of the regular NFL season. Obviously, based on these percentage factors, forty-three of them are won by underdogs.

What, then, makes the upsets mentioned above stand out from other games in which the favorite fails to prevail? One very important thing! These "upsets" were not upsets at all, according to one of the smartest gamblers in the business. They were the results of "overlay" situations, and the informed bettor, armed with certain past-performance statistics, might very well have predicted the results of the contests mentioned as well as many other similar upsets.

Not meaning to be condescending, we feel that there may be some readers not familiar with the term "overlay." The term is one used regularly in horse racing. Very often a certain animal is overlooked (for a myriad of reasons) by the betting public and goes off at odds higher than he should, considering his competition. An overly in football is exactly the same thing. Oftentimes, the oddsmakers will create a false favorite. When this situation occurs, the bettor who is able to recognize the discrepancy and jump on the underdog—taking the points—very often not only wins by the spread but watches his team win outright.

It may sound oversimplified and obvious, but it is axiomatic that in a football game, 99 times out of 100, the team that gains more yardage than its opponents and yields less scores more points. It follows, logically, that the team that scores more points wins the game. When that team is the underdog—and you don't have to worry about covering a spread—you win your bet.

Following are two charts that contain statistical data accumulated over two (1971–72) NFL seasons. The first gives the offensive performances of all NFL teams during this two-year period. The second lists all the defensive accomplishments of the twenty-six teams. Both offensive and defensive statistics are compared against a league average, providing us with a variance factor for each team. While not current, this information gives you some idea how to compare and use offensive-defensive performances.

Offensive Performances (1971–1972)
Offensive League "Norm" (1971–72)—294 Yds. Per Game (Average)

Team	Av. Yds. Gained Per Game		Total Yds. Gained	Av. Yds. Gained Per Game	Variance Position from League Norm
	1971	1972	(1971–72)	(2 Yr. Total)	
Dallas	360	319	679	340	+46 1st
Miami	315	360	675	338	+44 2nd
San Francisco	336	311	647	324	+30 3rd
San Diego	338	307	645	323	+29 4th
Oakland	304	339	643	322	+28 5th
Detroit	327	297	624	312	+18 6th
New York Giants	298	320	618	309	+15 7th
Los Angeles	302	311	613	307	+13 8th (tie)
Cincinnati	305	308	613	307	+13 8th (tie)
Denver	297	309	606	303	+ 9 10th
Washington	288	305	593	297	+ 3 11th
Baltimore	291	299	590	295	+ 1 12th
Kansas City	299	282	581	291	− 3 13th
New York Jets	233	342	575	288	− 6 14th
Atlanta	283	287	570	285	− 9 15th
Cleveland	276	265	541	276	−18 16th
Minnesota	239	305	544	272	−22 17th
Green Bay	280	253	537	269	−25 18th
Pittsburgh	227	302	529	265	−29 19th
New England	254	261	515	258	−31 20th
New Orleans	262	262	524	262	−32 21st
St. Louis	286	233	519	259	−36 22nd
Buffalo	238	267	505	253	−41 23rd
Philadelphia	255	247	502	251	−43 24th
Chicago	238	248	486	243	−51 25th
Houston	251	228	479	239	−56 26th

(*Explanation of Charts:* In the offensive variant, the plus figure remains the same. In the defensive variant, however, the minus figure should be changed to a plus before the two are added together to get the total variants.)

Defensive Performances (1971–72)
Defensive League "Norm" (1971–72)—289 Yds. Yielded Per Game (Average)

Team	Av. Yds. Yielded Per Game		Total Yds. Yielded	Av. Yds. Yielded Per Game	Variance Position from League Norm
	1971	**1972**	(1971–72)	(2 Yr. Total)	
Miami	262	236	498	249	−40 1st
Minnesota	243	264	507	254	−38 2nd
Washington	252	257	509	255	−34 3rd
Baltimore	204	308	512	256	−33 4th
Dallas	248	268	516	258	−31 5th
Green Bay	286	248	534	267	−22 6th (tie)
Cincinnati	279	254	533	267	−22 6th (tie)
Atlanta	271	269	540	270	−19 8th
Denver	273	275	548	274	−15 9th
San Francisco	263	288	551	276	−13 10th
Kansas City	269	288	557	278	−11 11th
Los Angeles	288	279	567	284	− 5 12th
Pittsburgh	303	269	572	286	− 3 13th
Oakland	296	280	576	288	− 1 14th
Detroit	276	301	577	289	− 0 15th
Cleveland	300	291	591	296	+ 7 16th
Chicago	323	280	603	302	+13 17th (tie)
San Diego	326	277	603	302	+13 17th (tie)
Houston	271	338	609	305	+16 19th
New York Giants	312	300	612	306	+17 20th
Buffalo	329	299	628	319	+30 21st (tie)
New Orleans	317	321	638	319	+30 21st (tie)
New York Jets	311	336	649	324	+35 23rd
St. Louis	312	339	651	326	+37 24th
New England	291	375	666	333	+44 25th
Philadelphia	330	338	668	334	+45 26th

With this data, let's now go back and take a look at the supposed upsets mentioned at the beginning of this discussion. For the two-year period, Cincinnati had a *plus* 13 offensively and a *minus* 22 (which actually is a plus) defensively for a total variance from the league average of *plus* 35. On the other hand, Pittsburgh was *minus* 29 offensively and a *minus* 3 defensively for a total of *minus* 26. The difference, then, between the two teams was 61 (*plus* 35, *minus* 26). This 61-yard total difference between the two clubs was worth at least 5 points since Cincinnati beat the Steelers by that margin, although the oddsmakers gave Cincinnati the points. The Bengals were a definite overlay in the contest and proved it by winning the game outright.

Against Kansas City, which was heavily favored, Cincinnati took its *plus* 35 variant into the game against the Chiefs' *plus* 8 (*minus* 3 offensively; *minus* 11 defensively equals *plus* 8). The variance against the Chiefs was not as great as against Pittsburgh (*plus* 8 Kansas City vs. *plus* 61 Pittsburgh). But it was still on the plus side and the Bengals came out on the plus side of the score as underdogs.

The Denver–Oakland game should have been no better than a pick 'em affair, although Oakland was installed a heavy favorite. According to our charts, the teams were not evenly matched. Denver was a *plus* 9 offensively and a *minus* 15 defensively for a *plus* 24 total variant, compared to Kansas City's *minus* 3 offensively and *minus* 11 defensively for a *plus* 8 total. The variance, then, was *plus* 16 in Denver's favor. Denver won outright by a touchdown and millions of bettors cried bitter tears.

What is pointed out here is the fact that, contrary to public belief, the oddsmakers aren't always "right on." Sometimes they're pretty far off. By utilizing this statistical data, you will not only be able to pick up certain overlay situations that will occur during he season, but you will be able to check to see whether published spreads are in line or not.

A serious bettor should keep these charts, as well as the others in this book, up to date season after season. This is rather easy to do and they are easy to use. Not much time is required to do so, and they just might win a few bets you might otherwise miss.

Pro Football Betting Cycles

The average professional football bettor more than likely is cognizant of the fact that odd "flip-flops" of form evolve during every season. There never has been a pro football campaign that wasn't filled with surprises nor is there ever likely to be one. The three seasons 1970–72 were no exceptions. A game-by-game study of these seasons in the NFL reveals that wagering was made which could greatly assist the football bettor in the future.

In order that the review be as analytical as possible, the three seasons have been broken down into categories based upon pointspreads. Every game played during this period has been assigned to a category based upon the pointspreads that prevailed in that particular contest. Studies were made of every game that involved a pick 'em situation; games where the spread was from 1 to 3 points; from 3½ to 6½ points; 7 to 9½ points; 10 to 12; 12½ to 14½; and all games in which the spread exceeded 15 points. The games have also been rated as to which team—home or visiting—was the favorite. This material was then arranged in tabular form as shown below.

Home Team Favored to Win

Year	Pick 'em		1–3 pts.		3½–6½ pts.		7–9½ pts.		10–12 pts.		12½– 14½ pts.		15 & over	
	H	A	H	A	H	A	H	A	H	A	H	A	H	A
1970	2	1	14	14	14	16	10	10	10	8	5	1	2	4
1971	3	0	13	7	8	18	8	12	10	7	4	8	2	1
1972	2	1	7	6	10	13	8	18	8	9	6	5	2	0
3-year Totals	7	2	34	28	32	47	26	40	28	24	15	14	9	11

Away Team Favored to Win

Year	Pick 'em		1–3 pts.		3½–6½ pts.		7–9½ pts.		10–12 pts.		12½– 14½ pts.		15 & over	
	H	A	H	A	H	A	H	A	H	A	H	A	H	A
1970	1	2	3	10	10	9	6	6	6	4	4	1	1	1
1971	0	3	4	7	14	8	7	14	11	10	5	2	0	1
1972	1	2	4	11	9	12	4	13	6	5	5	5	2	0
3-year Totals	2	7	11	27	33	29	17	33	23	19	14	8	3	2

It is safe to say that a careful study of this chart will reveal some startling discrepancies. At first glance, the chart appears to bear out what experienced football bettors already know too well. That is, it is extremely difficult (almost impossible) to beat the pointspread with any degree of consistency. The boys in Vegas do their homework just too well when making their weekly line so that just about every one—when the spread is considered—becomes an even match, and thus a "guessing game."

Let's take a closer look at the chart, however. If, during the 1970 season, for example, you had concentrated primarily on betting the home teams, regardless of the spreads, you would have made 111 bets (an inordinate number, but valid for this example). Of these you would have won 57 and lost 54. Needless to say, the "vigorish" or "juice" would have put you deeply in the red for the season. But since it is a known fact that footballs take funny bounces, if you had done the same thing during the next two seasons (1971 and 1972), you would have lost not only the "juice" but a lot more (31–33 for 1971 and 48–57 for 1972).

Obviously, then, a bettor should not make wagers on pro games without first doing some serious studying. The chart provides the statistical material necessary for this homework. From the three-year totals presented, it should be obvious that the home team "advantage" is really not all that it's cracked up to be. In fact, in all of the pointspread groups, only two stand out as good bets. They are pick 'em and 1–3 points. If the bettor had concentrated only on these very even (without the spread) contests over the period covered, he would have cashed 41 bets while losing only 30! This isn't too bad—but not all that great, either. But if we glance farther on in the chart, we see where it's really at. Namely, when the away team is favored by 7–9½ points, you cash just about twice as many bets as you lost (33 winners, 17 losers). Likewise, although you don't get nearly as much action, your winning percentage (close to 100 percent) remains the same in the area of 12–14½ points, away team favored. Here, however, by betting the home team, you win nearly twice as many bets as you lose (14 wins, 8 losses).

You should now have the idea. There is, of course, no guarantee these figures will hold up over every campaign. The fact that they did so in the three years 1970–72 has much to say, though, for their continuing to do so.

To make things even easier for you, following are the areas that seem to stand out as good bets as determined from the 1970–71–72 statistics:

1. In a game with no spread (pick 'em), the home team wins more than three times as many as it loses (7–2).
2. In the category where the home team is favored by 3½

to 6½ points, the away team overcomes this deficit and wins by the spread an ordinate number of times (32–47).

3. The best area on which to concentrate is the 7–9½ pointspread grouping. Here, regardless of who is favored, the away team seems to win an exceptional number of times, regardless of where the game is played. (Away wins 40 out of 66 when the home team is favored, and 33 out of 50 when it is favored for a total of 73 wins and 43 losses.)

4. The away team covers a 1–3 pointspread nearly three out of every four times (27 wins, 11 losses).

5. The away team fails to cover a 12½–14½ spread almost two out of every three games (8 wins, 14 losses).

An important word of caution: do not use the material in this chart blindly. Begin charting the results of the current season as soon as it commences. After several weeks you should see a pattern emerging which should coincide with the material in the chart. But, football being the game it is, your findings may not agree with the data gathered over the three season that were charted. If this is the case, bet the contests where the pointspread, for one reason or another, seems to be out of kilter. Eventually and over a lond period of time, the trends shown in the chart will prevail. But over the short haul, go with the tide.

Finally, remember this credo: the more you know, the better you understand, which leads to better chances for success.

High Score System

There are many betting systems, and for the most part, they are worthless. For this reason, we won't bother to mention them. However, there is one system we would like to describe, which has shown a great deal of promise. The angle upon which the system revolves is to follow up on the pro team which won its game by the biggest point margin the previous weekend.

The thinking behind the method is that a team which has just beaten a league rival by a very wide margin, regardless of the pointspread in the game, must have "put it all together" and could very well be able to do as well or even better the following Sunday.

Date	Game	Previous Week's Biggest Winner
September		
27	Detroit (−13½) 38—Cincinnati 3	Detroit 40
October		
4	Detroit (−12) 28—Chicago 14	Detroit 35
11	Los Angeles (−9½) 6—San Francisco 20	Los Angeles 27
18	Minnesota (−8) 54—Dallas 13	Minnesota 24
25	Minnesota (−3½) 13—Los Angeles 3	Minnesota 54
November		
1	Cleveland (−7) 10—San Diego 27	Cleveland 28
8	St. Louis (−18) 31—Boston 0	St. Louis 44
15	St. Louis (+1½) 38—Dallas 0	St. Louis 31
22	St. Louis (+4) 6—Kansas City 6	St. Louis 38
29	Cincinnati (−8½) 26—New Orleans 6	Cincinnati 27
December		
6	Cincinnati (+3½) 17—San Diego 14	Cincinnati 20
13	Dallas (−3) 6—Cleveland 2	Dallas 34
20	Minnesota-Atlanta (N.L.)	Minnesota 21
26	Dallas (+3) 5—Detroit 0	Dallas 42
January		
3	Baltimore (+1) 27—Oakland 17	Baltimore 17
17	Baltimore (+2½) 16—Dallas 13	Baltimore 10

We recently completed a check of the entire National Football League schedule using this approach and we learned that it produced a remarkable 14 winners as against only 2 losses, for a winning percentage of .880. After knocking off two successive wins at the beginning of the campaign, the first loss was suffered. The angle then picked two more winners before the second and last loss was sustained. The next 9 playable games all wound up in the victory column, carrying us through the regular season, the playoffs, and the Super Bowl.

Our first play came up on Sunday, September 27. Detroit had bombed Green Bay by a 40–0 count in opening-week action to rank easily as the play. The Lions were slated to lock horns with Cincinnati, and Paul Brown's eleven was tabbed as a 13½-point underdog. The Motor City team handled the Bengals easily, 38–3, to clear the bet by 21½ points and to get the angle off on a winning foot.

Thanks to the large (35 points) winning margin over the Ohioans, Detroit was once again the system play on October 4 in a home night game with its arch-rival, the Chicago

Bears. The spot at kickoff time was 12 points and the Lions squeezed through with a 28–14 win.

A losing play cropped up on October 11. Los Angeles was the key team, as the Rams were coming off an impressive 27-point victory just seven days previous. The Southern Californians were made 9½-point picks over their up-state rivals, the San Francisco 49'ers (who turned out to be for real this season). The notherners proceeded to keep the Rams from getting a touchdown en route to a well-earned 20–6 victory.

Things got back to normal on October 18, however, as Minnesota, a 24-point winner in its previous tilt, was our selection. This day the Vikings were pegged as 8 points better than the Cowboys and they went on to humiliate their guests by a score of 54–13. And, as you may imagine, this 41-point margin made the Vikes the play again the following Sunday.

The Minnesota–Los Angeles match-up, a Monday-night TV affair held in monsoonlike rains in Bloomington, Minnesota (where the Vikes hadn't lost a game in almost three years), saw the NFL champs rated a slim 3½-point choice. The home squad slipped and slid to a clever 13–3 victory, and once again the system won out.

Cleveland was the method's pick on November 1 as the result of its 28-point romp the week previous. But the lethargic Browns, a 7-point selection over San Diego, dropped a 27–10 decision to the in-and-out Chargers. This was the method's second miscue.

The next play under this angle cropped up on November 8 and was to be the start of a 9-game winning streak. St. Louis, a convincing 44-point winner on November 1, was rated 18 points stronger than the invading Boston Patriots and the Cards lived up to the expectations by routing the invaders by a 31–0 count.

St. Louis accounted for the next two wins also, then Cincinnati knocked off two in succession.

Dallas closed out its regular season by walloping Houston, and winning by 42 points. The Cowboys easily qualified as the pick over Detroit, but the books gave Dallas 3 points anyway. The Cowboys didn't need the points as they won a weird one, 5–0.

The principle behind this method of play is very sound, in that it steers the bettor onto a team that, in most instances, jelled just one week previous and is now hitting on all cylinders as regards passing, running, and defense. This is akin to a crack sprinter in horse racing which does wire-to-wire one week and, although picking up additional weight or moving up in class in its next start, is still vastly superior to its rivals. It's a good little angle that picks standout pro fooball winners at a much better than average clip, while requiring hardly any mental taxation at all.

In summation, the workings of this angle require only that the bettor know the scores of the previous week's games. He need only scan the results to learn which team won its game by the largest margin. He then wagers on that team in its next game, either giving or taking the points involved, as the case may be. (In almost every case, the team in question has to spot points to its opponent due to its convincing tally.) If easy-pick pro football methods are you cup of tea, you might want to give the High Score System a whirl.

Pre-Season Tilts

Come the end of July, the footballs start to fly through the air as part of the National Football League's pre-season schedule. And the gridiron bettors try to ouwit the bookies in the battle of the weekly pointspreads. It's a tough challenge.

Wherever NFL fans congregate at this time of the year, the conversation always turns to the merits of taking or giving points in clashes involving teams that stood out the previous season when they're pitted against perennial weak sisters. Many knowledgeable fans argue that the top teams don't go all out in these late-summer clashes either for fear of injury to star players or because the coach wants to try out green rookies at various positions.

Be that as it may, the general consensus at the conclusion of most of these gab sessions is to side with the favored team and give the points in most instances. The feeling is that the team that is strongest on paper will usually win many more games than it drops.

With the welfare of the average fan in mind, we ran a spot check on the NFL's pre-season schedules for 1970 to 1973 and found that, contrary to popular thinking, it is the *under-dog* that definitely fares better in these tilts. It seems that the coaches of the stronger elevens play their stars in the first half or the first and third quarters and then generally ignore the final score in favor of evaluating returning injured veterans, high draft choices, and free agents. This fact of football life holds true till the last or next-to-last game prior to the pre-season campaign. Then the "biggies" start playing a real, hard-nosed brand of ball in order to enter the season under a full head of steam.

But it is the topsy-turvy nature of affairs in pro football and what it all portends that keeps most of the bettors baffled. For while exhibition games don't mean anything at all in the official standings over the regular season, they usually make a mockery of the pre-season dope as forecasts by the oddsmakers in Nevada and other sports centers generally don't prove out when they "play for fun."

Is there another season of pro-football upsets in the offing? It would seem very much that way when one takes into consideration the results of recent years' exhibition play, which carry greater significance than most fans might imagine.

We advise players to bet with caution during the pre-season schedule and be leery of spotting points, because the teams with the best records the previous season will probably not be going all out in these games. And once the new season begins, you'll probably find that the teams with the best pre-season records often fare worse in regular play than teams with poor exhibition results.

Super Bowl Betting

The Super Bowl is our country's biggest single betting event. But four of the last six games have been won by underdogs, which should leave every so-called professional linemaker in the country a little red-faced. It's one thing for a team to beat the spread, but it is a completely different story for a team which was the underdog to win outright, particularly at the current rate.

The fact that the line on this game has been so far wrong in recent years is a mystery. We would have to guess that even professional linemakers stop thinking when they make the line on this one. They get carried away with a team's performance during the year and let that enthusiasm carry right over to the Super Bowl. Believe me, a championship game such as this is in a different world from any other game, regular season or playoff.

While the pros do their job week in and week out with little fanfare, they appear to get emotionally high for this one. This is for a big piece of change and lays a foundation for memories for years to come. There is something in the subconscious of a player that gets him ready for this kind of game. Thus, to begin with, the emotional factor in the Super Bowl makes the contest 50–50 right from the start. Either team has credentials to win, and this is something the sharp bettor will never forget. One could write a doctoral thesis on the emotion factor in this game, and what goes on in the mind of each performer.

Does this mean that every game such as the Super Bowl should be a pick 'em game? Absolutely not. It's just important that you never forget that there is more than past performance going into this contest. Emotion will play a big part in it and can equalize some of the supposedly better team's edges. That's all.

Before making your bet in this game, try to guess as much as possible what a team's game plan will be. You may have read in the newspapers that so-and-so's star running back will not see much action. Don't let that fact throw you. While the absence of any key player hurts a team, it won't necessarily affect the pointspread.

Never forget that any coach who made it to the Super Bowl is a thinking man. Without that ability, he would never have made it. If he has a key player whose ability to perform is in question, he is going to change his game plan to compensate for it. A change in game plan has killed many a bettor in big games.

The next factor we have to consider is just how the respective teams got to the Super Bowl. Did they have an easy time of it? Were they all out to win their playoff games? Did they build up a big lead in the standings early in the season and then coast into the playoffs? Did they slowly build momentum as the season stretched out, peaking near the end?

Don't bet a team in the Super Bowl because of what it did back in November. Bet if off what it did in the last two or three games before the big event. This will tell you the physical, mental and emotional condition of a team. By watching the last two or three games before a Super Bowl very carefully, smart bettors can determine who is peaking and who is already on the downhill side of his best form.

Before deciding which team will get our support with our bookmakers, it is important that we compare the relative strengths of the two teams, position-by-position. After we compare their quarterbacks, let's take a look at their field goal kickers. The Super Bowl game figures to be close and a kicker could mean the difference between winning and losing. Has the kicker been at his best? What is his percentage? Is he a money ballplayer? A good kicker is worth a point or two.

What about the running backs? Have they been used so much during the season that they are worn out? Are they a step or two slower than they were six weeks ago?

What about the receivers? This is an important department. The team with two good receivers certainly is going to have a big edge over the team with just one. That is worth a point or two.

What about the defensive front four? This is a group of men who play in the pits each week and are eligible to get hurt every week. In fact, most play with injuries the last half of the season. The punishment a pro lineman takes is fierce. Is this unit healthy, and not handicapped by injury?

We could go on and on, but our point is simply this: the Super Bowl is a game in which we have better than a 50–50 chance of winning via the pointspread if we will just stop and give it some serious thought. Don't rely on your friendly linemaker to give you the lowdown on this game. He has been wrong more times than he has been right, and this figures to follow through in any given year of the Super Bowl. If you are in doubt, take the underdog. The points in the Super Bowl are big ones.

Chapter 3

Betting on College Football

Betting on college football, like all other wagering, is a game of percentages. In order to be even moderately successful, you must take every edge that is available, and even that is no guarantee you will live rich.

One of the biggest pitfalls of football wagering is the bettor's lack of common sense. The average guy flips through his football sheet, quickly picks three or four teams, calls his bookmaker, asks for the line on those teams, bets his money, and then settles back for an afternoon of suffering. The only thing he really allowed time for was the suffering.

If you are going to bet college football—and millions of Americans do each week—then you're going to have to use a little common sense in your handicapping. You should spend just as much time selecting your teams as you allow for suffering. The odds say that if you do this your agony hours will be cut down considerably.

College Pointspreads

Every professional football linemaker in the country begins the season with just one thought: to make every team on which betting is conducted finish the season with 50 percent losscs and 50 percent wins against the spread. By doing this, he protects the bookmaker who, knowing he is going to get a 50–50 decision, conducts his business worrying only about the vigorish. His only concern is collecting the 11 to 10 when you lose and paying out even money when you win.

A fifteen-year study of pointspreads for the colleges demonstrates just how accurately the linemaker predicts the outcome of games via the spread. Over the fifteen years, the underdog has won just over 51 percent of the time, while the favorite has won just under 49 percent of its contests.

In analyzing the 1972 football season, in which the favorites won 202 games and lost 194 by way of the points, there is no way one can draw any conclusions which could easily tell the bettor whether to bet favorites or underdogs. The problem is just as basic in trying to determine if there is a relationship between a team's actual won-lost record and its performance against the pointspread. Stacks and stacks of statistics on this subject are available, but they prove nothing concrete. Teams which had good records did horribly against the spread, while others with excellent won-lost marks did well. Most teams with poor records didn't fare well against the spread, but there were even exceptions to that. For example, the top football teams in 1972 were Southern California, Nebraska, North Carolina, Tennessee, UCLA, Washington, Alabama, Arizona State, Colorado, Louisiana State, Michigan, Notre Dame, Oklahoma, Ohio State, Penn State, and Texas. It is interesting to note that the first five teams mentioned here had outstanding records and beat the spread consistently. The others had the kinds of records which keep the most difficult alumnus smiling, but knocked out the bettors. They just couldn't beat the spread.

Alabama was 10–1 for the season, and just 6–4 against the spread, with one game against a minor opponent carrying no line. Colorado was 8–3 for the fans and 5–5 for the bettor. Louisiana State, Notre Dame, Oklahoma, Ohio State, Penn State, Texas, and Texas Tech were particularly hazardous. They had an aggregate actual won-lost record of 68–11–1 but were able to win only 30 of 77 games against the spread. LSU performed the worst of any of these against the points, being 9–1–1 overall and 2–8 for the bettor.

On the other hand, Iowa, Miami (Florida), William and Mary, and Northwestern had miserable years for their fans but were pure whipped cream and sugar for the bettors. Iowa was 3–7–1 for the season but managed to be 7–3 against the spread. Miami was 5–6 and 6–3, William and Mary 5–6 and 2–0, while Northwestern was 2–9 and 6–5. It is interesting to note, too, that Pittsburgh, which was 1–10 in its actual wins and losses, was 5–5 against the spread.

As we have said, there is no way to draw any conclusion from studying the actual records of teams and their performances against the spread.

The linemaker is so sharp it also is next to impossible to stick with either favorites or underdogs, and win. The fifteen-year totals of these figures tell us that teams which were favored from ½ to 5½ points won only 44 percent of their games, while losing 56. Teams favored from 6 to 12 points were winners 47.6 percent of the time, while losing 52.4 percent of their contests. In the 14-point and over category, favorites won 56.3 percent of the time, meaning this was the only pointspread division in which favorites showed more than just a slight edge.

With college football, the bettor can often pick his spots better than when betting on the pro game. On the average there are at least thirty college games to choose from each weekend throughout the fall, and through careful scrutiny, a smart bettor can usually come up with at least three pretty solid wagers.

Bookmakers are wise to this, too, but sometimes they do not do their homework as well as the wide-awake and informed bettors. In other words, a bookie may not be aware that the quarterback of any given club has come up with an injury during practice before the game and the bookmaker may not take that particular game off the board. That's when he gets hurt because the bettors who subscribe to out-of-town papers or to a football telephone selection service know the score and may beat the bookie betting the other way. This happened several times in recent years when the flu bug was running through some eastern teams, wrecking backs and receivers and bookmakers. Reports out of New England revealed that a couple of bookmakers in Boston went into hock because they kept certain games on the board while one of the teams was playing at half strength. They (the bookies) were slaughtered by the smart bettors.

Occasionally a "hot" college game may be taken off the boards by bookies throughout the country. Don't suspect that there is any funny stuff going on. You can bet that a couple of key players are out with injuries and that's the only reason the bookies remove the game. A perfect example of this was the South Carolina–Virginia Tech game scheduled for October 6 at Blacksburg, Virginia, during the 1973 season. The opening Las Vegas line made South Carolina a 6-point favorite. However, for an unexplained reason, the game came off the board in most of the country two days later on Wednesday afternoon. One could still bet the game in New York on Thursday, but by Friday no one in the country could bet on the contest. An exhaustive search finally revealed that South Carolina coach Paul Dietzel was in the hospital and would not be on hand for the game. This was enough to make the bookmakers nervous, and down came the game. South Carolina ended up winning the game as the favorite, but by only 3 points, not covering the spread.

Form is very important when figuring a college bet because if a college team has a good defense the defense will stand up against most of the teams it faces. This is not always so in the pros because almost any good, fast-firing quarterback can punch holes in any defense. All he needs is a little bit of luck and a quick release of the ball. Actually this is what makes the difference between a pro and an amateur. The college kid has not learned "quick release" and his reflexes aren't as sharp as the pro, who is older and more experienced. The college kid will hold the ball and seek out a receiver. Usually he waits too long and is smeared from behind.

This generally works two ways so your bet is reasonably safe if you are betting on, say, Columbia, and the Lions are meeting a team like Brown. Usually those teams are so bad and make so many mistakes that no matter which club you bet you are bound to get a break during the game. You would be better off if you stayed away from weak teams entirely and bet the better clubs, especially if a better club has stronger statistics.

Another insight that might help a bettor is "laying the points" and when he should do it. In dealing with the colleges, if a team has the reputation of piling it up, don't hesitate to lay the points. Nine chances out of ten a "points" team will always beat the spread. Of course, the secret is to find out which coaches like to run up big scores and pick that team minus (or sometimes with) the points each week. On a given week the biggest spread will be from 25 to 30 points, but for some teams 45 to 50 would be more like it, as they steamroller 75 percent of their rivals week after week.

Take, for example, Penn State University. The Nittany Lions coach, Joe Paterno, is an innovator of various offenses who believes that the way to win games and guarantee a top ten finish is to score lots of points. In recent years the Lions ran up some incredibly one-sided scores in keeping with Paterno's doctrine.

While coach Joe Paterno has a reputation for rolling up scores, he is by no means the only coach who subscribes to that philosophy. Frank Kush of Arizona State, "Shug" Jordan of Auburn, Paul "Bear" Bryant of Alabama, Bo Schembechler of Michigan, Woody Hayes of Ohio State, and Ara Parseghian of Notre Dame have been known to pile it on weaker opposition, too. The reason for rolling up big scores in most instances has to do with weekly ratings. The ratings, a weekly promotional gimmick instituted by the two major wire services, Associated Press and United Press International, have become an important issue at major football schools and one way to get there is by winning big.

The college football bettor also can take an edge by knowing which coaches beat the spread. It will be a simple matter to follow them, for their number is small. Fewer than twenty-five coaches have winning records against the spread during the last ten seasons. At the head of the list is Bob Blackman of Illinois, who has been coaching for twenty-four years. He is followed by Bo Schembechler of Michigan, Joe Paterno of Penn State, Vince Dooley of Georgia, and "Shug" Jordan of Auburn.

Here is a complete list of coaches who have consistently beaten the spread for the last eleven years.

Coach	School	Lifetime Record	Against Spread Last 11 Years
Bob Blackman	Illinois	163–69	52–33
Frank Broyles	Arkansas	113–43	55–39
Paul Bryant	Alabama	210–67	60–45
Jerry Claiborne	Maryland	74–48	52–33
Bill Dooley	North Carolina	42–35	41–31
Vince Dooley	Georgia	73–32	63–43
Ralph Jordan	Auburn	162–75	55–42
Frank Kush	Arizona State	111–31	42–31
Johnny Majors	Pittsburgh	30–35	31–28
Ben Martin	Air Force	92–84	49–41
John McKay	Southern Cal	88–29	55–50
Ara Parseghian	Notre Dame	144–51	58–40
Joe Paterno	Penn State	75–13	55–30
Pepper Rodgers	Georgia Tech	39–34	38–31
Jim Root	William & Mary	29–25	3–1
Darrell Royal	Texas	142–45	59–41
Bo Schembechler	Michigan	88–23	52–28
Bill Yoeman	Houston	79–43	43–31

Bookmakers are wise to which coaches like to win big, too, and most of them will take the ten highest pointspreads off the boards. Naturally, the bookmaker is always looking to protect his pocket and by taking games off the board he is doing himself a favor. The more action he gets on fewer games the less chance he has of losing his vigorish (point edge in his favor).

The bettors are becoming wise to this practice and they're getting fed up with tight bookmakers. There have been reports coming in to us that bettors are now demanding action on certain games no matter what the pointspread is. This is a healthy sign because no bookmaker should have the right to make it next to impossible for a bettor to win. A bookmaker has the right to protect himself, true, but by eliminating any chance for a bettor to win, he is almost stealing the money.

Take enough time to study the top games each weekend. Don't automatically decide to wager on a certain college because you "like" it. Bet with your mind and not your heart. When you're nearly ready to bet, call your bookmaker, but don't ask him only for the lines on the teams you intend to bet. Why declare yourself to him before you bet and let him juggle the spread a point or two in his favor when he knows that you lean toward favored teams? Also, if you think you like Notre Dame over Purdue, don't ask him the line on the "Notre Dame–Purdue game." Ask him, "What's Purdue?" Always try to keep him honest. He's got the 5½–5 edge anyway, so why give him any more?

An analysis of the statistics covering the pointspreads in various categories of college football has revealed that betting *against* the favorite can be profitable under certain circumstances. A close study of 400 decision (no tie) games played during recent years shows that the underdog was the winner according to the pointspread or otherwise 54 percent of the time, which ought to give the astute player the insight necessary for him to turn losing action into profit by simply learning which underdogs are actually hidden favorites and, thus, good bets.

During the survey period, the established favorites won 184 times and lost 216 for an average of only 46 percent. Favorites have had a winning season only twice during the stretch. The record for each game site category was as follows, with the record of the favorite listed: *home favorites* (107–121); *visiting favorites* (64–78); *neutral site favorites* (13–17). These records are based on opening lines. It also indicates that there was no strong trend or margin in any category except visiting favorites, although the underdog came out slightly better every time.

These pointspread records are invaluable in handicapping college games because they reveal "what's happening," they uncover certain trends as they develop and before the general public latches onto them, they indicate which teams are overrated and underrated by the oddsmakers and so-called football experts, and help to turn up many sleepers.

Our survey indicates that one of the strongest categories in wagering is taking ½-point up to 5½-point underdogs, in which the dog has been a consistent winner every year except twice when the choice won only one and four games more than the underdog. Over the time span, the underdog in this category has won 56 percent of the games, pointwise.

While on the subject of points, if a college or pro team has the reputation of using a running game, such as Tennessee, Ohio State, or LSU, that means the team is less likely to run up big scores. Therefore, it might be wise to take the big points against a team like this. Chances are this club will drop a few games during the season but will win by 10–7, 12–7, 9–3, and so forth.

When you're giving points, study both offense and defense. Both are of equal importance regarding the outcome of a game. Consider how the teams do on first down. A team that gains little or no yardage on first down—consistently—isn't going to do well. It needs four- and five-yard gainers on first down to sustain drives. Consider, also, third down and short yardage. A team with a power back who can grind out the necessary yards has a potent weapon.

Newspapers have a tendency to call continually winning clubs "powerhouses" and other lively sounding pseudonyms, but how big a powerhouse is a defense-oriented club that wins most of its games by only one touchdown? Take the points against a club like this. Speaking of newspapers, here is one thing to avoid: don't look for betting information in the sports section of a team's home newspaper. Most sportswriters get carried away by civic pride and would have you believe that a team is a winner when, in reality, it doesn't stand a chance. This leads to one of the most important points to consider before betting a football game. Never let emotion influence your betting. Use your head, not your heart.

Remember that the spread which is published early in the week (the early line) doesn't necessarily mean that one team is a certain number of points better than its opponent. The linemakers' primary concern is to bring out money on the underdog. He may feel that the two teams are an even bet, but if public opinion strongly favors one, a point handicap is necessary. Regardless of how you bet, weather is always an important factor. If you're a taker, it behooves you to bet as early in the week as possible since you'll get your most favorable spread then. However, if the game is being played where there is a good chance that the weather will be foul by game time, and you feel that this will adversely affect your team, you should wait as late as possible to see what the weather conditions will be before making your bet.

Keep in mind that pointspreads are a risky factor in all football games, but much more so in college contests than in the pros. Although there are a few college coaches around who will run up a score against any opponent, as we mentioned earlier, most of them don't like to humiliate a fellow coach. They're also inclined to take out their first team in order to give their reserves experience, once they've run up a comfortable lead. Another consideration is the college team that has a big game coming up next week.

One other thing: if you think your bookmaker is taking too many games off the board, tell him so. If he tells you to take it or leave it, leave it and find yourself another sports accountant. There are plenty around—if you live in the New York City area there's something like 10,000 active books in operation according to the latest estimates. Remember that betting college football is not unlike playing Russian roulette, even for the experienced bettor. For the beginner, it can be total disaster. However, it can be a bonanza to the person who devotes some time to developing a working knowledge of the top collegiate elevens—in particular, knowing who the traditional rivals are and when, during the season, these usually hard-fought games are played. As we recommended in Chapter 2, smart football bettors also will arm themselves with all the data and statistics available. In fact many of the factors such as injuries and home field are about the same for both the college boys and the pros. However, here are some additional factors you must keep in mind when betting on college football.

The Football Schedule

The advantage of knowing the various teams' schedules is that the bettor can apply one of the least-employed, but most reliable, betting methods in existence—the "look ahead" method. Its premise, ironically, is as simple as the method is reliable.

Let's look at a hypothetical situation: Team A is a power-house ranked right near the top of the Associated Press Top Twenty poll. It is fighting for the national championship and a prestigious bowl bid. Team B is ranked just below team A and it too is seeking national recognition and a trip to one of the major bowl games. The two teams are scheduled to meet next weekend. This weekend, however, while team B is sitting out an open date, team A is taking on team C, a lowly, un-worthy opponent that should be defeated by at least three touchdowns. In fact, team C has been installed as a 24-point underdog by those making the weekly line. So what happens?

Team A goes through light scrimmages all week so as not to abuse its players, looking ahead to their meeting with rival team B two weeks hence. Meanwhile, team C has been drill-ing as if this Saturday were a bowl game, knowing that this is its one chance to break into the national limelight by knocking off big, bad team A.

By game time, everyone picks team A to romp—the book-ies know it; the bettors know it; and of course, the personnel of team A know it. The only one not in on the secret is team C, which has a secret or two of its own. This team fights like hell to make the game competitive. Team A, once they've taken a two-touchdown lead, replaces its regulars with second- and third-stringers to keep the starters healthy for next week's encounter with strong team B. As a result, team C much more often than not winds up beating the spread by a mile. In fact, they often end up winning the game outright.

Although hypothetical, this situation is not a dream, nor is it unusual. You will find it happening with amazing regularity every Saturday in the fall.

The reasons for these upsets are many. For instance, in games involving both college football haves and have-nots, the underdog with nothing to lose often plays with wild aban-don and pulls off a big upset, either by the points or outright. Also, the score of today's game may depend on last week's:

that is, whether it was won or lost; whether or not it was a rough, tough, hard-nosed affair that left the team injury-ridden, weary, and dragging. Knowledgeable college football bettors usually learn of these physical and mental letdowns on the part of the favorite through various inside connections, however, and they seldom get burned. But not so the man in the street. For this reason it is always better to give odds rather than points on a college game, assuming, of course, you can find someone who will bet you that way.

More often than not, it is true that college clubs aren't too concerned with beating the point spread—at least not to the degree that pro teams are. If a coach has a game with a top club or an arch-rival coming up and "gets in soft" the week before the game, he's very likely to pour second- and third-stringers into the game to preserve his starters for the big one next week. And naturally, the line doesn't usually reflect the fact that team A's third-stringers will be playing team C's first-stringers.

Another reason is the advance scheduling that takes place in collegiate football. Schedules for undergraduate grid squads are made up years in advance of the actual playing dates. Very often, by the time the games are played, the teams competing are mere shadows of their former greatness, having been decimated by graduation coupled with a lack of incoming talent. For example, teams such as Army and Navy had been on Notre Dame's schedule for many years because of the great teams the two service academies fielded during the late thirties and early forties. But the Blanchards, Davises, and Bellinos are gone and the games are now mere shells of the great rivalries they once were. Thus, the soft spot—the breather on the powerhouses' schedules which gives them an opportunity to go at half speed (or slower) when a big game is in the offing.

Extending this fact logically, it is also true that it is tough, if not impossible, for a team to be emotionally "up" for all its games. A smart bettor can turn this schedule quirk to his decided advantage by picking the spots when some clubs are in too soft. It's easy enough to spot these games. All you need do is get hold of a college football schedule and start searching for the week's mismatches. Once you've done this, then do what the coaches do—look ahead to the following week's opponents and check the advance spreads. If you see a potentially tight game upcoming, in which one team appears to have a decided edge (and this is borne out by the spread), you have yourself a good bet this week.

Before the 1973 season began, for instance, it would have been wise to get in some practice utilizing this "look ahead" theory. For openers, Texas—being touted by many as the 1973 national champ—got two excellent breaks in its schedule. It opened the season against a have-not eleven, Miami of Florida, on September 21. One week later, however, it met arch-enemy Texas Tech. And in the next two weeks it followed a similar pattern when it played a very poor (according to expert opinion) Wake Forest team, followed by a real toughy against Oklahoma. Texas, then probably counted on taking it a bit easy against both Miami and Wake Forest, but was the heavy favorite in both contests. These two underdogs turned out to be good bets because the pointspread was enormous. This was just one real example. One needs only to scan the entire schedule to pick out these potential "overlay" situations.

Examining the schedule produced a winner, here, too, as Miami upset Texas 20–15. The Longhorns' minds were on Texas Tech, and they were blown out of the Orange Bowl by the Hurricanes in what must be considered a stunning upset. When Texas came up against Wake Forest, the bookmakers took no chances and did not offer a line on the game. Texas won that one 41–0.

One word of caution, however! There are some coaches, as we stated previously, who never take it easy, who *never* let up. Naturally, you should shy away from these teams if you're looking to cover a point spread as an underdog. And occasionally, there's a mismatch in which the favored team's coach will put in his second- and third-stringers later in the game, and they will continue to destroy the opponent as did the starters—this is what happened in the Nebraska–Army game a few seasons ago. The final score was 77–7, in favor of Nebraska.

Nevertheless, in most cases the "look ahead" system will provide you with many good plays. In life, it's always better to plan ahead—and it's no different in betting on college football.

Is Momentum a Factor?

The dictionary defines "momentum" as the "quality of motion; the property of a moving body which determines the length of time required to bring it to rest when under the action of a constant force or movement." Can we then assume that a football team which supposedly has momentum is a team on which we can wager with confidence?

Momentum, as related to athletic teams, is a very deceptive thing, and the definition of the word itself offers insight into exactly what it means. A football team with momentum is doing only one thing, for sure, and that is moving. It is in motion. However, there is no guarantee of how long it will remain that way. Most footbal bettors believe that a team which wins and wins and wins will keep winning, and they are right. However, they fail to take into consideration the neutralizing factor—the points.

If you're looking for teams with momentum, they are easy to find. Just look at your daily newspaper and find which teams are nationally ranked by the Associated Press and United Press International. All of these teams have momentum and are winning. The problem is that you pay the price for this so-called momentum in the amount of points you have to lay on them. On the surface it is quite questionable whether it is worth it. Bookmakers are extremely cautious individuals and approach their business as if everybody was out to cheat them. They know all the edges and take them. And they hate the teams with momentum.

First of all, teams with momentum are usually heavy favorites—probably 20- to 25-point choices over their opponents. Bookmakers are nervous about any game in which the spread is that great for they feel that luck, more than anything else, determines whether you win or lose. They are not interested in giving you or anyone else a chance to get lucky. It is an element over which they have no control and they don't like it. So, don't be surprised if you find it almost impossible to bet on teams that have momentum. As each season gets under way, there are very few big bookmakers in the country who are taking any action on any game in which the spread is over 20 points. These games all spell trouble for them, and trouble they don't want.

While we have been discussing the negative aspects of momentum, it also has its positive sides and can be translated into winning some bets. For instance, you can use momentum in your favor when one of these teams is playing on the road. When a nationally ranked power such as Alabama or Michigan goes on the road, it takes with it its thirty-three best players. This means the bettor is going to get a top performance from these teams, for their second and third strings are almost as good as their first teams. However, if they are playing at home, coaches Bear Bryant and Bo Schembechler are going to suit up every available player and then let them all play.

While these reserves are in the game gaining experience, the other team will function better, for it brought only its thirty-three best players, and might close the gap and beat the bettor. Thus, we would say, bet the teams with momentum only when they are on the road. You can take a big edge with them, knowing they have nothing but their best players with them.

Momentun can be translated into winning, too, when you find a team which has won four or five games in a row going against one which has lost two or three in a row, or three out of its last four, and so on.

Psychology plays an important part in the life of a college football player. A coach can psych his players up to a point where they perform way over their heads. However, if they get beaten three of four games in a row, the hoopla the coach has been pouring out begins to fall on deaf ears. The losing syndrome sets in and there is no magic formula to get rid of it.

Contrast this to a team which has won four or five games in a row. It has no reason to doubt the hoopla. The coach keeps the team stirred up; it keeps winning and operates in a positive frame of mind. Thus, when teams like this meet, the contrasts are enormous. When that offensive tackle from the losing team starts getting knocked around by the defensive lineman from the winning team, he begins to back off a little bit. After about a quarter, he is whipped physically and psychologically, and asks himself, "What's the use?"

The entire losing team eventually does this, accepting the loss as if it were a way of life. The effect is just the opposite on the winning team, and we can see dozens and dozens of 45–0 scores.

Traditional Rivalries

College football, in many respects, is totally different from the relative sameness of the pro games, and for the bettor it can be as unpredictable as a Pete Liske aerial. The outcome of a college football game very often defies all logic. A team which is a three-touchdown underdog can be driven by sheer emotion to perform unbelievable tasks and the result can be a harrowing experience for the man who gave the 21 points. Those of you in the over-forty age bracket can remember back to the famous Columbia–Army game of the late 1940s when unbeaten and unscored-upon Army, led by Glenn Davis and Doc Blanchard, was upset by Columbia, 21–20, after being tabbed a six-touchdown favorite.

Such things happen ferquently even today in traditional college football rivalries where pride is often a more rewarding attribute than talent. And because of intangible things like pride, betting on college football can be a rough task for even the veteran speculator who has a ream of information at his fingertips. Frequently, however, it pays to look deeply into the history of important traditional games, such as Michigan State–Notre Dame, Alabama–Auburn, Tennessee–Kentucky, Southern Cal–UCLA, Florida–Florida State, Texas–Arkansas, Auburn–Tennessee, etc. These key games have long, rich histories, and rivalry is fierce. The games are more than contests. In some areas—most in fact—they are emotion-packed wars. It is of interest to note that the underdog usually beats the spread in games like this.

There can be no clearer example than a recent Auburn–Tennessee game in Birmingham, Alabama. Tennessee rolled into the Deep South with a national rating and victories over Georgia Tech and Penn State. Auburn was coming on a 14–7 win over Chattanooga. The game was played on a neutral field—if there is any such thing as neutral ground in Alabama—and Tennessee was installed a 15-point favorite.

It is unbelievable that anyone would give 15 points in an emotional contest like this. The rivalry is bitter and Auburn had won the game three out of the last four years. Not only did Auburn beat the spread, it beat Tennessee. Oh, what a brief look into the game history would tell us.

Revenge Angle and College Football

Even the most casual observer of the grid scene realizes that the pig-skin sport, especially on the college level, can be a highly emotional thing, with teams "getting up" for a particular game for various reasons. It could be the injury to a key star, the death of a veteran coach, or any one of a multitude of factors which can inspire a team to heights greater than their talent appears capable of on paper.

One factor that smart football bettors look for all the time is the revenge angle in the college sport. That is, they seek out games in which one team either whipped the other squad badly the previous year, cost the opponent a conference crown or a trip to a bowl game, or actually scored a stunning upset to ruin the rival's otherwise brilliant campaign. When these sharpies uncover such a contest, and they're able to get points or give very few in the process, they jump on the bandwagon of the team that suffered the setback the year previous. An excellent case in point was the Ohio State–Michigan game a few years ago. For an entire year Ohio State had "pointed" for this game. They were determined to avenge a 24–12 shellacking they received the previous fall by the Wolverines—a game which not only embarrassed Ohio State but also deprived them of a deserved league championship and a trip to the Rose Bowl. In 1970, Michigan did not have the incentive of the Rose Bowl to stir them up, and everyone in the nation who follows college football knew that Woody Hayes's boys were out to scalp the Michigan team. Although Michigan was a 6-point favorite, Ohio State—being as high as any team can be for any game—beat the spread easily, winning the game 20–9.

Keep in mind also that a college team is not playing for money but merely for the honor and glory of Alma Mater. Stay away from the first two games of each new season so that you can get an "actual" rather than "projected" view of how certain teams stack up. This will help greatly as the season progresses for, very often, a team that "figures" on paper will disappoint on the field and vice versa. That is, so-called early-season upsets are, in reality, usually not unexpected to the betting pros who keep charts from year to year and are wise to the vagaries of both linemakers and overzealous collegiate publicity men. The betting public as a whole eats up all the propaganda put out by the daily press, radio, and TV outlets regarding the week's big contests and does not take the time or effort required to dig beneath the veneer and come up with the straight scoop.

College Coaches

When it comes to selecting winners in the college football ranks, smart bettors usually follow a set formula. They stick with winning teams that are playing at home and at the same time are not too heavily burdened in the pointspread department.

This is a sensible approach to wagering success in the gridiron sport. But there's another solid plus factor to take into account when you're narrowing down your weekly selections. That factor is the long-term success, or lack of same, registered by the various head coaches. As in most sporting endeavors, winners continue to win while losers continue to lose.

If you find yourself in the latter category when it comes to make selections, get on the winning side of the ledger this semester by learning which mentors produce victories when the chips are down. In fact, try to limit your play to the teams led by the coaches who annually win many more games than they lose.

The top college coaches in the nation—including the 1973 season—based on winning percentages are as follows:

Coach	School	Years	G	W	L	T	Pct.
Joe Paterno	Penn State	8	88	75	13	0	.864
Frank Kush	Arizona State	14	143	111	31	1	.775
Darrell Royal	Texas	18	191	142	45	4	.743
Woody Hayes	Ohio State	26	235	174	54	8	.736
Paul Bryant	Alabama	27	292	210	67	15	.719
Charles McClendon	Louisiana St.	10	110	79	27	-4	.718
Ara Parseghian	Notre Dame	21	201	144	51	6	.716
John McKay	Southern Cal	12	123	88	29	6	.715
Bob Blackman	Illinois	23	218	155	55	8	.711
Frank Broyles	Arkansas	15	159	113	43	1	.711

Each one of these men has a record of winning better than 7 out of every 10 games and most indicators point to the fact that they'll all stay "up there" this time around with maybe only Blackman having a tough time of it. It's wise to study coaches' records, and then stick with the perennial winners.

Keep in mind that consistency is a key word in betting college games. If a club like Penn State is great one season you can bet it will be almost as good the next season. Therefore, it is wise to go with a winning team the following year because that team usually meets the same opponents the next time around. The turnover through graduation is seldom that great and through strong recruiting most of the better teams are able to attract top high school players.

Team Relations

There are other factors the college football bettor will have to contend with, factors he did not have ten years ago. The college kids today seem to be concerned more with taking over the campus than the goalpost. Upheavals, rather than touchdowns, must be considered today when handicapping a team. And that's not all.

The ugly specter of racial dissension is spreading from the campus to the teams and that's not healthy for the bettor. How can he ever be sure the black lineman will block for the white quarterback or that the white lineman will protect the black running back? Make no mistake, these things must be considered if your inclination is to bet the collegians.

With all these problems staring at them, the most confused people in the world will have to be the bookmakers. How will they rate the teams? What kind of pointspreads will they lay out? Temperament must be considered but is temperament worth a full point or a half-point? And what about harmony? Is Notre Dame worth 6 points over Texas on harmony? If you think silly things like harmony and temperament won't be considered by the pricemakers, then you deserve every losing bet you make.

College Football Trends

With college football wagering on the increase every year, persons who like to speculate on that type of activity will be interested to know that the rah-rah boys are actually outperforming the pros in the scoring department. According to the latest available statistics, often referred to as "trends," the nation's average college eleven is scoring 22 points per game, an increase of almost 6 points per contest in the past 12 years. This scoring is done on an average of 75 plays a game.

Against these figures, the pros are averaging about 19 points per game and only about 60 plays a game. So the play-for-pay boys are actually scoring 3 points a game less than the college teams. And, what is more significant, they run 15 plays per game less than the colleges. In other words, the college football fan gets more action for his dollar—considerably more—than the pro fan, and the colleges have the potential of racking up even more points this season.

Pass attempts per game have risen to well over 52 per tilt, yet the percentage of completions is up 4 percent. This is understandable as sharper passers and better receivers are coming out of the high schools every year. Running the ball accounts for 52 percent of all yardage gained. And with more running quarterbacks operating the now highly popular wishbone option series, we at *Sports Action* feel that this figure can only rise as times passes.

Another area in which the college football bettor requires up-to-date information is the comparative strength of teams from each area of the nation. In this department, we found that the powerful Big Eight Conference now ranks as tops in the nation, one point stronger than the Southeastern Conference, which had been number one for six consecutive years. These ratings are based on each loop's numerical power ratings, determined by averaging out the strength of all teams in every conference.

20 Strongest Conferences

1. Big Eight	111	11. Pacific Coast Athletic	85
2. Southeastern	110	12. Gulf States	78
3. Pacific Eight	107	13. Southland	76
4. Big Ten	104	14. Ohio Valley	73
5. Southwest	100	15. Lone Star	68
6. Mid-American	95	16. Big Sky	68
7. Western Athletic	94	17. Southwestern Athletic	65
8. Atlantic Coast	92	18. Southern	61
9. Ivy League	87	19. Yankee	53
10. Missouri Valley	86	20. North Central	50

The ratings reveal that an average Big Eight Conference team is considered to be 7 points stronger than an average Big Ten Conference eleven. This does not mean that in a game between, say, Oklahoma and Purdue, that the Sooners are an automatic 7-point choice. It does indicate, however, that if the game is rated a toss-up or one team is a very short favorite, the bettor who wagers on Oklahoma can be considered to have a "hidden" 7-point advantage in his favor prior to the opening kickoff.

Keep up to date with the trends in college football and you may be much farther ahead of the game at the end of the year when you take stock of your income and outgo for the season.

Checklist for College Football Bettors

Here is a brief checklist that college football bettors would do well to keep in mind all season:

1. Shop for as many outlets as possible. The official line is not the only line available to the bettor. Often bookmakers will raise or lower their lines to encourage or discourage betting on certain games.

2. Bet privately when you can, as you will have certain advantages when laying or giving odds.

3. Know your quarterbacks! As important, or more so, than knowing the pitchers in baseball, know every quarterback as well as possible.

4. Find the best possible outlets for scouting information available. And if it is at all possible, develop your own private sources of information. We understand, for example, that some fans have organized a co-op type of information exchange, with at least one member keeping close tabs on each team. You could join, or even start with your own scouting club.

5. Finally, if you have good scouting information, you won't have to match wits with the psychology expert. The "ups" and "downs" of teams will be a matter of record, rather than assumptions.

We feel it is important to elaborate a bit on point 1. If you could purchase a new car for $4,000 from dealer A and exactly the same car from dealer B for $3,800, would you make the deal with the latter? There isn't any question about it. All things being equal, $3,800 is a better price for the buyer than is $4,000. The average citizen wants to save himself money anytime he can and shops around for the best price, whether it be for that new car or a sirloin steak.

The only time a seller has a good chance of overcharging

the buyer is when the buyer doesn't have enough knowledge of the product to know actually what he is, or is not, getting. This problem hits the bettor every week, and he isn't even aware of it.

Regardless of what the line might be on a particular game in New York, there is a good chance it is different from the one being offered players in Chicago, or Detroit, or San Francisco. In fact there is a good chance the line is different in all four cities. The situation, however, gets even a little more basic than this. There are certain games in a single city which are offered at a dozen different prices by bookmakers. The variations are not necessarily small, either, as the line sometimes varies 2 or 3 points.

All of this leads us to note that you absolutely must shop around for the best price when you bet football. If you are to take an edge and protect yourself as a bettor, you need to have more than one accountant. And if you play the weekly football cards, you owe it to yourself to get them from five or six sources, for the prices on these cards vary drastically.

Matt Nevada, who has forgotten more about sports handicapping than most will ever know, points out that the 1973 Tennessee–Army game at West Point, New York, tells the shopping story clearly. The price was up and down all over the country. Note the variations:

City	Spread	City	Spread
New York	Tennessee −18	Kansas City	Tennessee −19
Boston	Tennessee −17	Memphis	Tennessee −21
Dallas	Tennessee −19	Houston	Tennessee −20
Los Angeles	Tennessee −19		

As is obvious, Tennessee was a heavy favorite in this game and the money poured in on the Volunteers to rout Army on that cool, overcast afternoon. Were the points important? Indeed they were. Tennessee won the game 37–18, which meant they were a 19-point winner. Those who bet on the Volunteers in New York and Boston and gave the 18 and 17 points, respectively, won. Those who wagered in Dallas, Los Angeles, and Kansas City tied, neither winning nor losing, while those who bet on Tennessee in Memphis and Houston lost.

We have a good friend who travels the country, hitting a different city every other day. He is a student of betting and keeps up-to-date on pointspreads in every city to which his job takes him. He also makes a fortune betting football and basketball by shopping around for the best line.

He and five of his traveling friends happen to live in six different cities. They get the lines in their respective cities and then get on the telephone and compare prices. If a team they like is offered at a better price in another city, they have their friend bet for them, or vice versa.

This friend happened to like Tennessee against Army and put all his action down in New York. But, had he liked Army, he would have bet the Cadets in Memphis with another friend and he would have won. These people shop around every weekend for the right price and it gives them tremendous edges in dealing with their bookmakers.

There are weekends in which they bet $1,000 on a particular game, $500 of it on each team. What they are doing is betting the game both ways at the best price, hoping the score falls within the varying spreads on which they are betting, permitting them to collect both ways. The worst they can do is be out $50, and they stand to win $1,000. What man wouldn't like to bet $1,000 on a game and actually risk only $50?

For instance, let us say they bet $500 on Tennessee, giving 17 points in New York, and then turned around and bet $500 on Army, taking 21 points in Memphis; they would have collected both ways. If they hit only one way, they would be out only the $50 vigorish they had to pay on the losing bet.

Football bettors should remain ever alert to these variations, which occur primarily on college games. Both professional football and basketball lines stay pretty much the same from coast to coast. The college line varies because of deep regional prejudices. In the case of the Tennessee game, most of the money would go in that direction. This situation occurs every weekend of the college season.

For instance, when Louisiana State and Alabama meet, or when Mississippi and Alabama get together, there will be a great variation in the line offered in the respective states. Bookmakers in Birmingham, Montgomery, and Mobile might make Alabama an 8-point favorite in hopes of stimulating some interest for LSU. Just the opposite would be true in

New Orleans and Baton Rouge. Bookmakers in those cities would make LSU as unattractive as possible. The more heated the rivalry, the greater the variation.

Be a smart bettor and become a good shopper. It would step up the player's winning percentage considerably if he would capitalize on those traps the bookmakers try to set for him.

Football Systems

As we said in Chapter 2, there are many systems for picking winners. While it would be impossible to mention all of them, here are two that are quite popular in college betting circles.

Pointspread System

Simply put, football is a game predicated on mathematics. The field is 100 yards long, no more, no less. To gain a first down, the ball must be advanced 10 yards. Here again, no variance exists. Six points are warded for a touchdown; three for a field goal; two for a safety; extra points are worth either one or two points. Using these figures as a basis, we would say that the pointspread can be beaten often enough, through the course of a season, to allow the average bettor to extract a profit—something that many fans are incapable of doing. A lot of fans subscribe to various services that offer worthless drivel disguised under the term "hot info." This inside information is available to the pricemakers and compensations have been made in the readjusted pointspreads.

Here's how one of the many methods operates. But it will be necessary to keep a list of the major college teams' scoring records. Concentrate on clubs that have played *at least* four games. Here's how the pointspread mechanism is determined.

1. Divide the number of games played into the total points scored by the club. Example: Team A has scored 137 points in 4 contests. Four into 137 is 34.3.

2. Divide team A's opponent's total points by the number of games that squad has played. Example: team B has scored 98 points in 5 games. Five into 98 equals 19.6.

3. Subtract from the higher club's average total the average total of the lesser club. In our example:

Team A	34.3
Team B	19.6
Difference	14.7

4. Your personal pointspread is determined by referring to the Bonus Points list.

Bonus Points	Bonus Points
0–5 = ½ point	25–26 = 7 points
6–9 = 1 point	27–32 = 8½ points
10–13 = 2½ points	33–37 = 10 points
14–16 = 3½ points	38–41 = 16 points
17–19 = 5 points	42 or more = 19½ points
20–24 = 6½ points	

Since team A has a per-game average of 14.7 points more than team B, team A is 3½ points better on average than team B. The home club is awarded an additional 3 bonus points. Let's assume that team A is the home club. Adding its home field advantage, its figure now stands at 6½.

5. To determine the pointspread, multiply this last figure by the club's winning percentage. If team A had a record of 2 wins and 1 loss, its winning percentage would be .666. Multiplying .666 by 6.5 we would come up with 4.329. After this figure is determined, divide it by two, then multiply by ten, for your personal pointspread. The answer in our example would be 21.64. In other words, using this mathematical method, team A should defeat team B by 22 points or more.

If the pointmakers' line lists team A as a 22-point favorite or less, team A would be a bet, for we have determined that the club should win by at least 23 points. If the pointmakers say that team A is more than a 23-point favorite to win, the underdog club, team B, would be bet.

As was stated earlier, this is one of many pointspread systems. However, it is one of the simplest, yet it should prove highly effective. If you have last year's results, a paper check should offer you some room for thought next time you consider making a football wager.

Two Touchdown Spot Method

Most college football bettors like to operate by using a simplified method of selection each weekend throughout the fall. A tried and true college grid betting angle which has been used successfully by big-time bettors down through the years is the Two Touchdown Spot Method.

The method performed up to its usual standards of approximately 75 percent winners in 1973, for example, with a total of 21 winners, 7 losers, and one betting standoff. We look for about the same results each season, so perhaps you might care to give it a whirl. Here is the way it works.

You carefully scan the college football betting lines just prior to the time you would normally send your action in. Whenever you find a team favored by 14, 14½, or 15 points (no more, no less), you place a bet on the choice. That's all there is to it! If you're seeking a lot of action each and every weekend, this angle is not for you, but if you're after three or four really solid wagering propositions every weekend for more substantial wagers, this angle should be right up your alley.

Over the course of the fall regular season, you should find about thirty to thirty-five playable games each year and, as we stated earlier, you should reasonably expect to win about 75 percent of your wagers. This has to place you in black ink if you regulate your wagers properly.

Right about now you're probably asking, "Where do they come up with these particular points—14, 14½, and 15—to wager on? Why not take favorites spotting only 2, 3, or 4 points? Wouldn't my chances of cashing in a bet be that much stronger?"

From the standpoint of the average bettor these questions seem extremely valid, but they can be quickly "shot down."

Sports statistics gathered over the years tend to show that bookies as a whole are overly optimistic about favorites in games that figure to be rugged, hard-fought affairs, while, on the other hand, they tend to be pessimistic about choices in games that really should be no-contest. It's been shown that underdogs being spotted anywhere up to 5 points are one of the finest bets on the gridiron, whereas teams that are chosen to win by the two-touchdown figure (plus a point in some cases) usually clear the points by 9 or more over and above the spot.

It's been learned through the years that as the season wears on, the number of games on which one can bet becomes less and less. The bookies start to wise up to the good and bad teams as far as realistic pointspreads are concerned, and stand-out teams start becoming 20-, 21-, and 22-point choices or are taken off the board completely, which signifies no betting action one way or the other.

As a general rule of thumb, we recommend that selections be played with a feeling of more security during September and October and that the size of your bets be reduced as soon as the November winds start to whistle through the leafless trees.

Football Handicapping Services

As football betting boomed, so did the number of handicapping services which offer to those willing to pay for them weekly selections of both college and professional games. There are over one hundred football services in the United States which send out a weekly publication in which games are analyzed and handicapped. Most of these sports analysts charge about $75 per season for their publications. Few of them are worth a dime. Then, there is a second group of handicapping concerns, all of which operate by telephone. We are going to discuss briefly three such services, Sports Sensational, Sports Life, and the Nevada Hotline. All three are telephone services, and all operate differently.

First of all, let's discuss the Nevada Hotline, which might be the most unusual of all sports services. The Nevada Hotline, which operates from New York, is the only service in the country which offers a money-back guarantee.

"It's the only way I'll operate," says its mastermind, Matt Nevada. "This business is full of swindlers and guys who don't know what they're doing. I tell all of my customers right from the start, they only pay for winners. If they don't do any good, I send their money back to them. Fortunately, I have done so well I don't have a half-dozen refunds a season, and those are guys who usually go for just one game to try me, lose, and ask for a refund.

"Most of my customers have been with me for several years, and most of them do very well. The guy who loses money with my selections is a bad bettor, because I do pick winners, and lots of them. So far into the 1973 season, five of my six college selections have won. In the pros I'm four out of six."

Nevada says he is strictly a "best bet" service. He picks his best bet in the colleges each week and his best bet in the pros, which means the most games you can get from him each week is two. He operates the same way in college basketball. Because of his high win percentage and his great following, Nevada gets a high price for his games. A single game cost $50 in 1973. However, he did give the players a break if they paid for more than one game at a time. For instance, he sold 5 games for $200, 15 for $500, and the entire season for $750.

Sports Life also is a telephone handicapping service. It picks both college and professional football, charging $50 per week or $150 per month, for its services. This very reputable firm also operates out of New York.

Sports Sensational is also a bit unusual in that it charges $25 for each winner that it gives out, but you don't have to pay until the game wins for you. Its operators say an unusually high percentage of those who call for its weekly selections pay, which goes to show there is a bit of honor among gamblers.

All of the above-mentioned services are full-time sports operations. They work at both football and basketball on a full-time basis, which is uncommon. Most sports-handicapping services are run by individuals who are doing so as a sideline to their regular occupations. Many business and professional people are in the handicapping business throughout the land. Unfortunately, we, and most bettors, don't know who they are. Before casting your bankroll and fate to any handicapping service, you owe it to yourself to determine whether its operators have any credentials or are just taking your money, hoping to get lucky. Unless you're with a pro, you're better off on your own.

A new element to betting football was introduced to the public in 1973 in the form of a gadget known as the Las Vegas Football Betting Calculator. The calculator, which sells for $25 and is available from the K2 Publishing Corp., 475 Northern Boulevard, Great Neck, New York 11021, was three years in research and development and, as stunning as it sounds, has picked over 80 percent winners over four years. The calculator is based on a theory of mathematical logic and is easy to use. We have examined it and feel it is better designed for college football than the pros, but it does work equally well for both. However, it would not turn up more than eight or nine pro bets during the entire season. It comes up with five to ten during each week of the college season.

After you have fed basic information into the calculator, it will tell you whether a given game is a "bet" or a "no bet" contest. The calculator, in simplified form, is designed to exploit the overpowering advantage of a team which is winning when it plays a team which is stumbling and struggling. For a team to qualify for play on the calculator, it must have won four or more consecutive games and be meeting a team which has lost two in a row or two of its last three. There are other rules used with the calculator but the above-stated are the basic ones. The calculator also has rated every college and pro football field in the country as to its point advantage to the home team. For the player looking for limited action, the calculator is a valuable aid in handicapping.

Football Betting Cards

The football betting card is a multimillion-dollar American institution that sweeps the factories, offices, and campuses of the nation each fall, as its users once again dream of instant wealth via some "easy" picks. The harmless-looking piece of paper, generally run off by back-alley printers, contains a list of teams and homemade pointspreads. It snares, but mostly disappoints its users. For anything from a dollar up a person can participate in this "cheap" racket every weekend.

In spite of the fact that the football parlay cards ("pools" as they have come to be known) are, perhaps, one of the worst bets one can find anywhere, they are extremely popular in the United States and their purveyors do a land-office business. All one has to do to realize that these cards are one of the worst gambles a sports bettor can possibly get is to note the odds on them. They are not even remotely near what they should be. These cards come in, literally, hundreds of shapes, colors, and sizes but the odds payoffs are basically the same on them all.

In addition to the odds payoff being so far out of line, there are other tremendous disadvantages to the bettor who risks his money on this type of wager. For example, on the football cards, all ties lose, which, of course, means that if you pick five teams and four of them win (by the point-spread) and one ends up in a tie, you collect nothing. With a bookmaker, all bets are off in the case of a tie. On the football cards, you will find that the pointspread much more often than not is completely out of line with the line being quoted by the books. This gives the pool operator another large advantage. All things considered, the football pool is something that everyone—no matter how experienced a bettor he is—should stay away from.

Undoubtedly, the huge popularity enjoyed by the pool is brought about by its simplicity. It is easy to buy and just as easy to play. The bettor doesn't even have to fill in the names of the teams he selects. All he need do is circle his selections. In most cases, the middleman in the operation, the seller, receives about 25% commission on the cards he distributes, which is another indication of how profitable this business is. Without question, parlay cards are a business of tremendous magnitude, and with their enormous popularity, the difficulty in winning, and the unreasonable payoffs to those few lucky individuals who do manage to win, the percentage of profit is astronomical.

The initial boom in football pool cards, as previously stated, started in the twenties and it swelled during the World War II years. Although proportionately less popular now, the cards still touch millions of lives and account for the exchange of up to $50 million a week.

Today, on most cards the lowest bet consists of picking three teams. For that feat the winning bettor will receive $5 for every dollar bet, or a supposed 5 to 1 payoff (really 4 to 1). The actual odds are 7 to 1 that you don't pick three teams. (And as all ties lose, the house has almost an extra 30 percent in its favor over the course of the fall.)

When the bet is on ten teams, the winning customer stands to pick up $200 for every dollar placed. However, the real odds are in excess of 1,000 to 1. Of course, the operator can get in a bad bind when a late-week shift in odds draws the high rollers in for heavy action. For instance, if Notre Dame's star quarterback's ankle should snap in a Thursday practice and the Irish suddenly lose 6 points on the spread, then the "smart money" comes cascading into the card operator. As his cards are printed on Monday and he must hold to those odds, he can sometimes take a real clobbering ... but don't count on it.

The early-season games are also a bit hairy for the operator as he has little more than pre-season publicity handouts, coaches' quotes, and perhaps some inside information to rely on for odds. Consequently, cards aren't put on the market until the second game of the season in some areas of the country. Despite occasional big payoffs to sharp customers, card operators continue to prosper. And despite the short odds, card players continue to play.

For those not too familiar with them, let's take a minute and explain how the football card is set up. The typical card consists of twenty-six college and/or professional football games scheduled to be played on a particular weekend. The favorite is listed first while the underdog appears on the opposite side of the card along with the pointspread. For instance, the two top lines on the card might look like this:

1. Ohio State vs. 27. Pittsburgh plus 19

If you were interested in this game, and you especially liked Ohio State's chances, you would put a circle around "1" on your portion of the card and, likewise, circle "1" on your portion of the card and, likewise, circle "1" on the tearoff portion of the card which is given to the man who's supplying your action. If you liked Pittsburgh with the 19 points, you'd circle "27" in both places on the card, etc.

The typical card gives you nine options of play. You may select three games out of three for a payoff of 5 to 1; four out of four for 10 to 1 odds, and so on up to 10 out of 10

Football Cards Odds

No. of Winners Selected	Payoff Odds	Mathematical Odds	Operator's Take-out
3 out of 3	5 to 1	7 to 1	37½%
4 out of 4	10 to 1	15 to 1	37½%
5 out of 5	16 to 1	31 to 1	50%
6 out of 6	30 to 1	63 to 1.	53%
7 out of 7	50 to 1	127 to 1	69%
8 out of 8	75 to 1	255 to 1	71%
9 out of 9	100 to 1	511 to 1	80%
10 out of 10	200 to 1	1023 to 1	80%
9 out of 10	30 to 1	101 to 1	71%

for 200 to 1 odds. Some "super-duper" cards also feature a 20 out of 20 deal where the winner (and we use that term advisedly) collects 500 to 1. In almost every case, however, all ties, as already noted, cancel any card, thereby giving the operator a clean sweep.

One may make as many selections as he or she desires, but remember that the more winners you try to pick, the greater your chances of losing. A person with a rudimentary knowledge of math need only glance at the table entitled Football Card Odds to see how great the operator's margin of profit really is.

Obviously, the player's best chance of winning is to pick three out of three and to settle for the 5 to 1 payoff. Mathematically true odds are 7 to 1, and even if you "hit," you really collect only 4 to 1 as $1 of the payoff was yours to begin with. In the three-for-three selection category as well as the four-out-of-four area, the operator's overall margin of profit is a beautiful 37½ percent. However, this is the lowest margin on the entire card and the player's only realistic area for cashing bets. But why should the player risk his dough picking four teams when he can pick three and just make a heavier wager?

"True," you might say in thinking this over, "but picking four out of four will give me a payroll of 10 to 1, or double that of picking three out of three. For only one more game it's well worth the wager."

It seems like a valid argument on your part, but we'll prove you wrong. Remember that we told you the *true*, or mathematical, odds for picking three out of three were 7 to 1, but that you were being cheated out of $3 on the winning payoff? Well, the true odds of selecting four winners out of the same number of picks are 15 to 1, or more than double that of picking three. And the 10 to 1 payoff (in reality only 9 to 1) is costing you $6, although the operator's overall profit margin remains stationary at 37½ percent.

When a player attempts to pick five winners for a 16 to 1 payoff, the real odds against him are 31 to 1 and the operator's take jumps all the way up to 50 percent on every dollar wagered. And so it goes up the scale.

The folly of attempting to pick ten out of ten winners is evidenced by the fact that even if you perform this feat you'll be rewarded with only $200 for your original ace, while in reality, the odds are 1,023 to 1 against you right from the second you start drawing those little circles on your card. It's in the nine of nine and ten out of ten categories that the operators enjoy their greatest profit margin—80 percent of all the intake.

As the cards are strictly a seasonal operation, the law enforcement agencies rarely conduct serious hunts for card people. As with most good things, the syndicate is in the card business, so you know that it has to be a moneymaking deal ... for the house!

If, despite the overwhelming odds we have pointed out, you still want to invest a couple of bucks each week there are a few simple guidelines we offer.

First, and foremost, just concentrate on the three strongest bets you can find and put down what you can afford on them. Don't start shooting for the moon with giant parlays. The price you're taking on these three picks is short enough without cheating yourself any further.

As to your selections: We can't tell you whom to bet but there is one type of club that has fared well over the years. This is the team that is a heavy favorite—two touchdowns or more. Usually, the higher the spread, the more likely the favorite covers. Don't be enticed by a pile of points. Stick to the top-heavy choices.

A final note: *don't bet early*. Take your time. The sheets come out in the early part of the week and there is still time for things to develop that can affect the outcome of a game. An injury, as we stated earlier, may be revealed later in the week or some other information may become known, Dissension, weather changes, anything can pop up. Check to see if the pointspread later in the week differs sharply from the price line on your sheet. You might have an overlay on your hands because some fact wasn't known early enough to fit into the early price. So, stick to your top three. If you get lucky, and we do mean lucky, you'll be paid off at 4 to 1 odds plus your dollar back. It seems pretty easy pickings, but take it from us—it's not!!

One-hundred-Square Sheets

An even worse sucker bet than the football card is the 100-square sheet which floats around the offices, factories, and campuses each week. In this gimmick you give the person conducting it a buck and scribble your name into one of the 100 open blocks. When all the blocks are filled in, numbers 1 through 10 are drawn twice and assigned in the order drawn around the edges of the sheet for both teams, giving you a final projected score of, say, 2 to 7. This means that team A (2) must score 2, 12, 22, 32, etc., points while team B (7) must wind up with 7, 17, 27, etc., for you to win the $100 prize. The odds are 99 to 1 against you right from the start, plus the fact that if you draw relatively "odd" final football score numbers such as 2, 5, 8, and 9, your chances of scoring are, theoretically, even smaller.

6-Point Bet

Stealing a page from the nation's racetracks, which are ever on the lookout for various new wagering schemes to separate the player from his hard-earned dough, quite a few bookmakers, most of them in the East, have fashioned a new betting scheme aimed at emptying the pockets of inveterate gridiron gamblers.

The bookies, in hopes of acquiring still larger profits, have come up with the betting plan used on college and pro football selections. The crux of the plan surrounds the deployment of two-team parlays. That is, the friendly bookies offer you an opportunity to lay a 6 to 5 line and select any two teams for parlay action. But here's the hooker: the player can adjust the pointspread line on both games by 6 points, in any direction he wishes.

For example, let's assume that Auburn is a 6-point underdog against Alabama, and Northwestern is favored by 15 points over Indiana. If the unwary bettor wishes, he can adjust the potential parlay to suit his particular fancy. He could make the Auburn–Alabama encounter a pick and select the favored Crimson Tide team, or, if he wishes, he could add an additional 6 points to Auburn's spread and make the Plainsmen a 12-point underdog. In this case, the underdog Auburn would appear to be a more attractive proposition, and it does look attractive, doesn't it?

In the Indiana–Northwestern battle, the player again holds the options. He could add another 6 points to Indiana's spot, thereby making the Hoosiers some 21-point underdogs. If he wishes, he could lop 6 full points off the spread, reducing Northwestern's spot to 9 points and swing along with the Wildcats.

The plan was inaugurated in the middle of the 1972 season and met with widespread acceptance. The suckers seem to feel the bookies have declared every day Christmas. Nothing could be more removed from the truth. Given enough plays, the method must eventually *break you*. Here's why.

For one thing, the books have increased their vigorish from an already favorable 5½ to 5 to a loftier 6 to 5 price line. Your initial investment must be necessarily larger and your losing potential is increased. Snared by the attractiveness of the plan, the bettor rushes full-steam ahead, only too happy to give the book an additional half-dollar.

Now for the clincher. The eventual payoff (if you win, that is) does not come at parlay odds, but merely even money. Not only is your original bet increased along with a larger vigorish edge to the book, the eventual payoff is incorrect. No parlay-type payoff exists. The book will insist that this must be so to overcome the "advantage" you have with your adjustments of the point. Sorry—you do not get paid off at a parlay rate.

If you're lucky enough to win at all, expect to receive $5 for every $6 you've invested. Pretty thin soup, don't you agree? No one—repeat, no one—can stand that type of breakage without eventually going broke. The best football handicapper in the country will see his profits reduced by the initial increased outlay. A serious losing streak will eventually spell his doom.

Analyzing the method, it's obvious that the bookies, looking for even more powerful methods of ensnaring the bettor, concentrated on the often fascinating pointspread aspect. This unnerving creature is a fascinating thing to watch. Football bettors are sensitive to every change, minor or major, in the weekly pointspread line. If a game opens at 3 points favoring a particular club and suddenly blossoms to 5 points, the bettors immediately go on the alert.

The game, in the minds of many, becomes suspect. We know of many bettors, several of the high-roller variety, who do nothing more in the way of football handicapping than bet the weekly "moves" of the pointspread. If a bookmaker offers you an opportunity to test the method, do not be misled. Avoid the plan and immediately label the purveyor as suspect. The book knows well that the method cannot be beaten. His suggestion that you try the method is an open invitation to drink financial arsenic. His suggestion can be construed as an outright and outrageous statement of distrust. It's as if he said, "Look, I know you can't beat me, but I'm going to make it even tougher for you."

We realize that the dissemination of this information will alert our many thousands of readers to the foolishness and perils of the plan. We hope the method will die. The plan may meet with acceptance by the less sophisticated wagerer, but his fate has been decided long ago. This type, doomed to failure at the start, doesn't have enough sense to seek out professional advice when it comes to wagering. This type has an almost masochistic desire to lose. His gambling "death wish" will certainly be granted. Thus, to summarize: stay away from the 6-point "sucker" bet!

Chapter 4

Betting on Basketball

There are dozens of differences between betting football and wagering on basketball games, the most basic of which is the amount of money an individual might be able to get down on a game. In football it is possible to bet hundreds of thousands of dollars on a game, if you have the bankroll, but it is difficult to find a bookmaker anywhere in the country who lets anyone other than his best year-round clients bet more than $200 to $300 on a single basketball game.

With the exception of bookmakers in areas such as Kentucky, Indiana, Ohio, and Chicago where basketball is *the* betting sport, those who accept wagers on the cage game are nervous about it. To them, basketball is a game of hidden information, which spells nothing but trouble for them. In the states just mentioned, basketball betting is such big business that bookmakers make it a point to know what is going on. They will take almost limitless action on area teams such as Louisville, Kentucky, Indiana, Purdue, Notre Dame, Loyola, Marquette, Michigan, and Bradley. They also let bettors go all out on games between other major colleges, but are not reluctant to take games off the board quickly if the action gets too heavy on one team or the other. They limit action on minor games, such as those between schools such as Western Kentucky and La Salle, because they do not take the time to really be up to date on them.

The dilemma of the bookmaker also is the dilemma of the basketball bettor. In football, bookmaker and bettor alike have a vast reservoir of information from which to draw. In basketball they have almost nothing, except the opinion of the linemaker, who has the impossible job of handicapping dozens of games seven days a week. They know he can't be right all the time.

Both professional and college football are covered more closely than the White House. Nothing can escape the nose of

the news media in football, whether it be the fact that someone's wife has the measles or that an individual just purchased a new car. The reporters keep the public informed as
to injuries, team morale, changes in the lineup, and myriad
other things which will affect the outcome of a game. Television has made football the nation's number one betting sport.
The public is interested in everything that happens to college
and professional football teams and the media supplies this in
abundance.

Basketball doesn't receive this kind of exposure on each individual game for two basic reasons: (1) there are fewer
than 100 college football teams on which bookmakers will
take bets, while the figure for basketball is over twice this
number; and (2) these same college football teams play an
average of 10 or 11 games per season, while each college basketball team competes in 22 to 25 games per season.

The pure figures of this situation mean that, not counting
professional teams, which are much easier for a linemaker to
handicap, the man who makes the pointspread for football
deals with approximately 600 games per season, and this figure is probably high. With basketball, he must make a line on
roughly 4,000 games per season. He can take an additional
edge with college football teams because the teams on which
he makes a line usually are competing against one another. In
basketball, they might be, or again they might not be. If one
reviews the South Carolina football schedule for 1973, we see
the school played such recognized betting teams as Georgia
Tech, Houston, Wake Forest, Louisiana State, North Carolina State, Florida State, and Clemson. Also on the schedule
were Miami of Ohio, Ohio University, and Applachian
State. The linemaker made a pointspread on the first seven
games, but did not make one on Miami of Ohio, Ohio University, or Appalachian State.

But when basketball season comes, he is confronted with
the problem of deciding whether to make a line on eight or
nine games in which any major school such as South Carolina competes. Many schools which do not have major status
as football schools have a name as basketball schools. The
number of teams that could be put on the board on any given
night taxes the decision-making capacities of anyone in the
business. For instance, on Saturday, January 27, 1973, there
were approximately eight major college basketball games on

the schedule. There was a line, nationwide, on fewer than half of them. Games involving California schools, for instance, were on the board in California but not in the East, and vice versa.

The linemaker had 20 to 25 bluechip games on which to make a line and at least 50 which had to make him nervous. In the latter category were games such as Kent State and Miami of Ohio, Seton Hall and Georgetown, Fordham and Rhode Island, Temple and Holy Cross, Syracuse and Massachusetts, Western Kentucky and Murray State, St. Louis and West Texas State, New Mexico State and Memphis State. We single out these teams because all, with the exception of Massachusetts, Rhode Island, and West Texas State, are major basketball powers. A line was issued on about half the games mentioned here and bettors were unable to get down on the rest.

The point we are trying to emphasize is simply this: the volume of basketball games among college teams is so great that the quality of the line is suspect, and this is no fault of anyone. Because the line is suspect, bookmakers have been knocked out of action and been forced to sell houses, cars, and legitimate businesses to pay off when a sharp bettor saw a hole in the line and backed his opinion with thousands of dollars. There is an old saying in betting circles that a dumb bookmaker is not a dumb bookmaker very long. He will be out of business so fast that the only thing he will have left is his reputation for stupidity, but a bookmaker he will be no longer. Any bookmaker who stays in business longer than a week has to be smart. The hustlers and sharpies are up every night dreaming of ways to beat the man on the corner, but they seldom succeed. However, there are occasions on which you can beat your bookmaker by just being alert and taking advantage of any mistakes he might make. For instance, for the weekend of January 6–7, a few years ago, a basketball card (basketball cards operate in the same manner and pay the same as football cards [see page 91] and should be avoided by the wise bettor for the same reasons) that came out in New York had a big mistake on it and permitted basketball bettors who work at the art to take advantage of a favorable betting situation. The card read:

Iowa State (H)   Wisconsin+2

While Iowa State was playing at home, it was playing Wisconsin State, a teacher's college in Oshkosh, Wisconsin, not the University of Wisconsin. This mistake gave the alert bettors a chance to take an edge right there. In some spots around New York, bookmakers were taking single action on the game as if Iowa State were hosting Wisconsin. Needless to say, they got knocked out of the box.

The players who used the cards each week had an automatic, bonus winner going in. There was absolutely no chance in the world that Wisconsin State (Oshkosh) was going to be close to Iowa State at the finish, even if the cheerleaders did the playing. The final score in that game was Iowa State 92, Wisconsin State (Oshkosh) 67. What a bargain. The mistake woke the bookmakers up to the fact that they had to pay more attention to what was going on in the world. It was tough for them to admit they had beaten themselves in this game.

There is a move afoot among gambling interests in the United States to find good regional linemakers in hopes of upgrading the quality of the pointspread. However, how do you find a "good" regional linemaker? There are no schools for them and most of the good linemakers prefer to remain in hiding, betting into the bad line and picking up the easy money.

The most famous basketball handicapper in the United States is a man who operates under the name of Matt Nevada. He claims to have broken more basketball bookmakers in this country than all other individuals combined. Many bookmakers have befriended him, letting him bet limited amounts of money with them and then taking the particular game he likes off the board immediately. "I started betting basketball in Stillwater, Oklahoma, back in the glory days of Hank Iba," Nevada said. "And, I've never worked a day since then. I just sit back and wait for the line to come out each day, look for a spot and bet, if I can find a hole in it. If not, I just wait until tomorrow, 'cause I know the man is going to make a mistake sooner or later."

Nevada has spent his adult life traveling the country studying college basketball. He claims to have been in the gymnasiums and playing arenas of over a hundred teams. He believes he knows more about the game than anyone else because he has made it a point to know how easy, or tough, it is to win in these coliseums. "Few years back, Mississippi

State and Bradley were the toughest places in the country for a visiting team to win," Nevada said. "But things are changing, with new gyms being built and the crowds being placed farther from the playing floor."

Nevada isn't convinced that the home court, per se, is the secret key to winning and losing bets on college basketball games. To him, it's a matter of knowing when to give the points on a team playing at home and when to take them. "To say the home court is the only thing that counts is foolish, because the points will, over the long run, neutralize playing at home," Nevada said. "Beating basketball is knowing when and where to bet, and when and where not to bet. I'm not going into a lot of detail because this is my game. I can't give away any secrets of the trade, but I can share one fundamental thought, which I use as the cardinal rule of all my basketball betting: *Never, under any circumstances, give points on any college basketball team which is on the road.*"

Nevada continued, "You are asking for trouble anytime you give the points on a team which is on the road. I've got records twenty years old which back up this contention. You'll pass up a few winners by not laying points on a road team, but not many. Pass *any* game in which you have to give points on a road team. You take points on the road—you don't give them."

While we have been speaking, generally, about college basketball teams, the pros of the National Basketball Association receive a high volume of coverage, but it still does not compare with the space and attention given professional football. Every team in the NBA is given excellent coverage in its own hometown, but fans in Chicago, for instance, have a difficult time staying abreast of the condition of teams from faraway places such as Seattle and Portland. The problem is magnified even more for the bettor in a place such as Wichita, Kansas, which is far removed from pro basketball. Regardless of his interest in the NBA, it is possible that his bookmaker will not accept any action on these games.

The corner bookmaker in many parts of the country restricts his action to either college basketball or pros, but not both. He figures it is impossible for him to stay atop the happenings in two worlds in which there is action almost every night. There are even some places in the United States where bookmakers are so nervous about basketball action that they will not let the bettor place a wager on a single game. He must bet on at least three, and win them all to collect. In betting situations like this, the bettor will have to give or take the points on each of three teams and then win all three to collect. For instance, let's say the bettor likes Providence over St. John's. Providence is a 5-point favorite, so he has 5 points riding for him in this game. Then, he selects Maryland over North Carolina and has to give 3 points. His final selection is Vanderbilt over Kentucky, and again he gets 3 points. He wins the Providence game outright, watches Maryland beat North Carolina by the spread, and then loses everything for the night when Vanderbilt fails to cover. Needless to say, the man was bucking great odds in trying to come up with three winners to collect a bet. The bettor is his own man and can do what he likes, but if his bookmaker insists he bet in this manner, he should drop him and find one who will give him a fair shake. If he can't find one, then he should take up golf or pool until he does.

One bets basketball in exactly the same manner as football. Most bookmakers will not take less than a $5 bet on a basketball game, and many will make you bet at least $25. However, as we have said before, big money is out of the question most of the time. You will be laying 6 to 5 or 11 to 10, just as you do in football. This means simply that if you lay $6 to $5, you owe your bookmaker $6 if you lose and win $5 if you beat him. By the same token, if his services are priced at $11 to $10 you get a much better break. If you lose you owe him $11 for each $10 you bet (on a $100 bet this would mean you owe $110), while he pays you even money, $10 for each $10 you bet, when you win.

With Matt Nevada's advice soundly written on our minds, it is important now that we begin to establish a foundation on which to bet basketball, both college and pro.

The Basketball Coach

To begin with, there is no sport in which the coach is more important than in college basketball. We say college basketball, specifically, because he is of much less importance in the National Basketball Association and the American Basketball Association. In the pros, one is dealing with superstars and accomplished players who already know the game and, by their very nature, work hard to improve it. In college, you have young men who are still learning, walking the fine line between being ordinary and being great. The good coaches make the ordinary great, while the bad ones can turn a great basketball player into a mediocre one.

In college basketball, the history of all winning teams is the history of a winning coach. It is important for basketball bettors to understand there are only about twenty-five outstanding college coaches in the game today. The rest are of varying degrees of average, but none of them have the consistent winning records which tell us they get the money, regardless of the handicaps. They don't make excuses. They just win.

As an example of this, consider Ray Mears of Tennessee. Mears built little Wittenberg into a small-college basketball power and then headed south to break Adolph Rupp's stronghold on the Southeastern Conference. Rupp had the championship reserved for his Kentucky Wildcats almost every year until Mears arrived. With good coaching, Mears built the Volunteers into one of the most powerful basketball teams in the country. He is a winner, period, whether it be at Wittenberg, Tennessee, or wherever life carries him. For the record, Mears has been coaching seventeen years and has compiled a record of 321 wins and only 106 losses. In nine of those years (three at Wittenberg and six at Tennessee) his teams won at least 20 games. In three other years, they just missed, winning 19.

We could say the same thing for Ralph Miller, now head basketball coach at Oregon State. Miller spent thirteen years at Wichita State, competing successfully with the great St. Louis, Cincinnati, Bradley, Drake, and Oklahoma State teams. He then went to Iowa, rebuilding the down-and-out Hawkeyes into another national power, winning Big Ten championships with them in 1968 and 1970. He also turned around a faltering basketball program at Oregon State. Because he is in the same conference with another great coach, John Wooden of UCLA, he has been hidden a bit, but he is still winning.

There are about two dozen other basketball coaches like this, and all of them are a bettor's dream. They beat the spread in almost every big game they play, either as underdog or favorite. By a *big* game, we mean one in which something such as a conference title or a tournament berth is at stake. They are the money coaches on which the bettor can count when the going gets a little rough.

The importance of the coach in college basketball is not

obvious to most. The public knows that some teams win, while others don't. They blame it all on a coach's inability to recruit good players. However, there is much more to it than this. Almost all coaches recruit outstanding players. They just don't know what to do with them once they get them. The players have reached a certain point in their athletic development when they arrive at college and it is up to the coach to carry them a little farther. If he doesn't have the ability to improve on a player's high school game, the competition will soon destroy him.

Coaches like Mears, Miller, Wooden, Gene Bartow of Illinois, Joe Williams of Furman, Chuck Daly of Pennsylvania, Norman Sloan of North Carolina State, Jack Hartman of Kansas State, C. M. Newton of Alabama, Roy Skinner of Vanderbilt, Bob Knight of Indiana, and David Gavitt of Providence have a talent for motivating people and then teaching them how best to utilize their physical and mental assets. In short, they bring out the best natural ability in their players and then add to it. They teach a man who can jump two feet off the floor to jump two feet and one inch. They take a player who can play full-speed for thirty minutes and discipline his mind to give its best for thirty-one minutes. They teach players timing, which is so important. They teach players to develop a new shot every season, knowing that the defense of last year will be ready to stop last year's offense. They do everything that gives every player that special edge.

Miller, for instance, has been known to recruit giants right off the nation's playgrounds and turn them into basketball players. In his opinion—and he has proven it—any tall player (6-foot-8 and over) can be taught two things which will make him an asset to any college team in the country: to jump and to play defense. Miller recruited a young lad named Gene Wiley and turned him into one of the great defensive centers of college basketball.

Wiley later played with the Los Angeles Lakers and spent his entire pro career as a defensive specialist and mortal enemy of Wilt Chamberlain (before he himself became a Laker). Chamberlain once became so frustrated at Wiley's defensive play that he stormed off the floor and refused to play the last quarter of a game. Wiley had no special talents except height and defense, but he contributed greatly to any team for which he played.

The case of C. M. Newton also tells us what an outstanding basketball coach can do. Newton, who was a member of the University of Kentucky basketball team which won the National Collegiate Athletic Association championship in 1951, was hired from a little college in Kentucky—Transylvania—to try to build a basketball winner at Alabama. One must understand that football was the only thing which counted in Tuscaloosa until Newton came along. Basketball was tolerated as a necessary evil, but treated as an orphan of the athletic program. The team played to as many empty seats during actual games as it did during practice.

Newton spent twelve years at Transylvania College and rolled up a 169–138 record, despite the fact that he was permitted few scholarships. In his first year at Alabama he saw his team go 4–20. But let's watch what followed: in the following years, he was 8–18, 10–16, 18–8, and in 1972–73 arrived with a 22–8 record and a trip to the National Invitational Tournament in New York.

What we are trying to say here is that the college basketball bettor must make an effort to find out just which college basketball coaches know what they are doing and which ones don't. While it is difficult to single out many coaches without leaving out some who also deserve to be on the list, the bettor can stick with the following winning coaches with confidence, knowing they win the *big* games and beat the spread in the tight ones. If any of them ever entered in a game in which his team was rated even with the opponents, we would have to give him the edge.

Here is a list of college basketball coaches who consistently come up with winners:

Jack Craft	Villanova	Ralph Miller	Oregon State
Denny Crum	Louisville	Bill Musselman	Minnesota
Don Devoe	Virginia Tech	Gerald Myers	Texas Tech
Lefty Driesell	Maryland	C. M. Newton	Alabama
Norman Ellen-		John Oldham	Western Kentucky
berger	New Mexico	Roy Skinner	Vanderbilt
Bob Gaillard	San Francisco	Norman Sloan	North Carolina
David Gavitt	Providence		State
Jack Hartman	Kansas State	Dean Smith	North Carolina
Don Haskins	Texas–El Paso	Carroll Williams	Santa Clara
Bob Knight	Indiana	Joe Williams	Furman
Frank McGuire	South Carolina	John Wooden	UCLA
Ray Mears	Tennessee		

Home Court Advantage

Is the home court advantage in college basketball a reality or a myth? If it exists, what can be done to offset it? Let's hear what a few of the nation's finest basketball coaches have to say about this:

John Wooden, UCLA: "The home court provides a definite advantage because the players are more familiar with the lighting, the floor, the background, and the baskets. Furthermore, they are not in unfamiliar surroundings as far as their sleeping and eating are concerned and they are accustomed to the routine. Then, of course, is the fact that the home crowd can inspire them and occasionally may subconsciously affect the officiating.

"However, many coaches make playing on the road even more difficult because they place fear in the minds of the players by talking about how tough it is going to be and 'crying wolf' when there is no wolf there. I believe in taking a positive attitude and continually impressing my players that all they need to do is to play their game without worrying about what could happen or making any excuses. Do not be defeated because worry prevents you from playing your game. Over 99 percent of all games are won because one team plays better than the other at that paricular time and that is as it should be. You may be surprised to learn that in the last ten years many teams have a home record equal or near equal to that of UCLA."

Jack Hartman, Kansas State: "The important factors connected with a home court advantage are: (1) enjoying the support of the home crowd, (2) playing in familiar physical surroundings, and (3) eating and sleeping under normal conditions and not having to travel.

"When on the road, we attempt to maintain as close to a normal daily routine for our players as they would have at home. I also feel that it is extremely important in offsetting a home court advantage on the road that your game be based on strong organization, discipline, and confidence. Another most important item in creating consistency, both on the road and at home, is to establish a strong defense as a foundation to your basketball team. Offensive output and efficiency will vary from night to night and from one condition to the next, but good defensive basketball can and should be consistent."

Ray Mears, Tennessee: "First, the advantage of the home court depends on the closeness of the crowd, particularly the student body. To win consistently on the road a team must be mentally tough. Experience and poise are the key ingredients to this mental toughness. We attempt to follow the same practice and day-of-game routine on the road that we do at home. Additionally, for the past few years, we have played three or four game-type scrimmages around the state at different high school and city basketball arenas. Because the crowds at these sites are friendly crowds, the team does not experience the on-the-road crowd, but it does get somewhat accustomed to playing in an unfamiliar arena."

Bob Knight, Indiana: "I feel that because of the new arenas that have been built on campuses throughout the country, the so-called home court advantage has been reduced in the last few years. In addition to this, I think officiating is much better because of performance and conference office selections from which they are assigned. We try to talk to our players about simply playing basketball whether on the road or at home. I think it is important to minimize their thinking in regard to a potential difference in playing on the road as opposed to playing on the home court."

Norman Sloan, North Carolina State: "I have always felt that home court advantage lay primarily in the inspiration the home crowd gave the visiting team. I do not believe the home crowd has a negative effect on the visiting team. As a matter of fact, a capacity, enthusiastic crowd, even though they could be one hundred percent for the home team, will inspire the visiting team. My primary concern in playing on the road is to remain active and avoid too much food and too much sleep. The biggest problem with away games is interruption of daily routine. If we can arrive by noon of the day of the game and avoid an overnight stay away from home, we will do so."

A five-year study of the home court advantage shows there is a direct correlation between beating the spread on the road and experience. By this we simply mean that teams made up of players who have had a year or two of varsity play under their belts perform much more coolly on the road than do those made up primarily of sophomores and freshmen. The upperclassmen have been there before, so to speak. They have heard the hostile roar of the crowd, experienced the bad lighting, learned to cope with the hazards and inconveniences of travel, including things as minor (although they actually are major) as bad water and tasteless food.

It is impossible to draw any specific conclusions that experience makes a team win any more games outright, although it probably does. However, there is no doubt that a veteran team beats the spread on the road more than an inexperienced team.

It would be impossible for the basketball bettor to get an age breakdown on 250 major college teams each season, but he certainly should be able to get a breakdown on teams on which he regularly bets. Information is available from almost every college publicity office in the country, if you'll shell out a dollar or two for it. During the season, journalists and commentators will stun you with statistical information about your favorite basketball teams. There is no reason to be overwhelmed. This same information is available to you in booklet form if you will but order it from the publicity offices of the universities and colleges in which you are interested. It normally costs between $1 and $2. The press booklet will give you a person-by-person, position-by-position breakdown on the team, plus additional data about some of its opponents.

If you are interested in a particular conference, it would be possible to get these press booklets from each school in it. For instance, those who bet the Atlantic Coast Conference, which from top to bottom probably is the best cage conference in the country, can purchase the brochures from almost all those schools. By doing a little reading you can determine the age and experience factors, plus other pieces of information which might help you.

There are several good basketball magazines which come on the market each year which also will give you insight into a team's potential. The finest of these is Street & Smith's college basketball annual. While it has its shortcomings, it is by far the best basketball publication on the market. At worst, it will give you a brief capsule rundown of every major college basketball team in the country and its potential for the season. The only thing to keep in mind when reading magazines such as Street & Smith is that most of the information printed on their pages is supplied by sports information offices at each of the schools and we've yet to see a press release from anyone which predicted anything less than a banner year for his team. But, even considering this element, the magazine is good.

Sports Action, which comes out every two weeks, also does an outstanding job of rating the top 150 college basketball teams each season, adjusting the power ratings of each as the season progresses. The power ratings are compiled by basketball analyst Matt Nevada and take into consideration every facet of a team's makeup, including age, experience, coaching, ability to win on the road, overall quality, class, height, defensive ability, offensive ability, and won-lost records.

Power ratings such as those printed in *Sports Action* are easy to use. Let us say, for instance, that Tulsa, which has a power rating of 80, is playing Missouri, which has a power rating of 91. The game is being played at Tulsa, where the home court is worth 6 points. This means that, by using the power ratings and adding the home court differential, Tulsa has a rating for this game of 86, while Missouri is 91, or 5 points better. Thus, the power ratings project a 5-point victory for Missouri.

It is interesting to note that UCLA, which has ruled college basketball for most of the last decade, finished the 1972–73 season undefeated, but covered the spread on the road only four times in twelve games. There is a reason for this, and UCLA is not alone in this situation.

The basketball bettor should remain forever aware of the fact that when a powerhouse, nationally ranked basketball team such as UCLA goes on the road, it is vulnerable. Every team it plays will pull out all stops to beat it, from hosting 72-hour pep rallies to throwing things at the visitors' bench during the game. Anything that will fire up the locals goes.

A down-and-out team is looking for a moment of glory and tries for it when a team of national prominence arrives in town. The underdog, hometown boys may be 4–15 in the won-lost column for the season, but they know everyone will forget it if they beat the champions. It is extremely tough to be number one, and the smart basketball bettors lay off the top teams on the road or take the points against them. The biggest problem with betting a team such as UCLA or North Carolina State when they are on the road is that you usually have to lay points, regardless of which teams you play.

The latter fact puts us in direct contradiction with what Matt Nevada says is the golden rule of basketball betting:

"Never lay points on the road." It's hazardous to lay the points on any road team, and doubly so if that team happens to be one which could give the home team a little recognition if it happened to beat it.

There are too many easier spots to win basketball bets than betting the giants on the road.

Are there any home courts in the country where it is almost impossible for the visiting team to win? Unfortunately, yes. A check of records for the past five years shows that it is almost impossible to beat the following teams at home and even more impossible for a visiting team to cover the spread against them when they are at home:

Arizona	Kentucky	St. Joseph's (Pa.)
Arizona State	La Salle	San Francisco
Brown	Louisville	Santa Clara
Butler	New Mexico	Stanford
Duke	Notre Dame	Wisconsin
Indiana	Purdue	Yale

There is much to be said about the statement made by Indiana coach Bob Knight that "because of the new arenas that have been built on campuses throughout the country, the so-called home court advantage has been reduced in the last few years." There was a time when playing at places such as Mississippi State during the Babe McCarthy era was an extremely painful experience, literally. The crowd at Mississippi State supported its teams with a dedication that defied words. It was unruly at best, doing everything it could to help the Babe win a game.

The playing floor was small, as was the bleacher area which surrounded it. Spectators sat within inches of the playing floor, and on it if officials didn't keep a wary eye. This crowd was so close to the floor that it never left room for a player to throw the ball in bounds. The crowd would, however, willingly make room for a State player when it had the ball out of bounds, but wouldn't budge for the visitors. When an official would make some of the students move, they would let the opposing player take his place to get ready to throw the ball in bounds and then would pull the hair on his legs. It was unnerving, to say the least.

Adolph Rupp, who retired as the winningest college basketball coach in history (he won 879 games, while losing only 190, for a win percentage of .822), faced more problems on a four-game road trip through the Southeastern Conference with his Kentucky team back in the 1950s and 1960s than most mentors would meet in a lifetime. Rupp, who learned his basketball under Phog Allen at Kansas in the early 1920s, worked for years to bring a powerhouse to the University of Kentucky. And, when he finally arrived, he became the most hated man in the SEC. He absolutely murdered his opposition in the conference, and the fans grew to hate him for it. A sellout crowd would show up anywhere Rupp's teams played in the South, and they all came to see him lose.

When he appeared at courtside, clad in the brown suit which was his trademark, fans booed, threw things, cursed him, and questioned his parentage. But Rupp weathered it all, remaining calm and cool, and won on the road just as easily as at home. He says the dirtiest thing that ever happened to him came when his team was in Starkville, Mississippi, to meet a McCarthy team in the little crackerbox they called a gym.

Rupp's team was involved in a fierce contest with one of the Babe's best teams. McCarthy, something of a basketball genius himself, had been hired to stop Rupp and he was attempting to do just that. And, to Rupp, the most insulting thing about it was the way he did it. McCarthy ordered his team to stall the ball, playing for the sure shots and keeping it away from Kentucky and its feared fast break. Rupp said this style of play ruined the game and, if everyone tried it, would empty the basketball arenas of the land (he's right).

As the game in Starkville wore on, so did Rupp's nerves. His team was getting beat by the stall and he didn't like it. He also was upset because both his starting guards had lost all the hair on the calves of both legs. Rupp felt extremely uncomfortable, but he didn't quite know why. He had lost before and hadn't felt quite like this. Then he smelled something. It was the most horrible, sickening smell that had ever hit his nostrils. "My God, what is it?"

Rupp looked to either side of himself, in back of him, and then under his chair. There it was. Some Mississippi State fan had placed a dead skunk beneath the chair on which Rupp sat. Rupp was furious and accused McCarthy of getting someone to do it. Rupp said he could not believe that anyone would stoop to such depths to try to beat him and he ranted and raved like a madman about it for months. But it is just an example of how tough it was—and still is, in some cases—to win on the road.

It is interesting to note that Rupp and McCarthy were reunited in 1973 when Rupp, as the top official of the Kentucky Colonels basketball team of the American Basketball Association, hired McCarthy to coach the team.

The small dimly lit quonset huts which used to be commonplace are now mainly something about which the old-timers reminisce. Most schools with major athletic programs now have beautiful, modern, well-lighted gyms which give the visiting team as much comfort and protection as possible. However, there are still a few places, for a host of reasons, which are extremely hazardous for a visiting team. The problems with these courts run the complete spectrum from bad lighting to vicious crowds. The bettor should keep this list handy and walk with caution anytime his favorite team is visiting one of these arenas. The home courts on which the visiting team is going to take all the worst of it at the present time include those of these schools:

Bradley	Eastern Kentucky	Jacksonville
Butler	Evansville	Marshall
Creighton	Florida State	Morehead State
Davidson	Furman	Ohio University
Drake		

While we have talked at great lengths about the hazards of winning basketball games on the road, we must keep in mind that we are not necessarily interested in "winning" on the road. We are interested in winning by the points, whether it be on the road or at home. Many teams—almost all of them with veteran starting units—play better against the spread on the road than they do at home. For instance, Auburn, which had one of its worst teams in 1972–73, was 3–4 against the spread at home but was 8–4 against it on the road. Brigham Young, which had one of the best teams in the country in 1972–73, was 5–7 at home and 7–3 on the road. Iowa State fielded a veteran five and was 3–4 before the homefolks and 7–2 traveling. Manhattan was 3–5 and 5–1, while Marquette was 3–7 and 6–3. Miami of Ohio was 3–5 and 8–3, Mississippi State 2–4 and 7–4. North Carolina State, which also went through the season undefeated, was 3–5 at home, but an amazing 8–2 on the road. Tulsa was 3–4 and 8–4, while a veteran Virginia five was 3–6 and 9–3.

All of these teams beat the spread consistently on the road and they had one thing in common—they were all seasoned fives which had been exposed, and hardened, to all the problems of travel.

Home and Neutral Court Records of the NBA for Each Season

| | Home | | | Neutral | | Total |
	Won	Lost	Pct.	Won	Lost	Games
1946–47	202	129	.610	—	—	331
1947–48	107	85	.557	—	—	192
1948–49	212	132	.616	16	16	360
1949–50	351	167	.678	43	43	561
1950–51	254	85	.749	15	15	354
1951–52	213	80	.727	37	37	330
1952–53	195	83	.701	73	73	351
1953–54	151	84	.643	89	89	324
1954–55	139	59	.702	90	90	288
1955–56	144	81	.640	63	63	288
1956–57	155	62	.714	71	71	288
1957–58	150	85	.638	53	53	288
1958–59	148	80	.649	60	60	288
1959–60	150	87	.633	63	63	300
1960–61	156	85	.647	75	75	316
1961–62	166	107	.608	87	87	360
1962–63	184	109	.628	67	67	360
1963–64	185	126	.595	49	49	360
1964–65	178	128	.582	54	54	360
1965–66	197	89	.689	74	74	360
1966–67	193	128	.601	84	84	405
1967–68	241	182	.569	69	69	492
1968–69	315	206	.605	54	54	574
1969–70	313	207	.602	54	54	574

There is little doubt that the home court means much less in professional basketball than in college. Basketball linemakers believe the home court advantage the pros enjoy is going down, while the edge enjoyed by the average college is going up.

Most professional coaches will deny that there is really much of a home court edge in basketball, explaining the problems of winning on the road as being the problems brought about by the aggravations and natural mishaps of traveling in the Jet Age. However, the pros do so much more traveling than do the colleges that they adapt to the rigors of playing in Boston on Friday night, catching a midnight flight after the game, and then playing Saturday night in San Francisco. Travel becomes a way of life for them, as they play 35 to 40 games away from home during the season.

The pros keep going back to the same places each year, too, and learn to know the towns they visit. This permits them to seek out restaurants they like and, when they check into a hotel, they've usually been there before and actually are not having to stay in totally strange surroundings. The college team visits several strange places each year, places in which most of the players have never been, nor will they ever be again. This makes adjustment much more difficult for them.

Another factor is the simple fact that professional basketball players are more mature and approach their game as a business. They may get tired of it for a day or two, but they know it is paying their bills and insuring their future just as the corporate employees know their company is, and they produce to gain the financial rewards. The average college player is torn between enjoying all the country he is seeing during the basketball season and actually playing basketball. There just isn't much on this in the pros. The players revisit the same cities over and over again. They see all of these cities they want to see and arrive in town with just one thing in mind—playing the game they get paid to play, whether they be in Boston on Friday, Houston on Saturday, or Los Angeles on Sunday.

There will be occasions on which the bettor can capitalize on a team's road schedule, but it won't happen often. It always is dangerous to lay the points on the road, regardless of whether it is in a pro game or a college game. An attractive betting opportunity could present itself for pro basketball fans when a team has been on the road for five or six games and is favored in the last one or two of them. The team has been traveling and everybody is anxious to get home. Maybe they just want to get the game over with and head for the airport. The longer a team is on the road, the less attractive it would be as a betting proposition. Anytime you find a team which has been on the road a while, and the team is favored, take the underdog and the percentages will be with you.

Here is a complete listing of what professional basketball linemakers believe the individual National Basketball Association home courts were worth in 1973:

Atlanta	3	Kansas City-Omaha	3
Boston	3½	Los Angeles	3½
Buffalo	3	Milwaukee	4
Capital	3	New York	4
Chicago	4½	Philadelphia	3
Cleveland	3	Phoenix	3
Detroit	2½	Portland	3
Golden State	3	Seattle	2½
Houston	3		

Playing on a Neutral Court

We have discussed in great detail the hazards and virtues of the home court, but what about the neutral court—the playing floor on which neither team has seen much action before? Can the bettor take an edge in a game such as this?

Madison Square Garden, home of the National Invitation Tournament, is the most neutral home floor in the country for college teams. Only Manhattan uses it as its actual home floor. The rest of the New York area teams play two or three games a season there, usually as part of a doubleheader involving Manhattan and another team. But come National Invitation Tournament time, a dozen teams from throughout the land are invited to compete on this neutral floor. Unless Manhattan is invited, which it is if its record merits, the tournament is made up of teams which do not call the Garden home. So what happens? The NIT is the most famous tournament in the country for underdogs. It drives the linemaker crazy, which gives us some insight into the natural hazards of a neutral floor. The linemaker doesn't know which way to go, so what chance does the bettor have?

In the 1973 NIT, only three favorites won in fifteen games. This means that twelve underdogs won during the tournament, and this included Virginia Tech, which upset (or was it an upset?) Notre Dame in the finals to win the championship. Virginia Tech rolled through the tournament unbeaten, and was never favored in any of its games.

A basketball bettor should stay away from any games in which he is not completely convinced of a team's ability to perform at 100 percent on a neutral floor. If his favorite team is at home, he knows how it plays. He also knows how it reacts on the road during the regular season, but there is no way to know in advance, in 90 percent of the cases, how a team will perform on a floor which really belongs to no one.

In the NIT, no one has ever been able to explain why underdogs do so well. Is it a bad line? Is it because tournament officials, looking and hoping for the most financially attractive final, play around with the pairings to bring about this situation? Do the officials get psyched to go with the underdog? Is it because the crowd is for the underdog, inspiring it to new heights of excellence?

There are no clear-cut answers to any of these questions, but teams playing on any neutral court are truly risky betting propositions. There are so many opportunities to win basketball bets that it is just good advice to stay away from such games unless you know you really have an edge—such as knowing that a starting center or another key player is going to miss a game.

As in all betting situations, there are exceptions to the rule. The National Collegiate Athletic Association (NCAA) tournament is much more predictable than the NIT. For the most part, teams in the NCAA classic have played on at least two neutral floors in preliminary rounds before getting to the championships. They are acquainted with all the hazards—and the emotional problems of playing before crowds which cheer and jeer both teams.

Other than the NCAA tournament, we would advise the bettor against getting involved in any holiday festival-type tournaments in which at least three of the four teams involved are competing on the neutral floor. If all four teams are in this category, it makes it even more hazardous.

Another situation of which bettors should be aware are the many tournaments which are held during the Christmas and New Year's holidays each season. These tournaments are usually located at the site of one of the teams—the host. Teams are invited to these tournaments on the strength of two things: (1) that they are name schools; (2) that the host school, which does the inviting, thinks it can beat all of them.

If you and I had a $1,000 bill for every host team which won its own tournament during the holidays, we would all be millionaires. The tournaments are, for the most part, setups to make the home boys look good. The host team will pair itself against the weakest of the four and then send the other two teams into battle to wear themselves out. The following night, the host team, which just toyed with its opponents the night before, is fresh for its showdown with the other team, which had to battle its guts out to make the finals. The results are easily predictable for the bettor. It is just a matter of beating the points to get the money.

As for the consolation games in these tournaments, they are sometimes interesting betting affairs. This thought is contrary to all popular opinion, which seems to be that a game for third place is one in which neither team really feels like trying. That certainly might be the case in the NCAA and NIT tournaments, but it is not the situation during the holiday classics. The season is still young, and every team is working on improving its record and its image.

For the most part, the linemaker doesn't make a line on third-place games in the NCAA and the NIT, but he does on most consolation matches in the holiday tournaments. The bettor need not be reluctant to wade right in and bet on these games, for you can be sure both teams are trying.

There are two other factors one should consider when thinking about betting teams on neutral floors, or betting on teams which are playing in tournaments on floors which are basically neutral. Coaching is a very important factor in winning games such as this. A good coach knows how to get his team ready for a contest in such surroundings. It is no accident that year-in and year-out the same teams show up and do well in holiday and post-season tournaments. They are in the hands of coaches who know how to get the money. The second factor is simply that of tournament experience. If you can find a team which has played in a classic such as the NIT before, you can bet it is a better wagering risk than one which is making its first appearance in this environment. Never overlook the importance of coaching or team tournament experience.

Pointspread and Basketball Betting

Matt Nevada says he stays away from professional basketball because "you've got to get too lucky to win, and I don't want anything to do with anything in which luck is the overriding factor." To him, and many other professional bettors, the game is so difficult to beat that the bettor who challenges it on a day-to-day basis has to wind up in financial difficulty. The bettor's only chance to beat the game is to be extremely selective in his betting, picking his spots and then betting with caution. There is no magic formula for beating any sport—and this is doubly true for professional basketball.

The linemaker figures the games so closely that few teams beat the spread more than 50 percent of the time—and that goes for the good teams and the bad ones. A review of the 1972–73 NBA pointspreads tells us that only six of the seventeen teams in the league beat the spread at home and on the road more than they lost to it. There were four other teams which beat the spread at home but faltered on the road.

The teams which had good overall records, winning both at home and on the road, were Boston, Capital (formerly Baltimore), Chicago, Detroit, and Los Angeles. Cleveland, Milwaukee, New York, and Seattle beat the spread at home more than half the time but failed to cover a winning percentage of time on the road.

A complete breakdown for the 1972–73 NBA season on how each team fared against the pointspread appears on page 121.

Incidentally, UCLA, which won all its games in 1972–73, had only a 10–12 mark against the spread (6–4, 4–8); the nation's other undefeated team, North Carolina State, was 11–7 (3–5, 8–2).

We have stated previously that the reason pro football's line is so hard to beat is the fact there are but twenty-six teams, and all of them are covered with a magnifying glass. Nothing is hidden from the general public. The press does its job. Consider, then, the position of professional basketball. There are but seventeen teams in the National Basketball Association, and all of them are examined through the same magnifying glass as football. The teams are located in major cities, with good newspapers and journalists which, at least, keep the public informed on the day-to-day operation of the team.

The linemaker can easily keep up with these seventeen teams, and the fact they play one another several times during the season gives him a solid line on all of them. It is not like college basketball in which the average team plays twenty-five games against twelve to twenty different opponents. The linemaker doesn't have to worry about the conditions of the playing floor, although an exhibition game was canceled in the new Omni in Atlanta in 1973 because of a leaky roof.

There are just very few unknown, or hidden, factors in pro basketball. The linemaker knows, for instance, when Atlanta meets Milwaukee on November 1, both teams face the same

Final National Basketball Association Pointspread Records 1972–73

Team	Home	Away	Overall
Atlanta	16–24	16–23	32–47
Boston	20–18	21–19	41–37
Buffalo	20–20	18–19	38–39
Capital	23–16	21–18	44–34
Chicago	21–18	23–18	44–36
Cleveland	24–15	19–19	43–34
Detroit	22–19	21–18	43–37
Golden State	18–22	18–21	36–43
Houston	19–19	18–21	37–40
Kansas City-Omaha	24–15	18–21	42–36
Los Angeles	24–17	24–16	48–33
Milwaukee	26–11	16–23	42–34
New York	22–17	16–23	38–40
Philadelphia	14–26	20–20	34–46
Phoenix	16–23	16–24	32–47
Portland	18–18	18–21	36–49
Seattle	21–19	14–24	35–43
TOTALS	348–317	317–348	

Best College Teams Against the Pointspread in 1972–73

	Against Spread	Against Spread at Home	Against Spread on Road
Air Force	10–4	5–2	5–2
Arizona	10–6	6–2	4–4
Auburn	11–8	3–4	8–4
California	12–7	6–5	6–2
Denver	10–5	7–2	3–3
Duquesne	10–6	5–4	5–2
Indiana	13–8	7–3	6–5
Iowa State	10–6	3–4	7–2
Kentucky	16–8	8–4	8–4
La Salle	11–4	8–3	3–1
Louisiana State	14–6	7–3	7–3
Louisville	14–8	8–4	6–4
Minnesota	10–6	6–1	4–5
New Mexico	13–6	7–2	6–5
Notre Dame	16–7	7–3	9–4
Ohio U.	10–4	4–2	6–2
Oregon	13–7	6–3	7–4
Richmond	12–6	7–4	5–2
Texas Christian	12–8	7–3	5–5
Texas Tech	13–8	5–4	8–4
Virginia Tech	10–6	3–2	7–4

basic situation they faced when they met on October 15. And, he knows when they meet again, the situation will still be the same. If we might use a wornout expression, making a pro basketball line is akin to shooting fish in a barrel, It's easy to make, and tough to beat.

In college basketball, playing conditions in such far-removed places as Blacksburg, Wichita, Lubbock, El Paso, and Bowling Green can change overnight and the linemaker will know nothing about it. He will make his line only on what he knows. The situation just doesn't exist in pro basketball. The linemaker is privy to everything that is going on and makes his line accordingly. And, he makes few mistakes.

If the line is so hard to beat—and never forget this has nothing to do with actually winning and losing games—can one take any edge with the pros? Yes, but even that is a risky one.

The bettor must keep track of which teams beat the spread at home and on the road. If the pro linemaker has a weakness, it is the time it takes him to react and adjust an NBA team's rating once he has assigned it. If he gives Atlanta a rating of 100 when the season opens, he might wait as much as a month to change it, even though the Hawks might deserve no more than a 96 rating during that period of time. It is during this period the bettor can capitalize on the point or two edge. If a team keeps beating the spread on the road and at home, you can bet the linemaker has underrated them.

The pro basketball bettor also can take an edge anytime a powerful team such as Boston, New York, or Milwaukee is playing a dog team, either at home or on the road. The differences in team quality among the haves and have-nots of the NBA are tremendous. Some teams just can't beat other teams, regardless of the circumstances. They might make a game of it for a while, but then just wilt under the continuous pressure from the better team. In the NBA, the better teams all have good benches (which is a key to their success) and the substitutes play just as well against dog teams as do the regulars. This means you will sacrifice nothing if the good team gets far out front and the coach decides to rest his first unit. The second-stringers will, in most cases, just keep right on running up the score. It is their time to shine, and they don't pass up opportunities such as this.

We would like to break the National Basketball Association teams into three categories to give the bettors some guidance in trying to determine which to bet and when to bet. The bettor should be forewarned, however, that nothing lasts forever and that includes great basketball dynasties. While these categories are reasonably accurate in 1973–74, they could well be changed for the 1974–75 season.

Outstanding Teams	Average Teams	Bad Teams
Boston	Atlanta	Cleveland
Capital	Buffalo	Philadelphia
Chicago	Golden State	Portland
Detroit	Houston	Seattle
Milwaukee	Kansas City-Omaha	
	Los Angeles	
	New York	
	Phoenix	

The bettor can translate these categories into winning bets in several manners. First of all, Boston, Capital, Chicago, Detroit, and Milwaukee have a so-so record against the teams rated "average." On any given night, the average team can knock them off, either as favorite or underdog. The fine line between the outstanding teams and the average teams is laser-thin and the slightest adjustment could reverse the roles. However, the difference between the outstanding teams and those listed under the "bad" category is so great there is seldom a chance that one of the top five will get beaten, either at home or on the road.

The outstanding teams also cover the spread a high percentage of times on the road against the real dog teams. You will have to lay plenty of points if you bet the outstanding teams against the bad teams, even on the road, but you will have an edge. The have-nots cannot adjust enough to compensate for the superstars of the haves, and in this lies a real betting edge.

Another situation the bettor must give consideration to comes when any two teams rated "outstanding" meet one another. When this happens, statistics tell us it is good to wager on the home team. This is one of the few times during a pro basketball season that psychology becomes a motivating factor. When an outstanding team meets an average team, or a bad team, its players go through a contest just doing their job. They all put out, but to them it is just another game.

They get paid to do a job, and they do it. However, when they face another outstanding team, something happens.

When the outstanding teams play, the good players like to strut their stuff against other good players. Some of the greatest duels in NBA history came when the superstar centers Bill Russell of Boston and Wilt Chamberlain of Los Angeles met. They stalked one another during the games, doing everything they could to take an edge on the other. They thought every minute, "How can I outdo this guy this time?"

There is an abundance of pride in the life of a good professional athlete and he loves to do his best against the best. Thus, when we catch New York playing Milwaukee at Milwaukee, the Bucks work hard to play their best before the sellout crowds they have for every game. Then, when the two teams come to New York, the 19,000-plus that see every Knickerbocker game bring out the best in their favorite team. The home crowd in such match-ups as these is very important, and maybe that is the edge. But, regardless of the reason, the outstanding team usually cover the spread against other outstanding teams at home. But, let us go a step further using the ratings. Anytime an average team plays an outstanding team, the game is strictly a "no bet" affair. The difference between average and outstanding pro teams is ever so slight, as we have said. You usually have to get lucky to win games such as this, and anyone who bets counting on luck to bail him out is bucking odds that would sober a fool.

In professional basketball's two loops—the old established NBA and the younger American Basketball Association (ABA)—there are eight teams which have shown decided winning tendencies over the years they've been in existence. Virtually every season these fives continue to win many more games than they drop and, for the most part, they are usually always solid bets especially when playing on their own home courts.

There are four teams in this group which annually snare more than six wins out of every ten games played. The always consistent Utah Stars of the ABA pace the field with a three-year total of 173–79 in 252 regular season games, for a brilliant .687 winning average. The NBA's Milwaukee Bucks and Boston Celtics hold down the second and third slots, while the ABA's Indiana Pacers are once again in the fourth spot in the pro cage won-lost hit parade. The all-time records of all professional teams are as follows:

All-Time Records of NBA Teams

	Regular Season		
	Years	Won	Lost
Milwaukee Bucks	6	331	161
Boston Celtics	28	1,304	779
Los Angeles Lakers	26	1,149	824
New York Knicks	28	1,059	1,020
Philadelphia 76ers	25	1,042	884
Atlanta Hawks	25	947	965
Kansas City-Omaha Kings	26	981	992
Phoenix Suns	6	220	272
Baltimore Bullets	21	651	867
Detroit Pistons	26	882	1,090
Golden State Warriors	28	1,030	1,048
Houston Rockets	7	218	356
Chicago Bulls	8	347	308
Seattle SuperSonics	7	237	337
Cleveland Cavaliers	4	99	229
Portland Trail Blazers	4	95	233
Buffalo Braves	4	107	221

All-Time Records of ABA Teams

	Regular Season		
	Years	Won	Lost
Carolina Cougars	5	215	205
San Antonio	6	247	245
Denver Rockets	7	288	288
Indiana Pacers	7	243	233
Kentucky Colonels	7	344	232
Memphis Tams	4	112	224
New York Nets	6	225	273
San Diego	2	67	101
Utah Stars	4	224	112
Virginia Squires	4	170	276

The Night-Before Blues

The biggest mistake the average basketball bettor makes is to give too much consideration to what a team did last night. If it won big, and beat the spread, he assumes the same thing is going to happen tonight. By the same token, if the team was badly beaten, he figures it will do the same again tonight.

Never forget, ever, that what a basketball team did last night has little to do with what it will do tonight. We are tempted to say it has nothing to do with what might happen tonight, but, as we have stated before, there are exceptions to every rule in betting sports. If a team was beaten 95–62 on Tuesday and is meeting the same type of team on Thursday, don't assume the result will be the same. The team could turn around and win 95–62—and it happens dozens of times during the season.

A basketball team cannot be up for all its twenty-plus games a season. A college team, for instance, could have its mind made up to play a good game, and then have a few calls go against it early, fall apart, and throw in the towel and get murdered. The next night they might approach a game in the same frame of mind, have all the calls break their way, and destroy the other team. Teams also have cold shooting nights and get wiped out. You can't win if you don't outscore the other team—no matter how good you are.

As an example of what we are talking about, one has but to examine the early play of the University of Kentucky basketball team during the 1972–73 season. Kentucky, which ended up in the NCAA tournament, opened the season by beating Michigan State 75–66, but then was upset at home by Iowa, 79–66. The Wildcats then suffered consecutive losses to Indiana, 64–58, and North Carolina, 78–70, before beating Nebraska, Oregon, Kansas, and Notre Dame and then losing to Mississippi. Then came a win over Mississippi State. Kentucky was favored in most of these games but covered the spread in fewer than half of them.

Kentucky fans had to be really disheartened when Iowa beat their Wildcats at home, but losing to Mississippi on the road was a hard pill to swallow, for the Johnny Rebs are looked upon with disdain by those who recognize good basketball. Had you followed the Kentucky team on a game-to-game basis, you would not have been able to come up with any particular pattern of winning or losing. On one night they played outstanding basketball, while on the next they could do nothing right. As a bettor, you must make up your mind to start the season anew every night. Forget about last night and just concentrate on tonight.

The Basketball Conferences and Betting

The verbal battle over which basketball conference in this great nation is the most powerful could go on for eternity. However, the controversy is really unnecessary, for the honor goes to the Atlantic Coast Conference by the length of the stretch. Next in line is the lesser-known Missouri Valley Conference, followed by the Big Ten, the Western Athletic Conference, and the Southeastern Conference.

With the lone exception of Clemson, the Atlantic Coast Conference teams—Duke, North Carolina, North Carolina State, Maryland, Virginia, and Wake Forest—play an outstanding brand of basketball. Year-in and year-out these schools have nationally ranked basketball teams which truly deserve the honors. They all get good coaching and play very tough schedules—and still win. We have searched long and hard for another conference which has the overall strength of the ACC, but there is none to be found.

Atlantic Coast Conference basketball is king and the bettor who follows its teams is going to step up his winning percentage. With the exception of Clemson, these teams have a chance every time they take the floor against a nonconference opponent, either at home or on the road. The only thing which prevents all of them from having outstanding records each year is the fact they all play one another twice, and someone must lose.

The overall quality of play in the ACC is so good that the bettor really has something going for him when these teams step outside the conference to play. After meeting their own family in competition, most of these nonconference affairs are breezes, even though their opponents might have high national ratings. Anytime an outside team tangles with an ACC five, either at home or on the road, it is in for a long night. Because competition within the conference is so fierce, every school works overtime just to remain average. Basketball programs are given heavy emphasis and leave nothing to chance, whether it be recruiting, scouting, or coaching. The conference is a bettor's delight for its quality, its consistency, and its good coaching.

A distant second is the Missouri Valley Conference, which really isn't located in the Missouri Valley at all, but stretches from Louisville in the East to New Mexico State in the West.

In between we find Bradley, Drake, Louisville, Memphis State, North Texas State, St. Louis, Tulsa, West Texas State, and Wichita. While some of these teams have their ups and downs, the overall top-to-bottom strength of the MVC is very good. Only West Texas State and North Texas State have trouble competing outside the conference.

Unlike the Atlantic Coast Conference, which also presents respectable football programs, the Missouri Valley emphasizes basketball only. All but one of the schools in the MVC (St. Louis) field football teams of varying degrees, but some are minor league in nature and do not even compete for the title. However, when basketball season rolls around, it is another story. The roundball is king in the MVC and its teams are famous for ambushing "name" schools. A road trip through the Missouri Valley Conference would give any opposing coach an early look at hell. The teams are tough, well-coached, and the fans are vocal and vicious. Teams such as Bradley, Drake, Louisville, Memphis State, St. Louis, Tulsa, and Wichita go to war and hold their own against all comers. The conference has its weak spots, but for a ten-team operation, the overall quality is excellent. As in the Atlantic Coast Conference, the one thing that keeps many of its good basketball teams from compiling outstanding winning records is the fact that they too play two games against one another and someone must lose.

Of vital importance to the bettor is the fact that the line-maker makes bad lines on Missouri Valley Conference teams and the bettor who studies and does his homework on them can take a big edge. Another fact of importance is simply that the MVC teams all seem to have a difficult time covering the spread on the road against one another. Even the best teams find it hard to win on the road, let alone cover the points.

The overall strength of the Big Ten also is excellent and will get better. Big Ten football is slowly going downhill because of regulations which limit the number of scholarships. Thus, athletic departments wanting to stay alive and important, are changing their emphasis to basketball. Big Ten basketball always has been good and if its rise in quality continues it will be on par with the Atlantic Coast Conference within a few years.

Another conference which has tremendous basketball teams from top to bottom is the Western Conference, which includes Arizona, Arizona State, Brigham Young, Colorado State, New Mexico, Texas-El Paso, Utah, and Wyoming. There is not a patsy in the group and these teams can compete at home and on the road against anyone. This conference, which doesn't get a lot of publicity because of its out-of-the-way location, is famous as a giant killer. Every team in the WAC specializes in ambushing nationally ranked teams at home.

Until North Carolina State came along in 1974, the only team other than UCLA to have won an NCAA championship in recent years was Texas-El Paso (formerly known as Texas Western). Of the eight teams in the WAC, only Arizona State puts greater emphasis on football than it does on basketball. The rest play football, but it is an athletic stepchild to most. They make their money and gain their national reputations on the hardwoods.

The fastest-rising conference in the land has to be the Southeastern Conference. Right now, its basketball strength lies in Alabama, Kentucky, Tennessee, and Vanderbilt, but the remaining six schools are working hard to put together good roundball programs. Until recent years, the only thing which interested most SEC schools was football, and then Kentucky basketball coach Adolph Rupp made them all discover basketball. He beat them all so badly that they began to build programs just to beat him. Rupp is now gone, but what he started remains.

Gone, too, are the days of bad officiating in the SEC. There was a time in its history when a nonconference, visiting team had two chances to win in the SEC—zero and none. But as the quality of play went up, so did the type of officials used by the conference.

There always is considerable dispute over the overall strength of the various conferences, and much of it comes from confusing name football schools with basketball schools. There are many schools which receive little publicity, but have tremendous basketball programs. Thus, when the bettor approaches basketball, he must realize that good football schools don't necessarily have good basketball teams. In fact, most don't. For reasons no one can seem to explain, there just doesn't seem to be room enough in anyone's athletic department for top teams in both sports.

While we have rated the conferences here, and listed each of their teams individually, there also are several independent schools (those with no conference affiliation) which emphasize basketball and have competitive programs in which the bettor can have confidence. Here is a complete list of these schools:

Major Independents

Boston College	Manhattan	St. John's (N.Y.)
Canisius	Niagara	South Carolina
Cincinnati	Notre Dame	Syracuse
Creighton	Oklahoma City	Utah State
Dayton	Providence	Villanova
Duquesne	St. Bonaventure	Virginia Tech
Holy Cross		

As far as relating the conference rating to betting, the wagerer should keep in mind that a good team from any conference is going to play excellent basketball against a good team from another conference. However, should you ever find teams from two conferences rated evenly, take the team from the conference with the higher rating. As in all things, class tells in basketball too.

National Rankings and the Bettor

One of the biggest roadblocks standing in the way of the basketball bettor is that of national ratings such as those distributed by the Associated Press and United Press International. Both wire services rank the top twenty teams in the country each week, creating mental havoc for the bettors who are hard-pressed to determine whom to believe.

First of all, the basketball bettor would be in front of the game right from the start if he completely disregarded the ratings. In our opinion they are without substance and are the worst possible guides for a person trying to decide which basketball team can beat another, and by the points.

The Associated Press poll is put together by sportswriters from member newspapers. The guy in Butte, Montana, who has not seen a basketball game in thirty years might gain the right to vote in the AP poll because someone in the wire service's management thought he was "a good ole boy." There are no professional requirements involved here. The biggest stiffs in the world vote in these polls and, in the process, give the basketball fan and the bettor an extremely misleading analysis of which teams in the country truly are the best.

United Press International goes a step further, but its poll isn't worth the paper on which it is written either. The United Press voters are college basketball coaches from throughout the land. They have seen few of the top teams play and the only knowledge they have of what is going on in other geographical locations comes from reading stories written by those same fellows who are voting in the AP poll.

The cases of the University of Houston, Southwestern Louisiana, and Oral Roberts are perfect examples of the folly of these polls. All were nationally ranked during the 1972–73 season, but none deserved the honor. However, because they all had impressive winning records, they got the votes. Those who are responsible for the weekly ratings said to themselves, "They're winning, so they must be good."

Houston received its national rating by beating such national powers as the New Orleans branch of Louisiana State University, Southern Mississippi, St. Mary's, Cal-Berkeley, Baylor, Rice, Hawaii, Houston Baptist, Corpus Christi, Trinity, Stanford, and Centenary. All of these teams were so bad during that season they would have had trouble finishing last in a respectable conference. But Houston was beating them and the pollsters gave the Cougars a lofty national rating.

But, let's look at Southwestern Louisiana. It compiled its tremendous record by tangling with the likes of Pan American, McNeese, Lamar, Texas-Arlington, Abilene Christian, Louisiana Tech, Arkansas State, Houston Baptist, and Hawaii. Totally disgraceful, but soft enough to give this team a place in the hearts of those who vote in the polls.

It was the same story for Oral Roberts, which beat everybody who was nobody, but came up short when it had to face somebody. It is interesting to note that Oral Roberts received an invitation to play in the NIT and quickly accepted. In the first round of play, Oral Roberts was paired with North Carolina of the Atlantic Coast Conference. Please keep in mind that North Carolina was considered the third-best team in the ACC, rated behind North Carolina State and Maryland. The pollsters had Oral Roberts and North Carolina rated closely during the season, but North Carolina destroyed the Oklahomans 82-65 without so much as taking a deep breath.

In examining the post-season tournament play of the University of Houston and Southwestern Louisiana it is the same story. Ironically, the two were paired in the preliminary elimination round in the NCAA. Playing on a neutral floor in Wichita, Kansas, Southwestern Louisiana beat Houston 102–89. The win was impressive and even the linemaker got sucked in the next time around, installing Southwestern Louisiana as a favorite over Big Eight winner Kansas State in the next round. But the Wildcats of Kansas State, tough, tournament-wise, and seasoned by one of the toughest schedules in the country, won 66–63 in what most considered an upset. To smart basketball bettors, it wasn't an upset at all, but a very predictable event. It presented to them the gambler's dream—getting the best team and points to boot. It was like stealing money off a dead man.

The hotdog teams with the weak schedules get beaten 99 percent of the time when they play good, tough basketball teams. Just because a group of sportswriters or coaches says a team is good, it isn't necessarily so. The polls show how ridiculous they are when a good team gets beaten by another good team. The beaten team sees its rating plunge just because it was beaten. Pollsters don't consider who beats whom—only that a team has lost. Most of the top teams in the Atlantic Coast Conference and the Missouri Valley Conference roll along unbeaten until they start to play one another. Then, as we have said before, someone has to lose. When an outstanding team from either of these conferences is beaten by another outstanding team, its stock starts to drop with those making the polls. As one can see, the entire setup is ridiculous and should be completely ignored by the bettor.

Defense and Offense

Is there a direct relationship between defense and offense and beating the spread in basketball? Let's look at the 1972–73 National Basketball Association season. The top five teams, with the average number of points scored against them in 82 games, were New York (98.2), Milwaukee (99.0), Chicago (100.6), Capital (101.6), and Los Angeles (103.2).

Additional statistics tell us that New York outscored its opponents an average of 6.8 points per game, while Milwaukee

NBA's Most Accurate Shooters

Rank	Player, Team	Season	FGA	FGM	Pct.
1	Kareem Abdul-Jabbar, Milwaukee	4	7,444	4,142	.556
2	Wilt Chamberlain, Los Angeles	14	23,497	12,681	.540
3	Walt Bellamy, Atlanta	12	14,537	7,523	.518
4	Terry Dischinger, Portland	9	6,836	3,457	.506
5	Jerry Lucas, New York	10	11,021	5,515	.500
6	'Walt Frazier, New York	6	6,791	3,388	.499
7	Wes Unseld, Capital	5	4,434	2,207	.498
8	Johnny Green, Kansas City-Omaha	14	10,091	4,973	.493
9	Dick Snyder, Seattle	7	5,829	2,870	.492
10	Jon McGlocklin, Milwaukee	8	6,682	3,286	.492

won by an average of 8.2 points. Chicago averaged 3.5 points per game more than its opponents, Capital 3.4, and Los Angeles 8.5. As we have said before, Capital, Chicago, and Los Angeles were among those teams which beat the spread both at home and on the road last year more than 50 percent of the time. Milwaukee and New York beat it at home but didn't cover once the traveling began.

Houston was the leading team offensively in the NBA in 1972–73, averaging 112.8 points per game. However, the Texans managed to give up 114.5 points each outing, which means the opposition outscored them 1.7 points per game on the average. As a result Houston was 37–40 against the spread in 1972–73.

While Cleveland was the worst offensive team in the league, averaging but 102.7 points each game, it happened to have an excellent record against the spread at home, 24–15. The worst defensive team was Philadelphia, which permitted an average of 116.2 points per game. The 76ers were 34–46 against the pointspread, while compiling the worst won-lost record in NBA history. Philly also gained the dishonor of being outscored by its opponents by the highest margin of points per game, 12.1. The second-worst team in this department was Buffalo, which gave up an average of 9.2 points more per game than it scored. However, the Braves still managed to be 38–39 against the spread.

There will be times in betting basketball that these statistics must be considered, but on a day-by-day basis they prove nothing concrete. While the 1973–74 stats were not available at press time, they failed to show any definitive pattern as the

Team Statistics—Offense

Team	G	Field Goals Made	Att.	Pct.	Free Throws Made	Att.	Pct.	Rebounds Off.	Def.	Tot.	Miscellaneous Asst.	PF	Stl.	Blk. Sh.	Turn Over	DQ	Scoring Pts.	Avg.
Buffalo	82	3728	7763	.480	1699	2221	.765	1150	2830	3980	2165	1875	786	600	1828	17	9155	111.6
Golden State	82	3721	8020	.464	1569	2018	.778	1379	3035	4414	1989	1893	668	450	1667	33	9011	109.9
Los Angeles	82	3536	7803	.453	1879	2443	.769	1365	2970	4335	2179	2032	794	653	1913	28	8951	109.2
Boston	82	3630	7969	.456	1677	2097	.800	1378	3074	4452	2187	1868	561	305	1796	22	8937	109.0
Atlanta	82	3602	7744	.465	1703	2264	.752	1240	2712	3952	1993	2073	758	332	1823	33	8907	108.6
Phoenix	82	3555	7728	.460	1737	2235	.777	1090	2723	3813	2052	2123	658	305	1666	48	8847	107.9
Houston	82	3564	7426	.480	1682	2071	.812	1063	2588	3651	2212	2104	727	407	1681	36	8810	107.4
Milwaukee	82	3726	7571	.492	1328	1741	.763	1133	2881	4014	2225	1864	726	519	1694	28	8780	107.1
Seattle	82	3584	8056	.445	1606	2095	.767	1323	2708	4029	2106	2074	689	294	1622	31	8774	107.0
Portland	82	3585	7684	.467	1591	2112	.753	1254	2598	3852	2106	2050	797	341	1823	23	8761	106.8
Detroit	82	3453	7515	.459	1654	2164	.764	1200	2681	3881	1958	1930	793	419	1763	19	8560	104.4
Chicago	82	3292	7376	.446	1784	2314	.771	1143	2616	3759	1868	1874	764	316	1690	17	8368	102.0
Kansas City-Omaha	82	3369	7342	.459	1628	2104	.774	1112	2554	3666	1744	1916	798	384	1791	22	8368	102.0
Capital	82	3460	7886	.441	1393	1869	.745	1286	2887	4173	1770	1746	703	441	1568	24	8353	101.9
New York	82	3478	7483	.469	1350	1738	.777	959	2725	3684	1937	1884	554	277	1463	14	8306	101.3
Philadelphia	82	3331	7702	.432	1633	2118	.771	1182	2626	3808	1799	1904	756	220	1665	25	8295	101.2
Cleveland	82	3420	7782	.439	1381	1788	.772	1275	2492	3767	2048	1925	598	293	1545	22	8221	100.3

Team Statistics—Defense

Allowed By: Team	Field Goals			Free Throws			Rebounds			Miscellaneous						Scoring		
	Made	Att.	Pct.	Made	Att.	Pct.	Off.	Def.	Tot.	Asst.	PF	Stl.	Blk. Sh.	Turn Over	DQ	Pts.	Avg.	Dif.
New York	3292	7377	.446	1496	1974	.758	1042	2790	3832	1580	1792	479	348	1555	13	8080	98.5	+2.6
Chicago	3336	7246	.460	1425	1847	.772	1136	2734	3870	1830	2200	614	408	1880	34	8097	98.7	+3.3
Milwaukee	3311	7799	.425	1499	1969	.761	1269	2487	3756	1909	1707	719	312	1554	12	8121	99.0	+6.1
Detroit	3376	7499	.450	1475	1932	.763	1173	2632	3805	1980	1996	772	410	1822	30	8227	100.3	+4.1
Capital	3498	7760	.451	1239	1639	.756	1206	2915	4121	1900	1840	651	350	1651	9	8231	100.4	+1.5
Cleveland	3440	7342	.469	1696	2163	.784	1137	2802	3939	2120	1853	630	343	1654	27	8576	104.6	−4.3
Boston	3561	8047	.443	1494	1938	.772	1131	2604	3735	1934	1858	540	309	1599	29	8616	105.1	+3.9
Kansas City–Omaha	3580	7514	.476	1512	1950	.775	1210	2650	3860	1916	1907	723	373	1765	22	8672	105.8	−3.8
Golden State	3619	7995	.453	1563	2054	.761	1227	2702	3929	2027	1826	714	465	1477	15	8801	107.3	+2.6
Philadelphia	3600	7685	.468	1617	2066	.783	1311	3107	4418	1930	1991	755	446	1830	23	8817	107.5	−6.3
Houston	3551	7433	.478	1719	2337	.736	1162	2619	3781	2122	1994	707	375	1737	29	8821	107.6	−0.2
Los Angeles	3667	8364	.438	1546	2044	.756	1525	2786	4311	2061	2135	797	430	1719	37	8880	108.3	+0.9
Seattle	3554	7675	.463	1875	2427	.773	1173	2932	4105	2255	2012	730	355	1796	34	8983	109.5	−2.5
Atlanta	3573	7628	.468	1878	2388	.787	1142	2754	3896	2028	2128	823	388	1846	40	9024	110.0	−1.4
Phoenix	3648	7809	.467	1843	2356	.782	1220	2773	3993	2180	2003	810	396	1637	25	9139	111.5	−3.6
Portland	3664	7571	.484	1825	2299	.794	1197	2678	3875	2308	1961	666	415	1713	20	9153	111.6	−4.8
Buffalo	3786	8106	.467	1592	2013	.791	1271	2733	4004	2256	1992	798	435	1763	37	9164	111.8	−0.2

season entered its final weeks. Simply put, a good basketball bettor should keep track of the offensive and defensive averages of the NBA teams he follows. Winning is strictly a percentage business, and there will be times he can turn these statistics into money.

The complete NBA team statistics for the 1973–74 season are on pages 134–135.

Other Statistics for the Bettor

All bettors refer to statistics, and the basketball bettor is no exception. However, one should be extremely careful when using statistics, and statistics alone, in trying to pick winners. As a politician once said, "Figures lie and liars figure." The same thing can be said when studying and analyzing figures and percentages earned by college basketball teams. We can take them and make them mean almost anything we wish. However, there are four statistical categories in which we can gain insight into a team's overall potential, or lack of it. These are the areas of a team's actual won-lost percentage, its offensive average, its defensive average, and its average scoring margins. One cannot use these figures alone to beat the spread, but they can serve as a past-performance sheet on a team.

The most important statistics are those relating to the average scoring margin. These statistics tell us just how many more points per game a team averages than its opposition. For instance, during the 1973–74 season, NCAA champion North Carolina State outscored its opposition an average of 16.7 points per game, while UCLA, which finished second in the college tournament, was 19.6 points per contest better than its opponents. The national leader in this department during the 1973–74 season was the up-and-coming University of North Carolina-Charlotte at 20.8 points per game. Rounding out the top five were UCLA, Long Beach State (19.1), Notre Dame (16.9), and N.C. State and Maryland at 16.7.

A good basketball bettor will keep track of this important figure on all teams he follows during the season. He knows just how much offense he can expect from his team and how much defense. If the pointspread falls somewhere in between these figures, he knows he has taken a percentage edge already. It does not require a degree from MIT to keep these statistics. All you have to do is keep a running total of the scores of each team, and a running total of the points run up against these teams. Subtract the second figure from the first, divide by the number of games, and you have the average scoring margin.

A complete rundown of these statistics from the 1973–74 season appears on page 139.

While on the subject of statistics, it is important to give consideration to the importance of defense to the basketball bettor. Almost all successful coaches, particularly those in college, work extremely hard on defense. They know their teams will play under strange and unusual circumstances every time they go on the road. The offense is less stable away from home, but the defense should be the same at home or away. You stop a man from scoring in Knoxville the same way you stop him in Portland.

Won-Lost Percentages

	(Top Streak)	W–L	Pct.
1. N.C. State	(28)	30–1	.968
2. Maryland East. Shore	(16)	27–2	.931
3. Long Beach St.	(12)	24–2	.923
4. Notre Dame	(12)	26–3	.897
5. Providence	(11)	28–4	.875
6. UCLA	(88)	26–4	.867
7. Pittsburgh	(12)	25–4	.862
8. UNC Charlotte	(9)	22–1	.846
9. Marquette	(11)	26–5	.839
10. Vanderbilt	(13)	23–5	.821
11. Indiana	(12)	23–5	.821
12. Maryland	(11)	23–5	.821
13. Michigan	(6)	22–5	.815
14. South Carolina	(8)	22–5	.815
15. Massachusetts	(9)	21–5	.807
16. McNeese St.	(11)	20–5	.800
17. Oral Roberts	(7)	23–6	.793
18. South Alabama	(10)	22–6	.786
19. North Carolina	(8)	22–6	.786
20. Pennsylvania	(6)	21–6	.778

Team Offense*

	Games	(W–L)	Pts.	Avg.
1. Maryland East. Shore	27	(26–1)	2664	98.7
2. Oral Roberts	26	(21–5)	2472	95.1
3. Va. Commonwealth	24	(17–7)	2266	94.4
4. N.C. State	25	(24–1)	2295	91.8
5. UNC Charlotte	26	(22–4)	2346	90.2
6. Utah	26	(19–7)	2334	89.8
7. Arizona	26	(19–7)	2315	89.0
8. Notre Dame	26	(24–2)	2312	88.9
9. Houston	25	(16–9)	2221	88.8
10. Illinois St.	26	(17–9)	2300	88.5
11. Purdue	25	(17–8)	2211	88.4
12. Georgia Southern	26	(19–7)	2295	88.3
13. North Carolina	25	(21–4)	2205	88.2
14. Austin Peay	26	(17–9)	2272	87.4
15. Mercer	24	(16–8)	2086	86.9
16. Southern Miss.	26	(11–15)	2244	86.3
17. New Mexico	26	(20–6)	2241	86.2
18. Middle Tenn. St.	26	(18–8)	2238	86.1
19. Canisius	26	(14–12)	2223	85.9

* Includes only regular season

Team Defense*

	Games	(W–L)	Pts.	Avg.
1. U. Tex. El Paso	25	(18–7)	1413	56.5
2. Temple	25	(16–9)	1417	56.7
3. Princeton	26	(16–10)	1520	58.5
4. Marquette	26	(22–4)	1540	59.2
5. Creighton	27	(21–6)	1624	60.1
6. Colgate	25	(15–10)	1522	60.9
7. Long Beach St.	26	(24–2)	1588	61.1
8. UCLA	25	(22–3)	1529	61.2
9. Pennsylvania	26	(21–5)	1607	61.8
10. Rider	26	(13–13)	1610	61.9
11. Colorado St.	26	(12–14)	1622	62.4
12. Drexel	24	(15–9)	1501	62.5
13. Massachusetts	24	(20–4)	1501	62.5
14. Penn State	26	(14–12)	1630	62.7
15. St. Joseph's (Pa.)	29	(19–10)	1820	62.8
16. Montana	26	(19–7)	1649	63.4
17. Navy	22	(9–13)	1398	63.5
18. Indiana	23	(20–3)	1470	63.9
19. Stanford	24	(11–13)	1534	63.9

* Includes only regular season

Average Scoring Margin

	Off.	Def.	Mar.
1. UNC Charlotte	90.2	69.4	20.8
2. UCLA	82.3	62.7	19.6
3. Long Beach St.	80.2	61.1	19.1
4. Notre Dame	89.9	73.0	16.9
5. Maryland	85.7	69.0	16.7
6. N.C. State	91.4	74.7	16.7
7. Va. Commonwealth	94.4	78.1	16.3
8. Massachusetts	78.8	62.8	16.0
9. Pittsburgh	80.8	65.5	15.3
10. Montana	77.5	63.4	14.1
11. Providence	86.9	73.5	13.4
12. Pennsylvania	75.7	62.6	13.1
13. Creighton	72.9	60.6	12.3
14. New Mexico	84.2	71.9	12.3
15. North Carolina	87.0	75.3	11.7
16. Indiana	76.9	65.3	11.6
17. South Carolina	76.4	65.4	11.0
18. Wisconsin	76.1	65.7	10.4
19. McNeese St.	84.8	74.6	10.2
20. Idaho St.	79.2	69.0	10.2

Defense can be the salvation of many teams on the road, although there are no conclusive records to indicate defensive teams beat the spread any more on the road than they do at home. However, if you know you have a good defense going for you, it is much easier to pick your spots on the road, particularly when you're getting a lot of points.

It is interesting to note that of the top twenty defensive teams in the country, only three, Colorado State, Navy, and Stanford, had losing records. Little Rider College broke even, but all the rest had winning records. However, of the top fifteen offensive teams in the country only Southern Mississippi had a losing record. Who is to say defense means more than offense?

How Important Is the Superstar?

Can one man make a basketball team a winner? This age-old question has sought a satisfactory answer for decades. We are inclined to say that one man can make a basketball team, but it is difficult to say that one man can help a team beat the spread more often than not. As we have discussed before, the linemaker makes his line knowing the ability and playing capacity of the superstar.

The importance of one man to a basketball team in either the colleges or the pros is related directly to just how much a team is built around him. For instance, as great as Bill Walton was at UCLA, there is little doubt in the minds of most basketball authorities that the Bruins would have done almost as well without him. Walton made a difference in big games, but UCLA would still have beaten most teams without him. UCLA did not rely on one man.

However, let's take the case of the Milwaukee Bucks of the NBA. The Bucks are tightly woven around superstar Kareem Abdul-Jabbar and they are a completely different team without him. In fact, so important is he to the Bucks' offense and defense that the team is almost inept anytime Jabbar has to spend too much time on the bench.

We could mention dozens of cases like that at UCLA and dozens that resemble the Milwaukee situation, but it is really unnecessary. The only time the bettor should be concerned about a superstar is when he is the main cog in a team's attack and he is going to be missing or play with injuries.

Every coach makes adjustments to compensate for the loss of a superstar. In the case of Walton, the adjustment could be made, while there isn't enough rearranging in the world that would compensate for the loss of Jabbar.

If a team's entire attack is built around one man, you can make money betting against that team when the man is hurt and not playing his best. With the man working at limited capacity, no one-man team is going to function smoothly or effectively.

Officials and Other Unknown Factors

The popularity of basketball in this country is growing at a rate faster than that of either baseball or football. It will be the sport of the future. If anything stops its growth, it will be the unbelievably bad officiating we have today. More teams have been beaten by officials, and more bettors destroyed by officials, than any other factor.

However, this is one factor a basketball handicapper has to contend with and there isn't any way for him to take an edge. The only way basketball will ever be given back to the teams is to install instant replay cameras to review all judgment calls.

While one cannot determine in advance how an official is going to call a game, neither can one know what kind of shooting percentage a team will have. It is impossible to know how fast key players will get into foul trouble. Nor can we predict when a dog team will decide to stall the ball in an effort to keep the score close. But these and all other unknown factors will forever be a part of the game. If you bet basketball, you'll just have to take these risks, but they are far fewer than you take on the racetrack with a horse.

Another Reason Why Bookmakers Don't Like Basketball

As we have stated, most bookmakers are honest, hardworking guys. They are in business, even though illegally in most states, to make a dollar and usually do. They operate their business with the assumption that every sport is honest and on the level. In fact, the average bookmaker works harder to keep betting sports on the up and up than do most people in the legitimate power structure of sports. All of them fear the fix, which could wipe them out in one night. Because of this fear, a bookmaker will limit payoffs on his horse action, limit the amount of money any player can bet on a single college basketball game, and take big action on football only from established players he knows personally. However, of all the sports in which the bookmaker fears the fix most, college basketball is at the top of the list. Past history tells him that college basketball is the easiest of all games to fix, and he is quite nervous about it.

Why is college basketball the one sport that seems to attract most of the crooked operators? The answer to this can be found in the nature of the game itself. Wagers on basketball are made by the pointspread method. When a person bets a basketball game, he doesn't merely wager that team A will beat team B. For every game played a line or pointspread is established. For example, team A may be favored over team B by 7 points. If A wins by 6 points or less, its backers lose even though A won the game. This method of wagering, then, is a natural for "point shaving." When the fix is on in a certain game, the players who are involved do the "shaving." It is their job to see to it that their team either loses the game outright or wins by fewer points than the published spread. This method of fixing games even enables the players involved to rationalize their actions on the court. "What's the difference," they ask themselves, "if we win by eight points or four? Just so long as we win." They (and in order for the fix to be properly carried out, more than one player must be involved) go out on the court and control the score of the game, making certain that they don't win by more points than the spread. The fixer is happy since he's made a killing by betting on underdog team B and taking the 7 points; the players are also happy with the "found" wad of dough in their pockets; in fact everyone involved is happy but the bookmakers who were had.

Another reason that college basketball is a fixer's delight is the fact that the fix is so easy to pull off even in front of a sellout crowd in Madison Square Garden. If you've ever attended a basketball game, you know how the crowd reacts when a player misses an easy "jumper" or "lay-up" or when a foul shot hits the rim and bounces away from the basket. They boo, and hoot, and yell "bum" and other unprintable invectives. The players involved in a fix, then, confine their "funny playing" to defense. One player who was involved in a fix scandal not many years ago was quoted as saying, "You simply play your best on offense, score as many points as you can—then make simple, stupid-looking mistakes on defense." Therein lies the secret of the fix. A player will let the man he is supposed to be guarding get a half-step on him—he breaks loose and scores. But who can say the defensive player wasn't trying to stop him?

A well-known coach of one of the nation's top basketball teams—Fordy Anderson of Bradley, whose team was involved in an uncovered "dump" involving eight players—said of the incident, "I've studied the films [of the games that were proven to be fixed] at least twenty times and can't find a single play which indicates the boys weren't giving their best effort every second." It should be obvious that if a head coach—an experienced technician of the game—reviewing films of games known to be fixed cannot find any purposely made "mistakes," how can the general public—watching the game live—be expected to pick up any? Therefore the fixer and his helpers go about their ugly business undetected in front of thousands of people.

Any dump coup, however, is worthless unless the fixer is

able to "get down" (bet) for large amounts of money. Book-makers may not be the smartest humanoids but they rate right at the top of the wariest. Thus, in order to bet large amounts on the fixed game without arousing the book's natural suspicious nature, the fixer must divert his attention. This is not easy to accomplish but it can be (and has been) done. How? The fixer will place a call to bookmaker "1" and bet, perhaps, $10,000 on each of two or more games. An-other call will then be placed to bookmaker "2" and every game but the fixed one will be bet the other way. Of course, the fixer can (and does) do this any number of times depend-ing on how many bookmaker connections he has. All it costs him, then, is the "juice"—the 5 to 10 percent fee the bookmaker charges for the privilege of wagering with him. (In betting basketball, one must lay 11 to 10 no matter which way he bets. If the team he chooses wins he gets even money back on his bet; if his team loses, however, he pays off at 11 to 10—$110 on the $100 bet, for example. The $10 is the juice charged on the bet.) Thus, if a fixer can get down five $10,000 bets on the sure thing in a fix, his return will be $50,000 from which he must deduct the juice on his losing wagers. Obviously he comes out way ahead—far enough ahead, in fact, to make enticing offers to the players he needs and still wind up with an incredible profit.

Almost every basketball fan still remembers the first large-scale crackdown on fixing during the 1951–52 season. Thirty-three players from seven different colleges admitted conspir-acy to rig the results of more than ninety games and, at the time, it was reported by the New York District Attorney's of-fice that these totals represented merely a *small part* of the entire fix ring's activities. And to show how difficult it is to uncover a dump mob such as that one, an official of the prosecutor's office working on the case was quoted as saying, "We discovered the fixing by virtually stumbling upon it dur-ing the course of other, nonrelated investigations. There is no telling how much more is going on that we haven't discov-ered." At the 1951–52 discovery it was learned that the same cast had been operating since at least 1948 (and probably longer) before they were caught. Salvatore Sallazo was named as the brains behind this coup and he, along with fourteen players, were tried and found guilty. Among them were Ed Roman of CCNY, Sherman White of LIU, Ed Warner of CCNY, Alvin Roth of CCNY, Connie Schoof of NYU, and Dick Fertrado of LIU.

There is, of course, little reason to believe that fixers are any more inventive around the New York area than they are anywhere else. Thus, the "Ostrich Award" must be given to Adolph Rupp, head coach at Kentucky University at the time, who, in the years since the 1951 affair, has become "the grand old man of basketball." While the New Yorkers were being arrested in bunches, Rupp was quoted as saying, "Gamblers couldn't get to my boys with a ten-foot pole. Our boys are under constant and absolute supervision at all times they are on the road—especially in New York."

The gamblers that Rupp was speaking of, unfortunately, didn't attempt to "get at [his] boys with a ten-foot pole." They used something much more practical—money! For, soon afterward, the nucleus of the Kentucky team—Ralph Beard, Alex Groza, and Dale Barnstable—admitted fixing the outcomes of many of their games. Trying to save face, Rupp again stuck his foot in his mouth with the statement "What these boys have done is not as bad as it sounds. The Black Sox actually threw ball games. All my boys did was shave points." Since this was the first large-scale fix discovery, the academicians who were playing out of their league got their feet wet in this business by heeding Rupp's casual dismissal of the charges. Thus the ground rules were laid for dealing with players tinged with the suspicion of fixing. These gentlemen—aloof and guarded in their ivory towers—hardly listened to those who recognized fixing as the serious offense it really was and who argued that those players involved should be dealt with as criminals rather than merely having their fragile wrists slapped.

As a result of this naïve, apathetic attitude taken in 1951–52, when the scandal of 1961–62 broke, the New York District Attorney's office stated in its brief against Jack Molinas—Sallazo's successor, and mastermind of the early sixties fixes—"It is safe to assume that even after the 1951–52 crackdown, basketball fixing did not cease but probably increased during the ensuing decade."

Charges against Molinas, who had played basketball at Columbia, were listed as far back as 1957 and the only reason they stopped there was because of the statute of limitations (which prohibits the prosecution of certain crimes after a fixed number of years has elapsed). At the Molinas trial, the New York D. A. made one of the most profound statements of all times. "I would suggest," he said, "that fixing basketball games is very profitable and the concept that you don't have to lose, but merely stay under the pointspread, is a great inducement to college players."

The fix that was brought to light in the early sixties involved forty-nine players, twenty-five colleges, and sixty-seven known fixed games. As shocking as this may seem, there were still those at the top who persisted in taking the matter lightly. One of these was Howard Hobson, head coach at Yale, who classically stated, "Don't forget the fact that more than fifty thousand college games have been played during the past five years and less than fifty are known to have been fixed. This small percentage is indicative of nothing."

Disregarding Hobson's inaccurate citing of numbers, this statement was akin to saying that a person shouldn't be afraid of being stepped on by an elephant since, although there are hundreds of thousands in the world, very few people have actually been stepped on by one.

So again the wise men at the colleges bought archaic advice and left the doors wide open for fixing to continue undisturbed. The eventual discovery of another large-scale dump ring is inevitable.

Aside from the ease with which a game can be fixed and the large sums of money to be made in fixing, the reason that the smart operators have chosen college basketball as their vehicle to quick—and relatively safe—riches lies in other areas. Placing of blame is like crying over spilled milk, but, without doubt, the situation still exists today and probably in an even bigger way than it did in the early fifties and sixties.

One of the "culprits" is the emphasis our schools put on intercollegiate athletics with the attendant battle for the high school stars; offers of scholarships and other inducements (a new convertible, "pocket" money, a house for mom and dad, etc.). Many of the "dumpers" get the first seeds of dishonesty implanted in their juvenile minds by the college recruiters themselves.

Another reason is the ultra-liberal feeling among today's generation that the individual is never to blame; social institutions, they feel, must be at fault since they have placed him in the position where he is vulnerable to the fixers.

The easily accessible and large number of betting sources (bookmakers) also enters into the entire scheme, but, without doubt, the single, most important thing that makes college basketball the "mark" it is for the fixer is the attitude of the college coaches. Coaching a college team today is a business, a livelihood, and, very often, a lucrative one. The men in it like to surround themselves with the aura of "educators" even though they are not. They are no different from professional coaches. Proof of this is the fact that the pro teams draw from the colleges and universities to fill coaching vacancies. The transition is a simple and natural one and is made with great ease. The same result is expected of a coach at both levels—build winners at any cost! Building character is left to someone else. A coach trying to build a winning team doesn't have the time to waste on moral issues. So if something is lost along the way—like learning ethical practice and recognizing decent values—that's unfortunate. After all, coaches have to make a living and in doing so they condition themselves not to "make waves." It is very easy, when one has a great deal to lose, to ignore even a fly on one's nose. In this fast-paced world of now, where the only thing that matters is the satisfaction of one's many appetites—the appetite for booze and broads and a knockout wardrobe and a swinging pad and, in many cases, drugs—the time is more than ripe for an escalation of basketball fixing. Today the seven-footers reign supreme in college basketball. An ordinary, mediocre team can become a powerhouse from one season to the next merely by acquiring the nation's 7-foot-2-inch high school phenomenon. But his price is high and often too high for the colleges and universities to pay. But if they want him badly enough, they'll look the other way and not ask questions when he turns up driving his $9,000 convertible with matching wardrobe and harem.

The point of all this is that, today, a fixer—unlike in previous years—need only get to "the big man" on a team to pull off a fix coup. This in itself paves the way for an upsurge in activity. Where before the fixer had to divide his "budget" among three, four, or even more players to buy a "sure thing," he now can make unbelievable offers to "the big man" on the team—offers that are extremely difficult to turn down, and logic dictates that more often than not they aren't.

It is the feeling at *Sports Action* that the fixing of college basketball games is probably more prevalent now than it has ever been before. It is also our feeling that it is so prevalent that someone, somewhere, sometime, is bound to uncover something that will make big ugly headlines.

The only question that remains in the minds of most bookmakers and many basketball bettors is "How soon?"

Ten Rules to Keep in Mind

Here are ten points of good advice to keep in mind when betting college basketball:

1. Always look to team match-up. Any disparities in speed, size and bench will show up on the scoreboard. Also know which coaches run it up and which play ball control. Don't lay too many points against ball-control clubs such as Army, Oklahoma State, and Fairleigh Dickinson.

2. Home court is one of the most important edges. Never underestimate the value of a home court in college basketball.

3. Stay with reliable teams, not erratic ones, and watch for hot and cold streaks. Teams that beat the points consistently should be your bread and butter—especially when they're hot. If a team's cooling off, wait until it gets back on the right track.

4. A team coming off a big win is usually due for a letdown next outing and may not cover. College basketball is played by kids and you can't underplay the value of emotions—positive and negative—that affect the players.

5. Don't go against a good team coming off a loss—either go with them or no bet. Don't buck the good ones. If they're upset once, they're going to be extra tough the next time they play.

6. If a good team is upset at home they usually win big in the return match. Revenge can be sweet, especially for the smart bettor.

7. Don't bet a team at home if it has already defeated an opponent on the road—they usually don't cover in the rematch. Our research has shown this to be an important betting point which can save a bettor a bundle of loot over the years.

8. Strongest home court advantage is in Western Athletic and Big Eight conferences. Statistics show that home teams cover consistently in these conferences.

9. There are usually two teams in every conference that never cover or win at home. As the season progresses these clubs are revealed. They are solid bets "against" since they

usually give points and lose outright—until oddsmakers catch on, and then the opposite usually happens.

10. The trend in the Missouri Valley is that good teams cover at home against each other almost all the time—a solid bet with which you probably won't be giving too many points. Invariably, the race in this loop goes right down to the wire and usually involves three or more teams.

College Basketball Systems

Trying to put together a system for picking basketball winners is a difficult task, at best. As with football, we won't dwell on systems since most are good only for their inventors. However, we like to give a mathematical formula that yields the *probable* victory margin of the winning club. Just as the football method (page 86) encompasses a number of mathematical computations, the basketball method requires a bit of work by its employer. As you know, nothing valuable in life comes easy. Unless you intend to devote some time to the plan, the method is not for you. You'd be better off to employ the services of a questionable "priceline" dispenser. Even better yet, picking winning names out of a hat could possibly suit you. If you have the patience (coupled with a modicum of mathematical expertise) to devote about twenty minutes a day to the plan, it will prove itself workable. Here's how it operates:

Do not consider any teams for selection unless the rival clubs have played at least three contests.

The first step in using the plan will be determining the *average* victory or losing margin of each club. For example, suppose team A has fashioned the following scores: 79–63; 81–47; and 78–76. Add the total number of victorious points and divide this figure by the number of games played. In the preceding example, our figures would be 16 (79–63), 34 (81–47), and 2 (78–76). Now add: 16 + 34 + 2 = 52. Divided by the number of games (3) our first obtainable calculable figure is 17.3. Thus, team A's average winning margin is 17.3. Now complete the same functions for A's opponents. Let's suppose team B has fashioned the following scores in five previous contests: 85–59; 49–40; 63–71 (a loss); 80–57; and 67–66. Our five figures are: 26 + 9 + 23 + 1 − 8 (the loss). In this example, our resultant total would be 51. Dividing this figure by the number of games played, we arrive at the average victory margin figure of 10.2. Our next step will be to subtract the smaller total from the higher figure. In this case, 17.2 − 10.2 = 7.1.

As has already been mentioned, some teams have a facility for performing well at home while suffering horrendous losses on the road. Any knowledgeable observer will attest to the fact that in no other sport is the home advantage more apparent than in basketball. Howling crowds, cramped playing conditions, vast differences in playing surfaces, lighting, and emotions all take a toll on visiting clubs. In our method, we will automatically add or subtract 4.9 points for the home court advantage (4.9 is an average figure that came about after many hours of research into the system's operation). It is to be used without variance. Do not tinker with the figure and expect the results to be fruitful.

Now, here's how to apply the home court advantage figure (HCA) to our current total. Let's assume today's game is being played on the home court of team A. Team A has a victory margin advantage (VMA) of 7.1 points. Adding the VMA and the HCA, our new adjusted figure is 12.0. Only two more steps are required in the plan.

It will be necessary to determine which clubs are more powerful on offense and defense. It has been our determination that defensive-minded clubs win more than their share of basketball contests. Use this table to determine a team's offensive and defensive capabilities.

Offense	Defense
40–45 = 0	under 50 = 9.4
46–51 = 1.5	under 48 = 9.8
52–58 = 2.1	
59–67 = 3.2	
68–79 = 4.3	
80 & over = 4.7	

Now it will be necessary to determine how many bonus points are to be awarded to teams A and B.

In its first game, team A scored 79 points; thus it acquired 4.3 offensive bonus points. In its second outing, it scored 81 points. This gives it an additional 4.7 bonus points. Team A scored 78 points in its third game for 4.3 more bonus points. Once again, add the bonus points together and divide this figure by the number of games played: 4.3 + 4.7 + 4.3 = 13.3

divided by 3 = 4.4. In its third game, team A held its opponents to 47 points. Referring to the defensive chart we find that this point total is equal to 9.8 more bonus points. Don't forget also to divide the defensive bonus points by the number of games played. Thus, 9.8 divided by three equals 3.3. Add together the offensive and defensive bonus points' averages. In team A's case, 4.4 + 3.3 = 7.7.

Now we perform the same function for team B. Here is a listing of its scores and its bonus points:

Team B
Defensive Bonus
Offensive Bonus

Team B	Offensive Bonus	Defensive Bonus
85–59	4.7	0
49–40	1.5	9.8
63–71	3.2	0
80–57	4.7	0
67–66	3.2	0
Totals	17.3 = 3.4	9.8 = 2.0
	5	5

Totaled, our resultant bonus points for team B are 5.4. Comparing this with A's total of 7.7 we can now determine that A's combined offensive and defensive skills are an additional 2.3 points better than B's (7.7 − 5.4 = 2.3). This additional figure is added to our previously adjusted victory margin forecast of 12.0 and we can now conclude that team A should defeat team B by approximately 14.3 points. Incidentally if B had fashioned a higher bonus average than A, these points would have been subtracted from A's current adjusted figure. Suppose that team B had acquired 1.6 more average bonus points than A. In that case, we would have subtracted 1.6 from A's adjusted total of 12.0 for a predicted victory margin of 10.4 points (12.0 − 1.6).

SYNOPSIS OF THE RULES

1. Rivals must have played a minimum of three contests.
2. Add up team A's victory margin and losing margin. Divide by number of games played. Do the same for team B.

3. Subtract the lesser figure from the higher to determine first adjusted figure.

4. Add 4.9 for team with home court advantage (HCA).

5. Award offensive and defensive bonus points to each club for each game played. Total bonus points and divide by number of games played.

6. Subtract lesser figure from higher bonus figure and apply to adjusted figure.

7. Resultant figure is predicted victory margin.

If the predicted victory margin of team A was 11.2 points and the club was picked to win by 9 points by the oddsmakers, A would be the choice since its predicted total superseded the odds. If the oddsmakers fashioned a winning margin of 15 points and A's predicted margin was 11.2, team B would become your choice.

The 200-Point System

Even in this era of racehorse basketball, a 100-point scoring effort still lifts many eyelids. More important, any college basketball team that is able to score a total of 200 points or more in its last two outings is really clicking in high gear. This is the basis of one of the more popular college basketball systems.

200-POINT SYSTEM RULES

1. Consider for selection any college basketball team able to amass a total of 200 points or more during its last two games.

2. Disregard home or away advantages or disadvantages. The method's underlying principle appears to be strong enough to negate the home court advantage.

3. Pass any game where both clubs amassed 200 points or more in their last two outings.

That's all there is to it. Glancing at the workout compiled during the first 4 weeks of a recent season's college basketball schedule, we find the method throwing off winners at the rate of 69.2 percent. In all 26 plays presented 18 were winners. And the method seems to produce selections at the rate of six or seven per week.

We'll offer you this example: early in the season, Butler was scheduled to play New Mexico at New Mexico's home court. Oddsmakers had installed the New Mexico team as 17-point favorites. In its two preceding games against Illinois and Virginia Common, Butler racked up point totals of 102 and 99 for a total of 201 points. New Mexico did win, but not by the required 17 points. The final score: New Mexico 94, Butler 86, an 8-point victory margin. Butler University, considering the pointspread, was the winner.

Here's another one: in the North Carolina-Creighton game, the Tar Heels were 6-point favorites. North Carolina's two preceding games showed totals of 109 and 101, easily exceeding the necessary 200-point figure. North Carolina won the game with ease, 106 to 86, for a 20-point victory margin. In

Workout of Results Obtained with the 200-Point System

Team	Opponent	Spread	Final	Result
Arizona State	Seattle	+7	84–89	Win
Butler	New Mexico	+17	86–94	Win
Drake	Iowa State	−10	87–63	Win
Florida State	Mississippi State	−19	117–84	Win
Holy Cross	Seton Hall	−4	59–49	Win
Kentucky	West Virginia	−5	106–100	Win
Louisiana State	Florida	−11	87–77	Loss
Loyola, New Orleans	Wisconsin	+16	83–94	Win
Mississippi	Texas	−6	89–84	Loss
Nebraska	Colorado State	+6	69–65	Loss
New Mexico State	Brigham Young	+3	75–86	Loss
North Carolina	Creighton	−6	106–86	Win
Southern Illinois	Texas	+5	100–107	Loss
Tulsa	Texas A & M	−16	103–71	Win
Utah	Washington	−10	89–78	Win
West Virginia	Army	−5	74–71	Loss
Wisconsin	Pittsburgh	+6	76–81	Win
Florida State	Jacksonville	+11	108–114	Win
Fordham	Columbia	+1	83–67	Win
Indiana	Butler	−16	111–94	Win
Kentucky	Indiana	−10	95–93	Win
Mississippi	Auburn	−4	108–96	Win
North Carolina	Virginia	−7	80–75	Loss
Southern Illinois	Arkansas	−13	99–78	Win
Florida State	Southern Cal	+6	85–94	Loss
Mississippi	Holy Cross	+4	99–93	Win

Winning Percentage—69.2%

26 Plays
18 Wins
8 Losses

the workout chart, under the column labeled *spread*, plus points mean a team was receiving that number of points from the oddsmakers, while minus points mean the club was spotting that total of points.

Basketball systems are complicated or very simple. If you have one that works for you, stay with it.

Chapter 5

Betting on Baseball

Baseball betting in this country is a multi-billion-dollar-a-year business simply because of the number of games played. Each of the 24 teams in the American and National leagues plays 162 games, which means the bettor has a potential 1,-944 betting opportunities during the six-month-long season. Even with nearly 2,000 chances to bet during the season, baseball definitely has slipped to the number two spot among sports bettors, ranking behind college and professional football.

While baseball people will dispute that the popularity of their game has slipped with the man in the street, bookmakers and sports-handicapping services say that the volume of money they now handle on the sport is about 70 percent of what it was ten years ago, and they say their clients are mostly in the over-forty age bracket. Does this mean that the young bettor is not oriented to betting baseball? We have a strange suspicion that it does, although we have no scientific facts to back up that thought.

First of all, the betting structure of baseball makes it an unattractive sport for the gambler because most of the time he is forced to put up a large sum of money to win a little. For instance, there is not a horse bettor alive who doesn't shudder when he bets on a horse which goes off as an odds-on (less than even money) choice. He knows it is suicidal to bet on horses such as that, for anytime you risk a lot of money to win a little you're opening the door for disaster. The same thing can be said of baseball. There is no point-spread to beat in baseball as all games are put on the board at different odds. The bettor either lays the odds or takes them, depending on whether he wants to bet the favorite or the underdog.

While baseball is an unattractive betting sport to many, it is the simplest of all sports on which one can bet. There are no elaborate scouting reports necessary as might be the case in football and basketball. There is no guessing as to what a team's game plan will be. There are few unknown factors to take into consideration. There are no position-by-position comparisons necessary. And, last but not least, there is no pointspread to haunt the bettor.

How Baseball Is Bet

Like other betting sports, baseball has an official line. Under it there are odds on all the baseball games to be played that day, determined by any one of twenty different individuals or sports services from whom your local bookie purchases his official line. It may read for a specific day something like this:

Mets 7–5 over Astros; Giants 7½–6½ over Phils; Braves–Reds pick 'em; Pirates 6–5 over Dodgers; Cards 8–7 over Cubs; Expos 9–5 over Padres.

Yanks 8–5 over Orioles; Tigers–Red Sox pick 'em; Twins 9–8 over Rangers; Royals 7–5 over Brewers; Angels–A's pick 'em; White Sox 8–7 over Indians.

There are definite class distinctions among baseball bookmakers. The $5 and $10 bettors (commonly called five and dime creeps by some bookies) are taking a hosing when looking for action. In effect, the small bettor is not getting the right price when laying down a bet.

To begin with, the margin of profit for most baseball bookmakers is rather small. They figure they're not going to make much money with the customary 1 point (and among really big bettors, the half-point) vigorish. Therefore, it has become their practice to quote different lines to different bettors.

The odds may vary from a 2-point split right down to the half-point margin if you are betting $1,000 and up. Meanwhile, the $5 and $10 bettor is taking it on the chin and there is little he can do about it unless he wants to spend most of the day shopping around.

There are really four categories of betting odds. Years ago they used to be referred to as the 40-cent line, the 20-cent line, the 10-cent line, and the 5-cent line. The 40-cent line is for suckers and small bettors, prevalent in small cities and towns, and serves as a cushion for greedy bookmakers. It is actually the 2-pointspread. For example: 9–11, 7–9. The bookie's favorable percentage, or advantage, on the 40-cent line runs from a high of about 11 percent to a low of just under 2 percent.

The 20-cent line (the most common line) is usually given to the more experienced bettor who knows when he is being trimmed on the price. This line is based on a 1-point odds spread, or a 20-cent spread when based on a $1 take price. The bookie's favorable percentage, or advantage, on this line ranges anywhere from a little over 1 percent upward to 6 percent depending on the actual bet. The 20-cent line deals mostly in fractions: 6½–7½, 7½–8½, 8½–9½.

Baseball's 40-Cent Line

Correct Odds on Favorite	Bookie Lays the Odds	Bookie Takes the Odds
5 to 5	5 to 6	6 to 5
6 to 5	5 to 5	7 to 5
7 to 5	6 to 5	8 to 5
8 to 8	7 to 5	9 to 5
9 to 5	8 to 5	2 to 1
2 to 1	9 to 5	11 to 5
11 to 5	2 to 1	12 to 5
12 to 5	11 to 5	13 to 5
13 to 5	12 to 5	14 to 5
14 to 5	13 to 5	3 to 1
16 to 5	14 to 5	18 to 5
3½ to 1	3 to 1	4 to 1

Let's take a look at two examples that show the 1-point differential and the 20-cent difference between the bookie's take and lay prices. As you know, when two ball teams are rated at even money, or pick 'em, it means that each team is considered to have an equal chance of winning. But in such cases you don't put up an equal amount of money with the book. When a baseball game is quoted as even money on the 20-cent line, the bookie quotes a price of 5½ to 5 pick 'em. You must lay $1.10 to the bookie's $1, no matter which team you select to win.

Referring to the official line given earlier in this chapter, you'll find, for example, in the case of the Twins and Rangers game that the Twins are an 8½ to 5 favorite. But the 20-cent price official line reads: "8–9 Twins favorite," which means that the bookie will lay on the Twins at $1.60 to $1 or take the Rangers if you wager $1.80 to $1.

Baseball's 20-Cent Line

Correct Odds on Favorite	Bookie Lays the Odds	Bookie Takes the Odds
5 to 5	5 to 5½	5½ to 5
5½ to 5	5 to 5	. 6 to 5
6 to 5	5½ to 5	6½ to 5
6½ to 5	6 to 5	7 to 5
7 to 5	6½ to 5	7½ to 5
7½ to 5	7 to 5	8 to 5
8 to 5	7½ to 5	8½ to 5
8½ to 5	8 to 5	9 to 5
9 to 5	8½ to 5	9½ to 5
9½ to 5	9 to 5	2 to 1
2 to 1	9½ to 5	10½ to 5
10½ to 5	2 to 1	11 to 5
11 to 5	10½ to 5	11½ to 5
11½ to 5	11 to 5	12 to 5
12 to 5	11½ to 5	12½ to 5
12½ to 5	12 to 5	13 to 5
13 to 5	12½ to 5	13½ to 5
14 to 5	13 to 5	3½ to 1
3 to 1	14 to 5	16 to 5

The 10-cent line is for the fair-sized bettor who is going for $100 and up knows his way around the fractions. That is, the 10-cent line operates on ½ of 1 point differential between the bookie's lay and take prices. In an even-money or pick 'em wager, you must lay the book odds of 5¼ to 5, rather than the 5½ to 5 odds of the 20-cent line. If a ball team is a 6 to 5 favorite, the bookie will lay you odds of 5¾ to 5 and require you to lay him odds of 6¼ to 5. The 5¼ pick 'em is really a $1.05 to $1 wager, while the 6¼ to 5 is $1.20 to $1. Incidentally, the bookie's percentage advantage on the 10-cent line is from just under 1 percent to over 5 percent.

On the 10-cent line you'll often note that the official line may read "Pirates favorite 120–130," or maybe just "20–30." This means that the book will pay $1.20 to $1.00 on the Pirates, and if you are to bet on the Pirates in their game against the Dodgers, for instance, you must lay the book $1.30 to $1.00. By the way, most 10-cent line bets are based primarily on the starting pitcher as recorded on the official line. If one pitcher doesn't start as indicated, all bets can be canceled.

The 5-cent line is dealt to bettors laying down $1,000 to $20,000 a game and is handled by syndicate bookmakers.

Baseball's 10-Cent Line

Correct Odds on Favorite	Bookie Lays the Odds	Bookie Takes the Odds
5 to 5	5 to 5¼	5¼ to 5
5¼ to 5	5 to 5	5½ to 5
5½ to 5	5¼ to 5	5¾ to 5
5¾ to 5	5½ to 5	6 to 5
6 to 5	5¾ to 5	6¼ to 5
6¼ to 5	6 to 5	6½ to 5
6½ to 5	6¼ to 5	6¾ to 5
6¾ to 5	6½ to 5	7 to 5
7 to 5	6¾ to 5	7¼ to 5
7¼ to 5	7 to 5	3 to 2
3 to 2	7¼ to 5	7¾ to 5
7¾ to 5	3 to 2	8 to 5
8 to 5	7¾ to 5	8¼ to 5
8¼ to 5	8 to 5	8½ to 5
8½ to 5	8¼ to 5	8¾ to 5
8¾ to 5	8½ to 5	9 to 5
9 to 5	8¾ to 5	9¼ to 5
9¼ to 5	9 to 5	9½ to 5
9½ to 5	9¼ to 5	2 to 1
2 to 1	9½ to 5	10½ to 5
10½ to 5	2 to 1	11 to 5
11 to 5	10½ to 5	11½ to 5
11½ to 5	11 to 5	12 to 5
12 to 5	11½ to 5	12½ to 5
12½ to 5	12 to 5	13 to 5
13 to 5	12½ to 5	13½ to 5
14 to 5	13 to 5	3 to 1
3 to 1	14 to 5	16 to 5
3¼ to 1	3 to 1	3½ to 1

The odds on the 5-cent line are, in effect, almost even money but not quite. No bookmaker can afford to stay in business by dealing even-money bets but with the size of the wagers, he can afford to make the odds very attractive in order to get the big action. Actually the 5-cent line operates on a quarter of a point differential between the price lines of two opposing teams. For example, in a pick 'em situation, you must lay the bookie odds of 5⅛ to 5 no matter which team you bet. As a rule, the 5-cent line is quoted in dollars and cents rather than in odds terms; the bookie quotes even-money games as $1.02½ pick 'em. The bookies favorable percentage runs from ½ to 1¼ percent on the 5-cent line. So he is making even money.

Meanwhile, the small bettor is taking a beating in hundreds of office buildings and factories around the country. He is, in effect, part of a captive audience. He can't very well leave his job to go shopping for a better price. Nor can he pick up the phone and let the Yellow Pages do the shopping for him. In most cases he's stuck.

The beautiful gimmick for the bookmaker on the 2-point-spread is that he's getting more for his money. Of course, while he gets more, the $5 or $10 bettor is getting much less and risking his hard-earned dough at a much higher rate.

For example, if the Yankees are a legitimate 8–5 over the Orioles a greedy bookmaker quotes his price as "7–9 Yankees favorite." This means if you want to bet the Yankees you have to lay the book 9 to 5. If you want the Orioles the book will lay you only 7 to 5. So no matter which way you bet the book has the spread in his favor.

To break it down further and to show how much profit the book is making, look at this: if one player laid $9 to $5 on the Yankees and another $7 to $5 on the Orioles, the bookie couldn't get hurt either way. He would break even on a winning 9–5 bet and be ahead $2 on the 7–5 bet if the underdog Orioles won. A classic example of why bookmakers most often root for the underdog, wouldn't you say?

At *Sports Action*, we have received many complaints from small bettors rapping the variety in baseball odds. Many of the small bettors wondered what would be the best way to combat the "cheap" or "chiseling" bookie.

One sure way is to know the real price. When a book-maker is operating on a 2-pointspread (7–9) the bettor should realize that the true price is 8–5 on the favorite. If the book-maker quotes the game as 8–10 you'd better believe that the true odds are 9–5. The middle figure between 7–9 is 8 (the true odds figure) and the second odds figure is always 5, therefore the true price becomes 8–5. In other words, know the true price and if the book insists his price is right, then by all means shop for another bookie. If you are part of the "captive audience" and can't shop around, then don't bet. Sooner or later the bookmaker will get the message and come up with true odds.

Remember that betting lines are very flexible. Often book-makers will raise or lower their lines to encourage or discourage betting on certain games. We had a letter from a reader in the Chicago area who said his bookmaker usually offered the home team as a one-run favorite—with the bookie winning on a tie (when the home team won by a run).

It's pretty obvious that the bookie was simply trying to discourage people from betting on the Cubs or to get in as much sucker money as possible on the local team at horrendously high odds. The bookie was well aware that he had few customers in his area who would take the visiting team.

Either way it was a bookie's bet—the favorite had to win by *two* runs for those who bet the home team to collect, and if you did take the underdog, you got no odds—just an even-up bet—in which the underdog had to win for you to collect since the bookie won on what he misleadingly called a "tie" (when the favorite won by a single run). Most bookies don't place their customers at such a great disadvantage because they'd lose them too fast. As a matter of fact, if you're clever enough, you might even be able to "dutch" your baseball bets (that is, cut down your chances of losing to almost nothing while giving yourself a possible profit margin throughout the season).

A quick example of how you can do this is in closely matched games. There are times when the price line may fluctuate just enough between several bookies so that you can bet both teams and win. Say the Yankees were playing Minnesota and one Bronx bookie was in an area that supports the Bombers pretty heavily. The Yanks might be quoted as the 5½–6½ choice. Across the river in New Jersey you might just get the opposite figure with the Twins being tagged the 5½–6½ choice. If you bet both teams with the bookies that rated them as underdogs you couldn't lose!

Say you were making $50 bets on each club. No matter which team won you'd get a return of $105 for the $100 you invested since you played each club getting underdog odds of 5½ to 5. The profit percentage is small in such moves (about 5 percent) but the income is as steady as and faster than the dividends you'll get at your friendly neighborhood bank.

Another good betting angle is to latch onto a hot team and keep laying the odds. It won't take a sharp bookie long to realize whom you'll be betting on. You'll do a lot better to deal with two, three, or four different bookmakers and vary your action so as not to bet the same team twice in a row with the same man.

There are some ways to get a bookmaker to give you the true price without his knowing it but you will probably never trick him into giving you better odds. So don't even bother trying. Actually, one of the best ways to get an even shake from a book is never to mention the name of the team you want to bet until he has quoted the prices. Ask him for a run-down on the games. If he says Yankees 9–11, you turn around and tell him you'll take the Orioles at 9–5.

Realizing he is caught in an odds trap, the shrewd book will probably then tell you, "Wait till I check the latest line." He will then make a fake phone call and come back and tell you the price is now 7–9 Yanks. You can then switch back to your Yankees bet (what you wanted in the first place) and thereby save yourself the extra 2-point burden.

The reason why so many bookmakers use the devious 40-cent line (2 pointspread) is that they, in a sense, are suckers themselves. A lot of people believe that baseball bookmakers reap fortunes by simply staying close to a telephone and recording bets. That's far from true. It might be true of syndicate bookies handling $25,000 per-game action but most of the small books have to rely on other forms of action to get a whiff of the sweet smell of success.

Our latest intensive survey shows that while the horse bookmaker can almost always unload if he has too much play on one horse, the baseball bookmaker is not that fortunate. If the 2 pointspread type of bookmaker wants to lay off some action, who can he turn to? He can only step up to the 20-cent-line operator who, nine times out of ten, will not give him any price. The reason for this is that "he's doing him a favor" by handling the action. That should serve as some consolation to the $5 and $10 bettor, knowing that the greedy bookmaker doesn't always survive in the jungle.

When possible, one always has an edge when betting privately by splitting the price. For example, if the official line is 7½–8½ Mets vs. Cardinals, and you like the Mets, you could lay 8–5 privately instead of 8½. The person taking the Cardinals will also be getting 8–5 instead of 7½.

Pitching and the Bettor

There are some who say baseball betting should not be called baseball betting at all, but "pitcher betting." In fact, many bookmakers quote the names of opposing pitchers, rather than teams, when running down a game-by-game price line for bettors. Connie Mack once said pitching was 80 percent of the game, but many feel the figure is higher than that. To them, the contest is 90 percent pitching, with the other 10 percent spread thinly over the other aspects of the game.

We can draw a comparison with horse racing. A horse is going to perform just as well for any average jockey. He is the thing that is important, not the jockey. It is an accepted fact that, when analyzing a horse's chance, the jockey makes up about 10 percent of the overall betting picture. In baseball, the pitcher is 90 percent of the game, the rest of the team 10 percent of it. As we have said before, there is no reason to be concerned with pointspreads in baseball. Almost all baseball betting is conducted on the basis of odds. But the odds you get will be based strictly on the ability of the pitcher, and the better the pitcher the shorter the odds. If a top hurler such as Tom Seaver were pitching, the price on a game woud most likely be 9–5, which means you would have to put up $9 to win $5 from the bookmakers if you wanted to bet on Seaver's team. Bookmakers, trying to take every edge they can, continually juggle the odds on baseball games. In fact, in the same game in which Seaver was pitching, the bookmaker might give you only 7–5 odds if you wanted to bet against him.

One doesn't have to be a mathematical genius to determine that the bookmaker who operates like this—and a high percentage of them do—has a tremendous financial edge over his clients. If Seaver wins, he pays his customers off at the rate of $5 for every $9 they put up. However, if Seaver loses, he pays off only $7 for each $5 bet.

In handicapping twirlers, in addition to knowing which guys dominate which teams, you must learn to spot the weaknesses in a pitcher's style. Some hurlers have mental blocks when going against particular pitchers and no matter what, some pitchers simply can't beat some clubs. Also, some pitchers excel in the daylight; others shine under the arcs. Some do best against teams with mostly right-hand hitters; others like to pitch to lefties.

It is important to remember that a team with a poor record will have a pitcher with a good won-lost mark and he might be a very effective hurler according to his ERA. Some typical examples from 1973 are Nolan Ryan of the California Angels and Bert Blyleven of the Minnesota Twins. Ryan was 21–16 for a team which lost 83 games, and on top of that he had a fine 2.87 ERA. Blyleven racked up a 20–17 record for a Minnesota nine that was only 81–81 for the campaign. But while the Twins were taking their lump collectively, Blyleven's ERA was a 2.52, second only to Jim Palmer's loop-leading figure of 2.40. A good rule of thumb to follow is that any pitcher with an ERA lower than three runs a game is usually a play, provided that you don't have to lay a superior team big odds. It is an extremely strong bet if you can get, not lay, odds with a good pitcher going for you against a rival pitcher who has a much higher ERA. There were 19 pitchers in the American League in 1973 with ERAs under 3.00; the National League had 18 hurlers in this category. So there are only a handful of pitchers that you really have to keep tabs on as far as ERA goes. If you want to narrow your field of consideration even further, you can confine your play to those pitchers with a 2.70 or lower ERA. There was a combined total of 24 of them in 1973 in both loops.

To prove out these comments, we analyzed the won-lost records of the Top 15 ERA pitchers in both leagues for last year. In the National League their combined record was 219–165, for a .570 average; in the junior loop it was 262–182, a .592 mark. Totaling up both leagues, we found a 481–347 slate, for a .582 average.

Cutting it even finer by figuring only the moundsmen with ERAs under 2.70, the National League had a 79–50, .609 mark, while the American was again tops, with a 44–26, .629 average. The combined total was 122–76, .616. It must be remembered that 1973 was *not* a good year for the better ERA itchers percentagewise.

The bullpen is sometimes a good bet. Most baseball people agree that using the same pitchers in more games isn't the answer to handling a 162-game schedule. The solution is in a team's bullpen where a manager can dip in and pull out an occasional starter. A smart manager uses those relief hurlers who have had experience as starters when he's pressed for a pitcher in the midst of a heavy schedule.

A smart bettor will jump on these hurlers as solid betting propositions in the clutch. Oftentimes, since these men have been in the bullpen, you can get good prices when they make an infrequent start. When you bet on starters coming out of the bullpen you've got a few things going for you. In the first place these men are generally experienced starters who have been relegated to bullpen duty for any one of a number of reasons. Promising rookies may have replaced them in the starting rotation or sore arms may have foced them into secondary roles.

Don't let these two strikes against these hurlers fool you. You've still got a good shot at expecting a fairly good performance when these men take the mound in a starting role. One reason is that these men are getting a "second chance." Remember, these men were once regular hurlers now relegated to bullpen duty. An impressive showing could mean another shot at a starting berth so they'll be in there trying to win just a little bit harder than a pitcher who's already got a spot in the regular rotation.

In addition, some of these bullpen starters are out of the regular rotation because of sore arms and other ailments they've been trying to work out since spring. But it's summer now and the hot weather seems to bring out the best in sore-armed hurlers, so they're worth a plunge.

All of the baseball buffs agree that one of the few times when it pays to bet the underdogs, regardless of who's pitching, is in doubleheaders—especially during the often nasty and unpredictable weather of spring and early summer when some of the top twirlers are not yet up to their hot-weather form.

Sports Action random suveys over 1972–73 revealed that there were only 13 percent twin-bill sweeps as against 87 percent splits. It's easily seen by this simple statistic that a good rule to follow in doubleheader play is to take the 'dog in *both* games of the two-ply battle. The percentages will be heavily with you because most of them will wind up in splits. And if you're taking the odds in a favorable situation, you've got to make money in the long run.

While on the subject of pitchers let us warn you: *name your pitchers*. When betting a ball game don't say you want the Dodgers over Atlanta—say you want Sutton over Reed. This will mean that there is no bet unless Sutton is the starting pitcher. The same goes if you want underdog Atlanta. Tell your bookie you want Reed—this way there's no bet unless he pitches.

Sometimes the option of picking pitchers is reserved for bigger bettors but, remember, no matter what you're betting your bookie won't offer you pitchers. You've got to ask for them. If you've got the smarts to speak up he's usually happy to oblige. If not, take your business elsewhere.

Spot Betting Baseball

Although baseball betting may not be as complex as football and basketball, it does take skill. The reason most people usually lose is that they are amateurs attempting to compete with professionals. In today's world one must devote so much time to his own profession that there is little opportunity to acquire more than a surface knowledge of anything else. For this reason any procedure that entails meticulous adherence to a given set of rules is fallible. This is especially true when it requires concentrated effort over long periods. The average person too often—through carelessness, forgetfulness, or inertia—fails to hold strictly to a prescribed pattern. Thus any system of betting that is based on the law of averages over an entire season's play can be defeated by the tendency of the bettor, himself, to err.

The majority of baseball fans have the urge, and the time, to bet on baseball only once or twice a week, usually on weekends. They are interested mostly in the games that are either broadcast or telecast on Saturdays and Sundays. All of them want to know whether there is some system they can follow which will prove profitable even though they make only an occasional bet. The man who bets on baseball spasmodically is called, in gambling parlance, a spot bettor—and he can win money, too.

Any spot bettor able to read the box score of a ball game and the batting and pitching statistics published weekly during the season should have no difficulty adhering to a set of rules which, during the past eight years, has accounted for the winner of 531 major-league ball games out of 603 selected—all suitable for *spot betting*. There are just eight rules to keep in mind:

Rule 1: Never make a bet prior to the first of June. Play during the first six weeks of a season rarely reflects the true ability of the contending teams. Some managers, still experimenting, have not definitely decided on their first-string lineup. Tailenders, with delusions of grandeur, often play over their heads. Many frontline pitchers get off to a bad start, not yet rounded into their true form. The weather in many big-league cities is atrocious. Muscles of older players need the lubrication that only perspiration, a byproduct of hot weather, can supply. Team rosters must be cut to twenty-five players thirty days after the season has begun; thus, by June first, the first-stringers have actually been on their own for only two weeks.

The period from the start of the season until June 1 should be used for study—not for betting.

Rule 2: Never bet on a team unless it is at least an 8 to 5 favorite. The official odds are a reflection of the research done by the professional gambling fraternity, usually the most accurate available estimate of a team's chances to win. When one plays the odds, he is backing the opinion of these expert researchers. Over the years it has proved more profitable to assume they are right, even though this involves a larger investment, than to assume they are wrong. The odds you take should never be less than 8 to 5, and preferably more.

Rule 3: Never bet on a team unless it has won its preceding game. This is a provision that the spot bettor should take from the Streak System. The mental attitude of a team is better after having won its preceding game, and it is wise to have this psychological factor working for you.

Rule 4: Bet on a team only when the starting pitcher pitched well the last time out. Most starting pitchers work every fourth day. Your gamble is always safer if you pick a pitcher who did well in his last game. (If he hasn't pitched in a week or more, however, don't bet.)

Rule 5: Be sure the key relief pitcher of the team you bet on did not work the preceding day. The key relief pitcher on a team is termed the "short man." His job is to pitch two or three innings, and he is usually called upon in the late innings of a close game to protect a scant lead.

Most good "short men" can pitch very often. Nevertheless, they are not always at their best when they work two days in succession. Don't pick a team whose relief man is overworked.

Rule 6: Consider carefully the ball park in which the game is to be played. Most teams play better at home than away. But a few are good on the road too. Others perform particularly well in certain parks, not so well in others. You must learn the peculiarities of the teams you sponsor in this respect.

There are two ball parks where, regardless of the team playing, the spot bettor should never act. These are Fenway Park in Boston, where the short left-field fence often makes a travesty of the game, and Candlestick Park in San Francisco, where the wind plays impossible tricks with the ball.

Rule 7: Check the past-performance record of the pitcher who is slated to oppose the team that you are backing. As previously stated, some pitchers pitch well against certain teams, poorly against others. Some teams hit better against right-handers, others against left-handers. Your study of the team or teams you plan to sponsor during the season will teach you these idiosyncrasies. Sometimes an average front-line pitcher can nearly always beat one particular team in the league.

A correct estimate of your team's effectiveness against right- and left-handed pitching is even more basic than the acquisition of knowledge regarding specific pitchers. Every team is just a little stronger offensively when batting against either right- or left-handed pitching. Obviously the chance of your team's winning is greater when it is pitted against the kind of pitching it prefers.

It isn't too difficult to classify the teams you plan to sponsor in this respect by the first of June. A team's power usually dictates your decision.

Rule 8: Make sure your team's first-string lineup is intact. Injuries to frontline players are inevitable at some time during the season. That is why good teams usually have a strong strength in the field. This is important because it also implies that the team's bench is at full strength and is available for defensive purposes or pinch-hitting as the game progresses.

These are the eight rules that will spell success or failure for you if you are a spot bettor. The number of bets you make during the season is relatively unimportant. Therefore, if the team you plan to back fails to meet any one of the requirements specified, don't bet.

The method you select to pick the team or teams you will back during the season is also vitally important. There are now twenty-four major-league teams. The pennant winners usually win about two-thirds of the games they play; the tailenders, one-third. Horse players will tell you that a stakes horse will always run more true to form than a claiming horse. By the same token a good ball club performs more consistently than a poor one. For this reason it is safest to sponsor the first-division clubs in each league, teams that usually win at least half of the games they play.

If the spot bettor wishes to insure having a successful season he must acquire an intimate knowledge of the teams he plans to sponsor and he must decide which teams they are to be by the first of June. It is our opinion that the average, avocational bettor has neither the time nor the capacity to gather the information he needs if he selects more than two teams. Aside from all other considerations, if he selects more, he subjects himself to too much homework and the whole thing ceases to be fun.

The teams you sponsor do not necessarily have to win their respective pennants; they may not even be contenders. They can both be in the same league if you so choose. As long as they are both first-division clubs they qualify. However, once you have made your selections you must restrict your betting to the teams you have chosen. If, as the season progresses, one of them goes sour you may drop it and substitute another club, but do not undertake to sponsor more than two at any time.

There are certain characteristics you should look for when you make your selections. A first-division team usually plays .500 ball, winning half or more of its games. Yet many of these teams lack certain vital essentials. When selecting your teams, there are four qualifications to look for (plus making sure the teams are of first-division caliber):

1. Ability to make the double play.
2. At least one reliable relief pitcher.
3. A team batting average of .260 or better.
4. A bench that includes one good right-handed and one good left-handed hitter.

A team batting average of .260 implies a little better than average offensive strength. With the lively ball and the short fences in many parks, most games require the winning team to score four or five runs. This means six of the nine men in the lineup are pretty good hitters, which usually indicates a team batting average of about .260. Hitting ability alone will not win a pennant, but it is extremely important to the spot bettor.

Most first-division teams seek both strength and depth on their benches. Injuries to frontline players at some time during the season are inevitable. Our basic rule is: make sure your team's first-string lineup is intact. Thus only the strength of a team's bench, not its depth, is important to the spot bettor. The caliber of the men on the bench when the team on the field is at fullstrength is your determining factor. Specifically, it is best to sponsor teams that have a good right-handed and a good left-handed hitter not in the regular starting lineup.

When sizing up American League games, there is another additional factor that must be taken into consideration. How good is the team's designated hitter? A successful designated hitter can mean a great deal to a junior loop club. In 1973, for instance, many baseball experts claim that it was the designated hitting of Tommy Davis that made the difference in Baltimore winning the AL East pennant.

In evaluating which team will win a specific major-league ball game, the manager is not a determining factor. He unquestionably plays a part in the result of an entire season's play and he contributes in some degree to the result of a series of games, but his effect on the outcome of an isolated game during the season's play is negligible.

Not too long ago the only way one could ascertain the odds on a major-league ball game was to contact a bookie. Today the odds on ball games are published in many newspapers. They also publish the past performances of the day's pitchers and name the team which, in their opinion, is the best bet. This is a relatively recent addition to the wide coverage given baseball over the years and stems from a reluctant desire to be of service to the many fans who bet on ball games. Nevertheless, betting on baseball is still a subject the average sports editor feels must be handled with kid gloves.

The old gambling axiom "Odds were made for suckers" really means that the average person wants to win more than he bets. Earlier, the advisability of playing with official gambling odds was mentioned, but if the team you want to bet on qualifies under these rules, don't let unfavorable odds dissuade you.

There are occasions, however, when the odds indicate that it may be profitable for you to back both your teams to win in a parlay. A parlay is when one bets his original stake, plus its winnings, on a second event. You will find that there are times when both your teams are playing exceptionally good ball. This usually happens in July, August, or September. During this period it is often profitable to back both your teams to win on the same day and there are occasions when a parlay is preferable to making two individual bets.

As teams round into form toward mid-season, the odds on the better teams lengthen. A game between the Yanks and Boston that was 9 to 5 in June may be 13 to 5 in August when the professional researchers have more actual performance data available.

Even if you haven't been a staunch rooter up until now, you'll find that putting your money on the national pastime will provide some great moments in sport. But let us sound a warning—the above applies only to the major leagues. So stick to betting only major-league games. Leave the minors to someone else.

Baseball Betting Systems

Keep all box scores and all other statistics that you can get your hands on ... and study them carefully. In this way you may uncover many surprising angles for betting on various teams. You might, for example, discover that a certain pitcher loses most of the night games that he pitches, or that another team never scores many runs in a certain ball park, etc., etc.

The value of this type of information cannot be overstressed. Can you imagine what it would be like to be the only horse player in the country who had access to horses' past performances?

Don't hesitate to be original when handicapping baseball teams. If you use the same techniques for evaluating a team as the sports offices, bookies, and all other bettors, then you won't have much success at this game. Be original, and you'll probably find yourself making a lot more winning bets on the diamond sport than you ever have before. But there are some baseball betting systems that you should know about.

High Run System

One of the most tried and true baseball betting systems, the Team Total Runs Angle, is once again putting alert hardball speculators on to some of the smartest wagers in the game. The method revolves around play on the five clubs which are collectively scoring the most runs on a seasonal basis.

Keeping tabs, at least weekly, on the top run-scoring teams in both leagues may help you to produce winners in baseball betting.

The Winning Streak Angle

Although the winning streak is hardly a new discovery, it is used by relatively few baseball bettors out of the millions who wager on the national pastime. This is probably so because most bettors are "action hounds" and must have many bets going every day in the week. They figure "more action, more winners," but as you well know, they're usually wrong. On the other hand, those people who follow this method to the letter usually enjoy excellent results over the course of the year.

Your first order of business in starting to make a steady buck on the horsehide-and-bat game is to keep accurate records of the twenty-four major-league clubs on a day-to-day basis, recording wins and losses as follows: Mets: W L L W W W W W W W L L W W W L L W W W W L W W W W W W W W W W W L L W L W W W W L W L.

Three days after the season is under way, the method is playable. When you find a team or teams—no matter if the club(s) is in first place, last place, or somewhere in between in its divisional race—has won or lost three consecutive games, it becomes a play in its next outing. It's immaterial whether the qualified club is playing at home or away, whether the game is a night affair or being played in the daytime, or whether a good ERA pitcher is on the mound. If it has won or lost three in a row, bet the team to continue the streak it's currently on, until the streak is snapped.

Reviewing the National and American leagues for 1973, we found that the angle produced as well as ever. Thus, it seems that a person playing it regularly can still expect to win upward of 67 percent of his wagers and might even be able to improve this percentage figure by adding in his own restrictive rules, such as playing a team on a winning streak only at its own home park and a losing team only when it's on the road, or if a streaking winner is pitching one of its top twirlers or a losing nine is starting one of its lesser lights, or if the team wins against right-handers and loses to lefties, and so on.

There are multiple variations that one can employ to make a profit under this basic winning angle. But win you will as long as you stick to your guns and the law of averages keeps working as it always has and probably always will.

Mathematical Betting System

In Chapters 3 and 4 we detailed a mathematical system for handicapping football and basketball teams. Here is one for baseball.

Once again, the method incorporates simple calculations that can be done by anyone with a rudimentary knowledge of math. There are no long, complicated formulas to contend with. If a fan can add and subtract, the method should be easy to handle. Although uncomplicated, the method will again force its users to keep some records. Frankly, we doubt if anyone can become expert or expect to extract profits from any vocation without applying the proper, necessary effort. Offhand, we would imagine that if one is willing to spend about ten or fifteen minutes a day jotting statistics into a notebook, he'll have little trouble in implementing the system. Let's take a look at the mathematical baseball system.

Rule 1: It will be necessary for the user to compile a daily list of major-league baseball scores. The best way to accomplish this task is to list the names of all major-league baseball clubs on separate pages in a notebook. At the top of the page, list the name of the club. Each time the team plays, jot down its winning or losing score. To avoid confusion always write the number of runs scored by the club before jotting down its opponent's run total. For example: if the team wins by a score of 3–2, naturally, the score would be written 3–2. If the team has been defeated by a 3–2 score, the score should be written 2–3. Although some fans may wonder why we've decided to spell out an obvious point, it's our contention that some individuals have a difficult time absorbing even the most rudimentary point of a mathematical method.

We now have a notebook containing the day-to-day scores of all major-league clubs. What do we do with this most important information? This question can best be answered by presenting rule two.

Rule 2: We will discount and eliminate any club with a record of less than .500. In other words, if a team has lost more games than it has won, it is eliminated from further consideration as a potential winning selection. Although the fans of the underdog may be disappointed by this ruling, the system is based on the fact that a concentration on winning clubs will afford us a higher winning percentage than can be gained by backing teams with losing records.

Rule 3: Determine the team's power winning average (PWA) by dividing its games-won margin into the squad's total number of victories. This point is quite unique among baseball systems we've seen and requires some explanation. The method can best be understood by citing an example. Let's assume that a team's current record stands at 42 wins and 33 losses. Its games-won margin is calculated by subtracting its losses from its wins. In this case, $42 - 33 = 9$. To determine its PWA, divide this figure into the number of recorded wins. To illustrate our example, we divide 9 into 42. The resultant figure is 4.67.

Considering the won-lost record of the scheduled starting pitcher leads us to our next axiom.

Rule 4: The scheduled starting pitcher's PWA must be higher than the team's PWA, otherwise the game is not considered for play. Here again, an example is in order. Suppose the scheduled pitcher has a record of 9 wins and 6 losses. To determine his PWA, again subtract his losses from his wins ($9 - 6 = 3$) and divide the resultant figure into the number of victories: 3 divided into 9 equals 3.00. In this case the game would not qualify for play since the pitcher's PWA of 3.00 is not higher than the club's PWA of 4.67.

In effect, what we are trying to find is a winning team whose scheduled starting pitcher has been outperforming his club. As we said, the method outlined to this point is totally unique.

Rule 5: Any team qualifying thus far is an automatic play against a club whose record is less than .500. At times we run into the situation where a qualifying club faces a squad which does not qualify due to the record of its scheduled starter, but which has a season's mark above .500, or above that of the qualified club. In that case—

Rule 6: If the opponent of the qualified club has better than a .500 mark, or a season's mark better than the qualifying club, it does not become a play unless it has won its last two games. At this point it will become clear to you why we advised you to keep game-to-game records.

Rule 7: If both of today's clubs qualify under the aforementioned rules, the game is passed unless one club's PWA is .75 points or more higher than its opponent's, or its starting pitcher's PWA is 1.25 higher than that of the starting pitcher of its opponent. Here again an explanation is in order. Suppose team A is playing team B and both clubs qualify for play under the preceding rules. Let's further assume that team A has a PWA of 4.86, while team B's PWA is 4.46. Without considering the starting pitchers' PWAs, the game would not qualify for play since the PWA difference is only .40. The rule states that one club's PWA must be .75 higher than the other's for the game to qualify for play. However, if the PWA of A's starting pitcher was 6.74 while the PWA of team B's starter was 5.42, A would become a play. It's obvious that the PWA of A's pitcher is 1.32 points higher than that of B's scheduled starter. In this case, A would become a play.

Rule 8: If a conflict results concerning the PWAs of either a team or starting pitcher the game is passed. To explain, here's another example:

A TEAM PWA: 6.22   A PITCHER PWA: 6.31
B TEAM PWA: 5.02   B PITCHER PWA: 7.74

It's obvious that A's PWA is more than .75 points higher than B's. Ordinarily, this would result in A becoming a selection. But note that B's pitcher's PWA is 1.43 points higher than A's starter. You may ask, "How could this occur?" If a solid club with an average pitcher were facing a so-so team with a superstar on the mound just such a conflict would occur. In this case it would be extremely wise to pass the game.

Obviously, the method should not be employed until the season has advanced into its third week. Otherwise, you'll be faced with a team that may be trying to work out the kinks—trying to organize itself—trying to establish its eventual starting lineup and the like. Likewise, the pitchers may or may not be in shape at this stage of the campaign. The wise selector will allow the clubs to get at least fifteen to twenty games under their belts before any intelligent prognostications will be attempted.

Baseball's Gimmick Bets

There are numerous gimmick bets connected with baseball and they vary in style and odds, depending on the area of the country in which you happen to reside. The gimmick bets are strictly guessing games but do give the small bettor the opportunity to have an interest in the sport. Some baseball bettors, in fact, concentrate the bulk of their baseball betting action on Run Pools, Six-Hit Pools, the Big 8, baseball cards and Homers.

Run Pools

The most popular gimmick bets are the baseball run pools, most of which are operated by small bookies in the offices and factories of the land. There are daily baseball pools and weekly baseball pools, both of which are based on total runs scored by a selected group of teams.

It usually costs 50 cents to participate in a baseball run pool and the payoffs run between $150 and $200 if you happen to be the winner. In the baseball pools, either weekly or daily, you select the four or five teams you think will score the most runs during a specified period of time. You will be competing against all other individuals in the pool and the person with the teams which scored the most runs is the winner. Some bookmakers also pay off consolation prizes for second, but not all do.

As one can see, the baseball run pools are strictly guessing games in which there is not much one can do to take an edge. Stick with the teams with the best batting averages and hope you get lucky. Luck will determine whether you win or lose.

Six-Hit Pools

Most baseball gimmick bettors, who feel that they're quite knowledgeable in the sport, go for the Six-Hit Pool because they believe (or perhaps know from experience) that they have a better chance of winning here than they do in team betting.

In the Six-Hit Pool you must name three players who will produce six (or more) hits among them in any one day. Of course, only individual games of doubleheaders count. If you can accomplish this seemingly easy feat, you'll be rewarded with odds of 8 to 1. If you feel even cockier, you can name four players who'll get nine hits among them and the book will pay you off to the tune of 15 to 1.

Although Six-Hit sounds like a fairly easy bet to case, it's not all that simple. First, your best bet is to pick slap or singles hitters such as Joe Morgan of the Reds or Roy White of the Yanks, instead of sluggers like Jackson, Burroughs, and Dick Allen. Second, if one of your players comes up sick or a game is rained out, you'll have only two or maybe even only one man working for you.

You must exercise extreme caution in selecting your trio of players when making a bet of this kind. Make sure that their teams are playing, make sure that the three players are playing, learn the weather conditions in the various cities so you'll have a normally sure chance that the game is going to be played, and, finally, play only *day* games to increase your chances of winning. Lights often play a very important role in the outcome of baseball games as well as performances by individual players. Batting averages in the major leagues at night trail daylight averages by 14 points! Pitchers average about 1½ more strikeouts a game under the arcs.

The Illuminating Engineering Society has deduced that illumination for night games directly affects "the quality of visual signals reaching the brain." There may also be psychological or physiological differences between playing at different times on the clock and "unknown" twilight effects occurring during twi-night games which start in dusk in late afternoon.

The chart on the next page offers a good guide as to the players to consider when selecting three daily for your Six-Hit Pool. Although this list will change somewhat after the new season is well under way, you'd be surprised as to how often the same names show up in the list year after year.

Players like Pete Rose, Lou Brock, Bobby Bonds, Billy Williams, Dave May, Joe Morgan, Roy White, Rod Carew, and Amos Otis are always solid bets for at least 150 hits a season. Also, when selecting players on a given day, choose the players from the list who will be going up against weak pitchers with high earned-run averages. Naturally, double-headers do not count. The pool is conducted on a one-game-only basis and if one or two of your men are rained out, you have only one man going for you.

Remember one thing: the bookie is never giving the bettor the best of it and even when you do hit him the 8 to 1 payoff is considerably less than the true odds of 10 to 1. Don't ever go for the four-players gimmick as the payoff odds of 15 to 1 are much less than the true 20 to 1 figure.

The Hot Hitters of 1973
(Based on 150 or more hits)

American League		National League	
Player	Team	Player	Team
Bando	A's	Baker	Braves
Bell	Indians	Bonds	Giants
Campaneris	A's	Brock	Cards
Carew	Twins	Buckner	Dodgers
Cepeda	R. Sox	Cardenal	Cubs
Chambliss	Indians	Cedeno	Astros
Clarke	Yanks	W. Davis	Dodgers
T. Davis	Orioles	Evans	Braves
Harper	R. Sox	Garr	Braves
R. Jackson	A's	Helms	Astros
A. Johnson	Rangers	D. Johnson	Braves
Kelly	W. Sox	Kessinger	Cubs
D. May	Brewers	Lum	Braves
Melton	W. Sox	Luzinski	Phils
Money	Brewers	Maddox	Giants
Murcer	Yanks	Matthews	Giants
Nelson	Rangers	Millan	Mets
North	A's	Morgan	Reds
Oliva	Twins	A. Oliver	Pirates
Otis	Royals	Perez	Reds
Rojas	Royals	Rose	Reds
Scott	Brewers	Russell	Dodgers
White	Yanks	Sanguillen	Pirates
Yastrzemski	R. Sox	Simmons	Cards
		Singleton	Expos
		Stargell	Pirates
		Staub	Mets
		Watson	Astros
		B. Williams	Cubs

The Big 8

The Big 8, or over-under, bet is one baseball gimmick that on the surface looked like a big money-maker for the bookies, but it turned out to be a big headache instead. It's really a simple bet. You pick a baseball team and bet that the club will score *over* eight runs or *under* eight runs. (Usually, if the team scores eight, there is no bet. But it doesn't hurt to make that perfectly clear with your bookie before you place your bet.) The price, in the beginning, was pick 'em. But, in the early 70s, the baseball moguls decided that to reverse the falling attendance trend and to give the game more interest, more runs must be scored. To accomplish this, the ball was souped up, the pitcher's mound was lowered, and a designated hitter rule was put into effect. As a result, there were a tremendous number of high-scoring games and it cost the bookies a fortune before they suddenly realized that their odds were out of line.

In an effort to save their hides, the bookies started to play with their prices. They then insisted that the player lay the price, and the line went from 6–5 to 7–5. Today the odds are 8½ to 5 or 9 to 5 and most bookies still tend to shy away from Big 8 bets, especially where any amount of money is involved.

"Over-under" betting has proved extremely popular for many reasons. "You're always in a game," one bettor confided. "Even if the score is 6–0 you're either hoping the runs will stop or a rally will get started, depending on how you bet. I've watched the end of many a 'dull' ball game hoping that my team would cover."

Another big reason is that many bettors feel this type of action is easy to handicap. "It's a lot easier than picking winners," a West Coast fan explained. "All I do is check the pitchers' Earned Run Averages and add them up. If they're over the spread I bet over. If they're under I bet under. Of course I don't always win!"

The truth is that there's a little more to successful "over-under" betting than the pitchers' ERAs. Our research staff has dug through a backlog of baseball statistics and come up with a few other factors that should be considered before plunging. Follow these few simple guidelines that we have found to be important and you may cash a few extra "over-under" bets.

Pitching has got to be your prime consideration when you're talking about how many runs are going to be scored in a game. What you're looking for is a consistent performer—both positively and negatively. A pitcher who is usually knocked out of the box after five or six innings can be an excellent "over" proposition, especially if his team has a weak bullpen that might let the game get completely out of hand.

Other good "over" bets are pitchers who go the distance but usually give up a lot of runs. These are the hurlers whom teams seem to hit behind so they manage to stay in and earn a 9–5 verdict. You find these players by matching up completed games with high Earned Run Averages. Jim Perry of

Detroit is a prize example. He wins, but both teams usually do a lot of scoring.

Another pitcher who offers a prime "over" bet has to be the gopher ball pitcher. Every time he takes the mound he's a constant threat to hang a curve ball that will be orbited for a couple of runs. Mistakes like this can be costly if you're betting the wrong way.

"Under" betting has its nuances also. The best "under" bets are no real secret. They're the league's strong men who are aiming for a shutout every time they take the mound. More often than not, they don't blank the opposition, but the score of the game is usually low enough to cover the spread. We have listed the most consistent shutout leaders in both the American and National leagues. They're usually solid "under" bets.

Shutout Leaders in the Majors

American League		National League	
Player	Team	Player	Team
Marichal	R. Sox	Gibson	Cards
Stottlemyre	Yanks	Pappas	Cubs
Lolich	Tigers	Osteen	Astros
McNally	Orioles	Sutton	Dodgers
Jenkins	Rangers	Carlton	Phillies
Cuellar	Orioles	John	Dodgers
Hunter	A's	Seaver	Mets
Palmer	Orioles	Niekro	Braves
Holtzman	A's	Koosman	Mets
Singer	Angels	Billingham	Reds
Wise	R. Sox	Dierker	Astros
Blue	A's	Downing	Dodgers
Blyleven	Twins	Rogers	Expos
Ryan	A's	D. Roberts	Astros
G. Perry	Indians		

A very good "under" proposition is the hard-luck pitcher. This is the fellow who is sporting a mediocre or weak won-lost record but has an extremely good ERA. You can usually count on something to go wrong for this guy when he's on the mound but the score will usually be tight.

As previously stated, it's true that pitching plays a great part in baseball but it's not the only betting basis. If you're looking for runs to be scored there are certain ball parks that favor the hitters. Good visibility, moved-in fences, and strong winds all combine to up the scores in certain parks. Soft pitchers are solid "over" bets when matched up in these parks, so don't miss out.

A quick note about artificial turf fields. It is the consensus of opinion that they make for a higher-scoring game. Ground balls fly through the infield for base hits, and the spring in the outfield "grass" makes every base hit a potential extra-base knock.

A final factor to be considered in "over-under" action is the weather. We've already hinted at wind conditions (Candlestick Park and Cleveland's Municipal Stadium are notorious examples) and how they can affect hitting action. But a bigger factor is rain. Rain means wet grounds, and a major threat of high-scoring games. Soggy outfields can lead to falling players and slithering hits going for extra bases. If the weather turns foul you may have some real solid "over" action.

Baseball Pool Cards

They are very similar to the college and pro football cards. What you do is pick three teams to win and get odds of 4 to 1. If you're a real baseball nut and pick four teams to win you get 5 to 1. If you're way out and think you can pick five teams to win the price is 8 to 1. But, before buying a card, take a look at the true odds given on page 93. For a four-team pick you should be getting 15 to 1 and for a five-team zaperoo you ought to get 31 to 1.

Homers

Although the odds of a person beating this particular bet are quite high, the payoff odds of 297½ to 1 (you heard right) make the gimmick extremely interesting to those who like the idea of a lot for a little. If you want to play the game you must select three different players to hit one home run each on a particular day. Of course, only single games of doubleheaders count, and the first or second game must be specified when placing your action. To make the bet even spicier, the bookies are offering double the payoff, or 595 to 1, if each of the three hits a homer and one of the four-bag artists gets two home runs in the same contest. (If one player hits one homer and the second or third hitter is shut out in the home run department, you lose and the bookie wins.)

It's a tough bet to win, but if you are going to play Homers it's imperative that you select your trio of swatters with some type of system or you'll be broke in no time flat. We have made the task of selecting your players much simpler by coming up with a list of the guys who produce home runs in duos.

Looking at the National League list, it's readily seen that the Atlanta tandem of Dave Williams and Darrell Evans is the strongest 1–2 punch on one team in all of professional baseball with 43 and 41 homers, respectively, for a total of 84. Add to this the fact that Hank Aaron—baseball's all-time home-run leader—had 40 homers, you can see the real punch that the Braves had for 1973. Willie Stargell of the Pirates, with 44 round-trippers, was actually the home run leader in the senior circuit, however.

Top Home-Run-Hitting Duos for 1973

National League

D. Johnson (43), Evans (41)	Atl.	84
Stargell (44), Hebner (25)	Pitts.	69
Bonds (39), McCovey (29)	S.F.	68
Luzinski (29), W. Robinson (25)	Phil.	54
L. May (28), Cedeno (25)	Hous.	53
Perez (27), Morgan (26)	Cinn.	53
Bailey (26), Singleton (23)	Mon.	49
Monday (26), B. Williams (20) or Santo (20)	Chi.	46
Collert (22), D. Roberts (21)	S.D.	43
Ferguson (25), W. Davis (16)	L.A.	41
Milner (23), Garrett (16)	N.Y.	39
Torre (13), Simmons (13)	St. L.	26

American League

R. Jackson (32), Bando (29)	Oak.	61
Otis (26), Mayberry (26)	K.C.	52
F. Robinson (30), R. Oliver (18)	Cal.	48
Burroughs (30), Sudakis (15)	Texas	45
Spikes (23), Hendricks (21)	Cleve.	44
Murcer (22), Nettles (22)	N.Y.	44
D. May (25), Briggs (18)	Mil.	43
R. Smith (21), Cepeda (20)	Bos.	41
C. May (20), Melton (20)	Chi.	40
Cash (19), Stanley (17) or Horton (17)	Det.	36
E. Williams (22), Grich (12)	Balt.	34
Darwin (18), Oliva (16)	Minn.	34

Major League Home Run Leaders for 1973
(25 or more)

American League		National League	
Player	Team	Player	Team
R. Jackson	A's	Stargell	Pirates
Burroughs	Rangers	D. Johnson	Braves
F. Robinson	Angels	Evans	Braves
Bando	A's	Aaron	Braves
Mayberry	Royals	Bonds	Giants
Otis	Royals	Luzinski	Phillies
D. May	Brewers	McCovey	Giants
		L. May	Astros
		Perez	Reds
		Bailey	Expos
		Monday	Cubs
		Morgan	Reds
		Bench	Reds
		Cedeno	Astros
		Ferguson	Dodgers
		Hebner	Pirates
		W. Robinson	Phillies

Over in the American League, Reggie Jackson (32) and Sal Bando (29) teamed up to beat Royal's duo of Amos Otis (26) and John Mayberry (26) by 9. Jackson won the home run title with 32 blasts.

Working from 1973's totals, it would appear that a Homers bettor should concentrate his action on Stargell, Evans, Aaron, Luzinski, Bonds, Burroughs, Jackson, and the like until new figures for the 1974 season start to become conclusive.

An interesting benefit to a person keeping home run records and betting on Homers is the fact that he can use these statistics to aid him in straight team betting, also.

Homers and the other baseball gimmick bets are sucker bait and should be shunned by any real sports bettor.

Chapter 6

Betting on Hockey, Boxing, Golf, Tennis, Jai Alai, Soccer

While the so-called minor betting sports of hockey, boxing, golf, tennis, jai alai, and soccer account for only 4 to 7 percent of total betting dollars, they are major sports to bettors who bet on them regularly. Let's take a look at these betting sports.

Betting on Hockey

Ice hockey, for years one of the most exciting spectator sports, has now moved to the position of big business in the betting department too. In the last few years betting action on ice hockey has risen faster than a Bobby Hull slapshot.

According to one source, it's estimated that nearly $35 million was wagered by Canadians alone last year. The handle for action in the United States was figured at almost $3½ million a weekend. But it still remains a fact that most American hockey bettors are unversed in the nuances of the sport. It can take a novice half a season just to figure out the off-sides rule and even longer before he can come close to successful handicapping NHL contests.

Sports Action, in an attempt to educate the American hockey bettor, has completed a four-season study of all the action in the NHL. We have come up with four critical areas that every potential punter should consider before putting his money on the line.

Home Ice Advantage

The home edge in most sporting events can often be used successfully by the alert bettor in his pursuit of the ever-elusive dollar. Hockey clubs playing on their home rinks are no exceptions and they can be extremely solid wagering propositions when the conditions are right. In fact, during the 1973–

74 season, the sixteen teams in the National Hockey League posted an aggregate total of 322 wins, 198 losses, and 104 ties at home, for a winning percentage of .641. Eleven of the sixteen clubs produced winning marks on the friendly rinks, with only California, Vancouver, Pittsburgh, and the New York Islanders dropping more decisions than they won. The St. Louis Blues had a 16–16–7 mark at home during the 1973–74 season.

Only Boston, Montreal, Chicago, and Philadelphia in the NHL had winning road records. All the other clubs in the league had losing marks on the road, proving once again just how powerful the home ice advantage is.

The reasons home ice is so advantageous are many. Familiarity with the playing surface is a big help. Although the basic specifications for hockey rinks are fairly standardized, each arena has its own peculiar quirks. In some rinks the pucks zoom off the boards while other boards slow the speeding disc down. A team that plays 35 to 40 games on one arena is able to know every nook and cranny and creates its own "lucky bounces."

The hometown fans affect both the players and the referees. Hockey arenas are small in comparison to giant football stadiums and the fans and officials hear every cheer and jeer. The players get a good psychological lift and referees have been known to be intimidated by hometown crowds. "Hockey fans are the same everywhere," says Bill Chadwick, who refereed close to 1,500 games in the National Hockey League and was rewarded by being inducted into the Hall of Fame.

"They all want to see the home team win," says Chadwick, now one of the broadcasters for the New York Rangers. "The referee is never right. But I figured a guy paying his way into the rink had the right to boo me. I didn't mind. It just rolled off my thick Irish skin."

Nowadays there are too few Bill Chadwicks tooting whistles around the NHL. Consequently, the fans are getting what they want. The home teams are winning with more consistency than ever before and this is partially due to the influx of young, inexperienced referees, who are often intimidated by the fans, the players, and the coaches. According to Scotty Morrison, the Referee-in-Chief of the NHL, the referees are not to be faulted as far as favoring the home teams. "The referees in the NHL are the most hard-working, honest guys on earth," says Morrison. "I think they do a terrific job. A hockey referee has the toughest job of any official in any sport because he alone must see everything that happens in every game he works.

"Boo the players," Morrison pleads, "but leave the referees alone. They're doing a difficult job well and they don't need 5,000 assistants."

The crowd, however, has little choice but to harass the refs when they are always disregarding what Morrison calls the two basic qualities he insists upon in a referee. One, that he must set the pattern or take charge from the opening minute of every game and, two, that he must be consistent in his calls. The referee, perhaps, is just a guinea pig who tries to do his best under adverse conditions. But the best is never good enough. Realizing that the outcome of every hockey game is in his hands, and his hands alone, only puts more pressure on the ref. It is inevitable that he becomes a puppet of the roaring, sometimes animalistic crowds that fill most every stadium around the league. Referees can be intimidated by the fans, the players, and the coaches, and they usually are. The result of all this is that the home team gets the benefit of the doubt on most hairline calls, which can only enhance its chance for victory.

NHL Goal Spread Records
(consecutive home games in November 1973)

Team	Won	Lost	Tied	Pct.
Chicago	5	0	0	1.000
Boston	5	0	0	1.000
St. Louis	4	0	0	1.000
California	3	0	0	1.000
Buffalo	2	0	0	1.000
Philadelphia	2	0	0	1.000
N.Y. Rangers	1	0	0	1.000
Montreal	1	0	0	1.000
Toronto	1	0	0	1.000
Minnesota	2	1	0	.667
Pittsburgh	1	1	0	.500
N.Y. Islanders	1	1	0	.500
Atlanta	1	1	0	.500
Detroit	0	1	0	.000
Vancouver	0	0	0	.000
Los Angeles	0	2	0	.000
Totals	29	7	0	.829

While it is common knowledge to almost all pro hockey speculators that the home team has quite a decided advantage in most games where it is not completely outclassed, the goal spreads imposed by the linemakers are often so tight that it's hard to squeeze out much of a profit at season's end merely by backing the home team. But by doing quite a bit of digging into results of previous years' contests, our figure bettors discovered that clubs which play at home for two, three, or more consecutive times are very solid wagering propositions with goals for or against taken into consideration.

Here's the way the method works. A bettor simply watches the schedule each week until he finds a club or clubs which have at least two consecutive home games slated. The first home game is not playable under this angle for the team in question is often forced to play after returning from a very rugged road trip and, although favored by the home ice in most instances, is sometimes not quite up to par. Therefore, the home club often doesn't cover the goals on its initial home game in a series. But by the time the second and third games come along, the home team is usually well relaxed, they are back to eating their regular food and beverages, and the partisan crowd never hurts, either. It is these games that the home club excels in.

Checking out this angle during the month of November 1973 in the NHL, we came up with 29 wins as against only 7 losses and not a single tie. The winning percentage was a fabulous .829.

Goaltending

Goaltending is the second most important hockey factor to keep in mind. The goalie is the last line of defense in hockey. When a goalie makes a mistake the red light goes on and a score goes on the board. Consistent goaltenders win more games and cash more bets than the occasional wonder who looks brilliant one night and leaks like a sieve the next.

Check for the goalies with the best goals-against averages. These are the guys who are steady betting propositions throughout the season. Actually, the winning hockey clubs almost always employ one or two top goalies. These are the men who, year after year, allow an average of fewer than 2.60 goals a match. They are also the fellows who the big hockey bettors want in the crease before they'll put their money on the line.

Just like the leading twirlers in baseball and the best quarterbacks in football, the cream of the goalie ranks always rises to the top and the same familiar names can usually be found in the top ten at the end of each campaign. Thus, if you're going to wager on hockey games like a pro, keep tabs on the net-minders, for their won-lost marks and goals-allowed averages will show the way to many a nice winning bet.

The Goal Spread

The price line is based on a differential of goals. For instance, the Montreal Canadiens are favored to defeat the New York Rangers and the bookmaker's line states: "Montreal favorite 1–1½ goals." This means that if you place your money on Montreal, you win only if they defeat New York by 2 or more goals. As with football and basketball, the bettor lays odds of 6 to 5 or 11 to 10 on either team.

We kept the NHL goal spread standings for the first month of the 1973–74 season and the results were as follows:

NHL Goal Spread Standings
(final month, 1973–74)

Team	Won	Last	Pct.
Los Angeles	11	3	.786
Atlanta	9	4	.692
Buffalo	8	4	.666
Pittsburgh	9	5	.643
N.Y. Islanders	9	5	.643
Detroit	8	5	.615
Philadelphia	7	6	.539
Boston	8	7	.533
Toronto	6	6	.500
Chicago	6	7	.462
Vancouver	5	6	.455
Minnesota	5	9	.385
Montreal	4	8	.333
California	3	9	.250
N.Y. Rangers	3	10	.231
St. Louis	3	10	.231

At this point in the season, it would have had been wise to shy away from the Rangers, St. Louis, California, and Montreal. These outfits won only three times out of ten or less and were generally very hard to figure due to the goals which a bettor must almost always spot them.

Of course, the safest bet of all is to play the teams that do best in the goal spread category when they're playing in the friendly confines of their own rinks. The home ice is always worth at least a half-goal. But be extremely leery of spotting anything over 2½ goals to even the weakest six, however, as you're generally taking the worst of it percentagewise. Stay with the clubs that are playing over .600 hockey, goalwise. Incidentally, the eastern division of NHL, as a whole, played winning hockey, garnering victories at an approximately 59 percent average during the 1973–74 season, while the western half was, naturally, winning at a 41 percent stride.

The importance a short-handed goal has on the outcome of a National Hockey League game is very strongly emphasized by the fact that a team scoring such a goal has almost a 5 to 1 chance of winning that game. The *Sports Action* study also broke the fourteen NHL clubs down according to their ability to score while having the man advantage. It was no secret that Boston, Philadelphia, and New York were the best teams at putting the puck in the net when they had a man advantage. They were able to score at a phenomenal clip of once every

NHL Power-Play Scoring Potential

Team	Scoring Frequency	Average Penalties Minutes Per Game
N.Y. Rangers	3.5	10.0
Boston	3.7	12.4
Philadelphia	4.3	22.4
Chicago	4.6	11.2
Detroit	4.6	11.7
Montreal	5.0	9.7
Vancouver	5.0	12.1
Buffalo	5.3	10.0
Toronto	5.5	11.5
Minnesota	5.6	10.5
Atlanta	5.8	10.7
Pittsburgh	5.9	12.1
Los Angeles	6.6	13.5
St. Louis	7.0	14.7
N.Y. Islanders	7.1	13.7
California	7.6	8.3

Power-Play Goals Against Average—Short-Handed Goals

Team	Opposition Scores Once Every	Short-Handed Goals For	Against
Philadelphia	8.6 times	20	6
Chicago	8.0 times	8	5
St. Louis	5.9 times	4	9
Buffalo	5.6 times	5	12
Minnesota	5.6 times	5	5
Boston	5.4 times	12	2
N.Y. Rangers	5.3 times	9	2
Pittsburgh	5.2 times	12	4
Toronto	5.2 times	5	7
Los Angeles	5.1 times	4	9
Atlanta	4.9 times	1	6
Detroit	4.9 times	8	13
California	4.8 times	6	14
Montreal	4.3 times	12	7
N.Y. Islanders	4.2 times	7	13
Vancouver	3.8 times	4	8

four times the opposition was shy a man. The rest of the NHL's top goal-getters were Chicago, Montreal, and Detroit. Their scoring frequency was a little under one out of every five times they had the man advantage.

The trick for the smart bettor is to try and get money down on these clubs when they're meeting some of the more penalized clubs in the league. Teams such as The Islanders, St. Louis, and California are especially soft touches when meeting strong power-play clubs. According to the statistics, California seemed to be the most vulnerable club in the league when it came to penalties.

The best defensive club in the NHL when a man down was Philadelphia. Opposing clubs got the puck past Flyer net-minders on the average of only once every 8.6 times they were a man up. The second stingiest club was Chicago, who held the opposition to a goal every 8.0 times they had a power play on.

One interesting aspect of our study was that Pittsburgh, one of the weakest clubs in hockey when they had a man advantage, were very dangerous when they played short-handed. The Penguins had scored seven goals against enemy goaltenders when they had a man in the penalty box! But to point out how weak Pittsburgh was on the power play, they had allowed the opposition to score ten times while they were a man up! California and Detroit have been caught for an unusually high number of goals while they were a man up. This situation usually results from the defensemen being too offense-minded and getting caught up ice when they're a man ahead. Teams like this are dangerous bets, even when playing highly penalized clubs.

In conclusion, keep in mind that penalties are going to be points on the board for teams that can capitalize on them and money in the pocket of the smart bettor who knows what to look for.

Scheduling

The final handicapping factor in hockey is scheduling. With the expansion of teams in the NHL it's not unusual for a club to be in Minnesota one night and two days later on a rough road trip up the West or East coast for several games in succession.

No team, no matter how well conditioned, can play at its peak throughout such a grind. Check the schedules a week or so in advance and see where the clubs are headed. If there's a big travel jump after a hard home stand bet *against* the club the second or third game of the road trip—no matter how classy they may appear.

Very often powerful clubs will "cheat" against what appears to be soft opposition. They will play second-rate or makeshift lines to give their regular players a "breather" for the tougher clubs. Sure, they'll win most of their games but they won't come close to covering the spreads. Also watch the penalties. If there was a lot of fighting going on in early games on road trips a team is going to be tired and physically spent for upcoming competition.

With hockey being such a low-scoring sport, one should look for every possible edge he can find in order to stay in black ink. You must keep records on how the various teams are doing at home, on the road, and against interdivisional rivals if you really want to have a better perspective on the spread in any particular contest. Find out which teams are patsies for the better clubs and tap out on that kind of game instead of racking your brain trying to pick between Chicago and Boston in a toss-up affair.

Betting on Boxing

Betting on boxing in this country has dwindled to the point where it is no longer significant. Those who book bets legally on the sport in Nevada estimate that less than $1 million is bet each year in the United States on prizefights, and they concede this figure probably is high.

There is no great amount of money bet on boxing because there is no public confidence in the sport. Boxing has been scandal-ridden for years and bookmakers refuse to take action on most fights. They still fear the fix and believe that to book action on a fight is to invite disaster. Bookmakers don't trust people who stage and promote fights, and won't let anyone bet on them.

If, however, you ever want to bet on a fight and can get a wager down with a bookie, the game is strictly one of odds. If the man you like is the 8–5 favorite, it means you will have to put up $8 to win $5 if you like the favorite. The odds will be shifted a point to 7–5 if you want to bet on the underdog, which means you will collect only $7 for each $5 bet if the underdog wins. By the way, most bookmakers won't handle any bets that have more than a 2- or 3-point price line spread. That is, if a fighter is more than a 4 to 1 favorite, most bookies will refuse to take action on the underdog.

Betting on Golf

Gambling on golf is now big business, with approximately $500 million wagered on golf matches and tournaments. For instance, at most invitational tournaments in California you can buy mutuel tickets on the field. The teams usually sell at $5 and, since the golf is unpredictable, the long shots draw the big play. The gambling is operated by the clubs, but most of them take no profit from the pot.

The Calcutta Pool long has been popular at the pro stops on the Coast. At the prestigious Bing Crosby tournament each January, the Calcutta is conducted by the Monterey Elks Clubs for its members and their friends. Before the actual golf contest, the participating players are auctioned off. The bids for the privilege of "owning" top players usually range between $1,000 and $7,500, though spirited bidding has revved the tag up to $10,000. After the Elks Clubs takes its 10 percent from the pool's total handle, the rest is divided as follows: 50 percent to "owner" of the winning player, 20 percent to holder of the second-place player, 15 percent to the holder of third-place, and 10 and 5 percent to the owners of the fourth and fifth finishing players. The pro golfers, of course, know nothing about this action, though reports often reach them as to who the betting favorite is.

At Las Vegas tournaments, the Calcutta Pool often drew bids of a least $50,000 but there's little Calcutta action there today since most local sports books can accommodate the punters.

The Tournament of Champions Calcutta in Las Vegas pointed up the dangers of the event and effected its ban in most cities. For example, when Stan Leonard of Vancouver won the event in 1959, it provided $95,760 for Carl Anderson, a Los Angeles car-loading mogul, who had bid in Leonard at $11,500. Anderson then gave $10,000 of his loot to Leonard.

Frankie Laine, the singer, found a good thing in Gene Littler in that period. He got Littler for $13,000 in 1955, and he paid off $72,900; Laine bid $16,500 in 1956 for Littler and grossed $68,120 as Gene won for the second time. He then hit the jackpot in 1957 when a $15,500 bid on Littler gained him $100,100.

Of more concern to the golf hierarchy, however, are the parlay betting cards, patterned after those used for pro football. Joseph C. Dey, the former pro golf commissioner, has spoken out bitterly against the cards and labeled them "a sucker's game." What Dey fears is a gambling scandal such as rocked college basketball in the 1950s.

"We are constantly reminding our players of two things," he said. "One is that they are not horses and the other is that there are stern regulations against gambling in our bylaws."

Regardless of the warnings, the cards are gaining popularity in the West as word spreads of payoffs approaching $1,000 on $1 bets. Actually, betting points up the honesty of a sport. You don't see any betting on wrestling, do you?

We are often asked, "Is it possible to fix a golf tournament?" No! You can't. That's the consensus of professionals and officials, who outline two main drawbacks any would-be fixer would encounter in an attempt to arrange a particular finish of a pro tournament: (1) there isn't that much gambling by the big-money boys on pro golf, as they prefer to bet on football, basketball, and baseball, and (2) there are too many players involved and things would get out of hand.

Almost all sports have had their scandals. Baseball had its Black Sox. There were the basketball point-shaving scandals in the New York colleges and elsewhere. Football, boxing, and flat and harness racing all have had their fair share of behind-the-scenes shenanigans, too.

Although millions are wagered on golf games on the amateur-club level, professional golf has a history comparatively free of any taint of scandal. But with professional tourists now playing for a minimum of $100,000 a week, ranging up to $250,000, it's unrealistic to assume that professional gamblers aren't lurking around. So watch your step when wagering on pro golf just as you have to have your wits about you when on the links so as not to get hustled out of all your gelt by the slickers who pervade our nation's links.

Many golf hustlers work doctors only. Some guys work fat-cat athletes, some guys work movie stars. One famous golfer once estimated that 40 percent of all golfers lie about their handicaps. The true percentage is probably about 90 percent of all golfers. When a hustler finds a pigeon, he may pull the "give the sucker the edge" bit.

As soon as he spots his mark, usually an older-type gent, and as soon as they agree on the price per hole, the sharpie goes into his routine: "Since I'm much younger than you and I have a better handicap rating I don't feel right playing you even up. I know I'm a better player than you are so I'll give you a break," he tells the pigeon. No duffer likes to be told he's a poor player, but he's interested in a money-making proposition.

Here's what the hustler says. "Since I'm a better player I'll let you play the best of any three balls you shoot and I'll play only one ball." The bird immediately thinks he's got a sucker and ups the ante. The cheat agrees and the deal is that the bird takes the best score on each hole.

On the surface it appears that the hustler made a bad move, but stop and think. The bird is older than the cheat, he's carrying a big corporation up front, and he doesn't look like he can go the route. In effect, the hustler plays only 18 holes of golf while the bird plays 54 and that's where the hustler gets him. Somewhere along the back nine his clubs become as heavy as steel girders, his legs become rubbery, and his game falls apart.

The sharpie picks up a very nice piece of change and the sucker never realizes that he played three times as many games. He's so mad at losing despite his "big advantage" that he almost cries for revenge and forces the cheat to make another date with him, same conditions except he wants to raise the ante even more. Pure murder!

Then, there's the "big-mouth drunk" approach. The cheat hangs around the club bar drinking a little, bragging a lot, and flashing a Philadelphia bankroll. The suckers soon start coming out of the woodwork. When he's playing the "drinking role" he insists on carrying his own bags because "I have a little something in there." That "little something" is a phony bottle of booze and a real one. Here's how he uses this bit to keep in big money and big broads:

Almost immediately after the hustler and sucker tee off, the cheat excuses himself, goes over and reaches into his bag and pulls out a pint. He pretends he's trying to hide the fact that he's drinking and the sucker's eyes start dancing. He's got it made! After the third or fourth hole the cheat is usually behind and starting to wobble. The sucker then hints that maybe they ought to increase the size of the bet. Naturally, the pro agrees.

By the eighth or ninth hole the cheat's wobbling pretty good, "drinking" pretty good, and starting to beat the sucker's brains out. "By the twelfth hole I'm way ahead, still drinking, and he's getting curious," related a hustler to *Sports Action.* "To put his mind at ease and to convince him that I'm only a 'lucky drunk,' I reach into my bag again and pull out the real bottle of booze and offer him a drink. The sucker is so blind with rage because he's being beaten by a drunk he refuses the drink but gets a smell and is convinced I'm really belting the rye pretty good. Actually the 'rye' is cold tea.

"Anyway, at the end of the eighteen holes, I'm still wobbling but 'sober' enough to see that he gives me an honest count when forking over the money or that he spells my name right on the check." And so it goes.

As a word to the wise, we suggest that you never bet on a golf match with a stranger, especially a man with a deep tan. Stop and think. If it's the middle of the week and the stranger asks for a game he should look like the sucker who spends most of his days in the office and is chalky white in comparison. A deep tan is a good way to spot a golf hustler because he's out "working" in the sun all day. Golf cheats working North Carolina, Florida, and the Islands in the winter often use talcum powder to cover their exposed skin, so check the back of a guy's neck around the collarline and his wrist around the watch before you put any money on the line.

But if you must bet on your golf fame, you had better be like a poker player and know the house rules before you start. Most wagers are won or lost on the first tee when the game is made up, so know what you are playing and, above all, know your opponents. Here is a brief guide to the types of bets you may encounter:

Nassau. The most common kind of bet. A match play three points are scored: one for the first nine, one for the second, and one for the 18. If a golfer is playing a "one-dollar Nassau," he has three individual one-dollar bets.

Bisque. A handicap stroke that may be taken on any hole at the player's option. Strictly speaking, a stroke that is given to an opponent must be taken at the hole indicated on the scorecard as being that particular handicap number. Thus, if a player is given "five strokes," he must use those strokes on the holes marked one to five on the card. The handicap numbers are usually circled to differentiate them from the hole numbers. A bisque, on the other hand, may be taken anywhere.

Skins. A skin is awarded to the winner of each hole, provided that he is not tied by another player. If two tie, all tie. A deadlier version of this game (and not one for those who play a steady, unspectacular game) is called cumulative skins. In this little hair-raiser, holes not won by anyone because of ties are accumulated and awarded to the first winner of a hole. Also called "scats" or "syndicates."

Greenie. This is a shot that ends up closest to the cup on par-3's. Again, the winner collects from the other members of the foursome.

Team Skins. Those loyal partners who do not wish to win greenies and skins from one another play for team skins. If either member wins a skin, it is awarded to the team and not to the individual.

Bingle-Bangle-Bungle. A fast-paced item with lots of action. Three points on each hole: one for the player who reaches the green first, one for the player nearest to the cup after all are on the green, and one for the player who first holes out.

Birds. Points scored for birdies on any hole; double for eagles.

Low Ball and Total. A four-ball team bet in which the best ball of each team wins one point, and the low total of the partners wins another. This game is a method of getting a good bet out of the situation in which there is one very good player with a poor one against two average players.

Low and High Ball. A four-ball team bet in which two points are scored on each hole; low score wins a point, and high score loses a point. If both partners score lower on a hole than their opponents, they can win two points.

Press or Extra. A new bet on the remaining holes. If someone wants to take a "dollar extra" on the 17th tee, he wants to play the last two holes for the dollar.

The best advice on betting is never to wager more than you can comfortably afford to lose, or else you may be putting yourself under unnecessary pressure that will probably hurt your game. Don't rush into an extra bet when you are losing unless you have been playing unusually badly and have suddenly discovered the cure, or you have been hitting the ball well but have been unlucky.

Betting on Tennis

Except for the famous Billie Jean King–Bobby Riggs match, and private wagering on an individual level, public interest in betting on tennis has never been too high in the United States. Even this "Women's Lib" match didn't create sufficient interest among bookmakers or bettors to have the event carried on the books except in Las Vegas, Los Angeles, and Houston.

While not a great betting sport in our country as yet, it's well covered by book in such countries as Great Britain, France, and Sweden. Here the wagering is usually strictly one of the odds, as in boxing. For example, if Stan Smith was a 7–5 favorite to defeat Arthur Ashe in a certain match, you would have to put up $7 to win $5 if you liked Smith. If you wished to bet on Ashe and he won, you would collect $6 for every $5 you put up. In some countries there are mutuel tickets on the field which operate in the same manner as the golf cards that are so popular in California and Nevada. Also, in Europe there are several handicapping systems employed in situations where one player is better than another.

With interest in tennis, especially at the professional level, increasing in the United States, it is just a matter of time before the sport finds its way onto the American book.

If you play tennis and like to bet on yourself, there is always the problem of hustlers. As in golf and other self-participating sports such as bowling, billiards, and pool, you should never play a stranger for money.

Betting on Jai Alai

At present, Florida and Nevada are the only states of our fifty where legal parimutuel betting on jai alai is sanctioned, and it draws capacity crowds. To point out just how great has been the growth of jai alai over the years, consider the growth of just one of Florida's seven frontons—the Dania Jai Alai Palace in Miami. In its inaugural season of 1953–54, a total of 232,566 fans wagered $2,746,664 during a 90-night meeting. By 1969–70 the mutuels handle had leaped 282 percent and attendance had jumped 76 percent. In the 1972–73 season, the handle was up almost 20 percent over the 1969–70 mark.

Whether you're a regular visitor or a first-time starter at a jai alai fronton, you've got to be swept away by the beauty, grace, and excitement of the sport. Hailed as the fastest game in the world, jai alai originated in Spain from a form of handball played by Basque priests with their parishioners two hundred years ago.

Today professional jai alai can be pictured as a souped-up version of handball with a basket (cesta) and a hardened goatskin-covered ball (pelota). The object of the game is to throw the ball with such speed and spin that it rebounds into fair territory in such a manner that the opposition is unable to catch it either in the air, on the first bounce, or return it from the back wall.

The object of the game for the spectators is to win money betting on the action. Betting is the same as for horse racing, with each player or team given a number and wagers taken on where the players will finish. In addition to the standard win, place, and show betting allowed there is also gimmick wagering. There are two daily doubles on the third and fourth events and on the tenth and eleventh. There is quinella and perfecta wagering on every match. Incidentally, on night cards there are twelve games, while matinees usually have only eleven.

To win the quinella the bettor must select the players of the teams that finish first and second in a given game. Either team may win, the other must finish second. Perfecta wagering, of course, is actually a quinella in which the bettor must select the exact order of finish for the first two places. Payoffs can be high in the perfectas—a $1,314.60 perfecta was hit at Dania—with $100 being common.

The Big Q was introduced several years back and was an instant success. The trick is to wager $2 before the start of the first game on two teams you think will finish first and second. If they win you exchange your winning ticket at no additional cost for your choice of the win and place finishers in game two. If you're a winner you can collect as much as $4,-168.20 or as little as $171.80—those are about the biggest and smallest Big Q payoffs at Dania during the last couple of seasons.

The reason for all this gimmick wagering is simple. "Big money will not be bet at jai alai because of the handicapping problem," admitted Gordon Hulbert, General Manager of Orlando Seminole Jai Alai. "That is the reason for the handle being almost entirely quinella, perfecta, and other gimmick pools. The win, place, and show pools are always small."

How do you handicap jai alai? Even the experts admit it's hard. "The difficulty is not in the nature of the game but due to the type of information available," revealed Dick Warnoff, General Manager of Dania's Jai Alai. "Information such as blood lines for horses and dogs is pertinent in racing, but has no relevance in professional athletic competition. Therefore, the only information used by the handicapper in jai alai is a player's past record which is not conclusive by any means."

Probably the best jai alai handicapper is the players' manager, who also serves as the matchmaker. He holds a position similar to that of a racing secretary in horse racing, having the difficult task of assigning the players the post positions and setting up the games for the evening's program. The leading players are assigned the higher numbered and more difficult post positions. Players in the lower numbered posts have an advantage because they have the earliest opportunities to serve or receive and pick up points. If you're betting jai alai and notice that a player has been doing well during the evening and has drawn an inside starting position, don't hesitate to back him up.

We have drawn up a few rules to help make a trip to the jai alai frontons a little more pleasant and possibly more profitable.

1. *Always bet across the board* (win, place, and show). Since most of the betting action at a fronton is done in the gimmick pools there are many overlays in the place and show pools. A winner can pay $6 to win and return close to $10 in the place or show spots. Don't miss out.

2. *Play established players vs. youngsters.* A few years back there was a strike of the jai alai players and the best players were dismissed from the frontons. The bulk of the players today are exciting to watch but lacking in experience. A veteran player has a distinct edge—especially in singles play. You can find out about a player's experience simply by looking through your program.

3. *Play perfectas, not quinellas, and reverse them.* Although a perfecta costs $3 instead of the $2 quinella price it is well worth it. For a $6 investment to reverse the perfecta (playing 1-6 and 6-1) you will get back between two and three times the quinella payoff. It's a wise investment.

Experience has shown us that following these three rules can minimize your losses and maximize your profits when you do collect. It is difficult to beat jai alai but it's no trouble to enjoy an evening of action and excitement.

One final note: Oftentimes you will hear talk about fixes and dishonesty. It is well nigh impossible for something like this to happen. The players compete for money prizes based on their performance for the entire season. It is difficult to do tricks when a ball is sailing up to speeds of 150 miles an hour. So, take in an evening of one of the world's fastest sports. Win or lose, you'll come out ahead.

Betting on Soccer

While there was very little betting on soccer in the United States in the early 1970s, both sports and gambling enthusiasts see it eventually becoming one of the major betting sports in this country. For the record, it already is the biggest betting sport in the world. At this time the United States is the only major country in the world where soccer is not a least one of the most popular spectator and betting sports.

It might seem absurd to predict that soccer will become a major betting sport in the United States, but the thought is based on some rather realistic facts. First of all, soccer is growing faster in popularity than any other sport on the campuses of Eastern colleges. Professional soccer is getting a strong foothold in major population centers and those behind soccer leagues are encouraged by what they are seeing. But the key to the future of soccer lies in the area of change. The attitudes of the American people are changing rapidly, particularly in the area of education vs. athletics at the junior high and senior high school levels. The cost of supporting athletic programs has gotten out of hand in many areas of the country, causing educators and parents to take a hard look at continuing to support them at the expense of the music and English departments.

Football, which is king of the betting sports now, is being de-emphasized in many areas of the country because of its high cost. High school coaching staffs, which in the past numbered five or six, are being reduced to two or three coaches. Schools no longer buy new equipment each year, and mom now has the responsibility of seeing to it that John's jersey is laundered before each game.

This is only the beginning. The cost of football will eventually cause its elimination at many schools, with money going to departments which educate all the students. Whether this is right or wrong is unimportant to us; we just know it is going to happen.

For these reasons soccer becomes an attractive sport at which students, both male and female, can excel. It is not costly. A major soccer program can be conducted for pennies when compared to what it takes to finance a competitive football team at the secondary-school level. With this in mind, athletic departments at the secondary-school level are changing their emphasis to soccer, which is every bit as exciting as football, and the colleges are following suit.

Soccer has become so popular at Ivy League schools that it is not unusual for a game between Yale and Harvard to draw more people than a football contest between the two schools. Those behind professional soccer in this country are well bankrolled and willing to operate at a loss for a few years. They believe their time is coming and that soccer will emerge as *the* sport in the 1980s.

As we have said, there is little betting conducted on soccer in this country at this time and what there is is usually on a man-to-man basis, with the money never seeing the hand of a bookmaker. The fans in Philadelphia are big soccer bettors. but are forced to bet with one another because the local accountants do not yet take wagers on their professional team, which played before crowds as large as 25,000 during the past seasons.

Most of the bets are simple. One man bets another, even-up, that Philadelphia will beat New York, or vice versa. The soccer bettor has not become sophisticated enough to demand a goal or two, even when he should. When betting soccer, review a team's past performance with a particular eye to just how it has fared against the opponent it faces today. Soccer teams are quite consistent. If Philadelphia beat New York on May 15, it usually is a good bet to get the job done on June 1. The only thing which can neutralize the situation is a pointspread, so don't be afraid to ask for a goal or two if you're betting the underdog.

Many of the rules of football betting relate to soccer. If you plan to bet a lot of money on a soccer game, take the time to check the weather. Wind and rain completely change game plans and style of play in soccer. You also should keep track of which teams play on artificial turf and those which compete on an old-fashioned grass field. There can be little doubt that a team which has a home field of natural grass and sod is going to have an edge whenever it plays at home against teams which have competed primarily on the synthetic playing fields. By the same token, that team would be at a disadvantage when it played road games against teams which played most of their games on the artificial turf.

In soccer, make yourself a checklist, never forgetting to study (1) consistency, (2) weather, (3) how a team has previously performed against the team it meets today, and (4) which team seems to have the edge because of the surface of the field, i.e. artificial turf or real grass.

Most soccer betting in the rest of the world is conducted on a pool basis and this type of wagering will eventually come to this country, whether it be in soccer, football, basketball, baseball, or hockey. To win a soccer pool, the bettor puts up his pennies, picks the results of fifteen to twenty games, and hopes. It is an almost impossible task to pick the winners of all the games on a European soccer sheet, but when one hits, the payoffs run into the millions of dollars.

Soccer pool betting is big business in the rest of the world for it is priced within the reach of those who have as little as two or three pennies to wager. Of course the game has its high-rollers, too, but its tremendous pools are made up for the most part by the nickel and dime wagers of Mr. Average Citizen.

Our advice to the American people is to start studying soccer. It's the coming sport. Let's get in on the ground floor and begin to lay those plans to deliver the knockout punch to the bookmaker.

Betting on Other Sports

Professional bowling, skiing, auto racing, and track and field have not yet attracted too much attention from the American sports bettors. Calcutta type pools are sometimes organized on stops of the Professional Bowling Association's tour, as well as at resorts where the professional skiers conduct their races. While these sports offer no bookie action at present, there is usually plenty of private man-to-man wagering available for the sports bettor at these events.

Chapter 7

Thoroughbred Horse Racing

Thoroughbred racing is fascinating, frustrating, and by far the most complicated betting sport facing mere man. On the surface, it appears the bettor has more information to guide him to the plus side of his profit and loss statement when, in reality, he has much less. The thoroughbred bettor can purchase the *Daily Racing Form,* which is the past-performance newspaper and bible of the thoroughbred industry, and see in black and white the history of every horse in the race on which he is going to bet. In theory, this should enable him to pick winners, but it does not. A statistical analysis of racing over the past thirty years shows that 33 percent of the horses the public sends off as favorites win, which means this same public, with all this information available, loses two of every three bets. It seems that the average individual, with just everyday luck, should be able to pick 50 percent winners in sports such as football and basketball by using a hatpin.

There are approximately 20 million people in the United States who will attend racing at a thoroughbred track in this country in any year. And with them, they will bring at least 10 million different systems and philosophies for winning—a fact which should give us some idea of just how complicated thoroughbred racing is. As in all other betting sports, the thoroughbred fan can use all his knowledge, expertise, and resourses to handicap a race and still lose. Regardless of how great an edge you take in racing, you still fight dozens of unknown betting factors. No one is trying to hide most of these factors from the public. The nature of thoroughbred racing itself, and nothing else, leaves the bettor at the mercy of the unknown factors.

The problem is basic. Horses cannot talk. They cannot tell us exactly how they feel on the day of the race. They cannot tell us if their minds are as much on running today as they were two weeks ago when they absolutely destroyed the same kind of competition. They cannot tell us they are feeling a little pain in the old ankle today and just might not feel like running hard. They cannot tell us they have an upset stomach. Most trainers know when a horse is feeling its best or is not well. However, even the best conditioners such as Elliott Burch, Cahrlie Whittingham, Willard Proctor, Allen Jerkens, and those of that quality cannot always know. Thus, the horse which set a track record two weeks ago might be up the track today for no other reason that it just didn't feel quite as well.

When a horse doesn't run the race the bettor feels it should, he immediately assumes he has been cheated—that the game is crooked, that the race was fixed, that the jockey pulled the horse, or that the trainer drugged it to slow it down and build up a better price for the next race. The thoroughbred bettor places himself in this position because he cannot accept the fact that he read the *Daily Racing Form*, handicapped the race, applied his own betting system, and lost. (For full information on how to read the *Racing Form*, write to Daily Racing Form, 10 Lake Drive, Hightstown, N.J. 08520 for a free booklet.) It is, indeed, an unacceptable state of affairs for him. In truth, however, he is so unknowledgeable of the sport on which he and his friends bet over $5 billion annually that he hasn't the faintest understanding of what has happened.

The key problem came when he accepted what he saw in the *Daily Racing Form*, or any other publication, as a picture of the complete horse, when these past-performance charts and histories actually told him about 25 percent of what he needed to know to insure his chances of winning. This figure will never improve, either, because very few bettors will ever know the actual physical condition of a horse at race time. A trainer doesn't usually knowingly run a horse if he knows the horse is not well, but he sometimes will, feeling the horse, though slightly subpar physically, still is good enough to handle the competition. These are decisions of judgment, and trainers are wrong as many times as they are right. Thus, the first thing the horse bettor must accept before he really gets seriously involved in wagering on thoroughbreds is the simple fact that racing is basically an honest game. Form reversals and upsets occur for reasons which usually are not within the control of anyone, except the horse, which at best is quite unpredicatable.

How to Bet

Any person attending a thoroughbred racetrack for the first time will most likely be fascinated and excited by the experience. The thrill of seeing the beautiful thoroughbreds and their brightly dressed jockeys thundering through the stretch to the finish line would turn on the most lifeless individual. Thoroughbred racing makes one's heart pound faster.

The difficulty, however, the new bettor faces once he gets past all this excitement is wading through the tons of data which is supposed to help him pick a winner. His first problem is basic: he doesn't identify with racing and horses and feels uncomfortable around them. He can identify with the Los Angeles Rams because he has personally thrown a football around since he was a child. He can even visualize himself trying to block one of Wilt Chamberlain's shots, for he has played basketball many times. Baseball is easy, too, for his father put a baseball in his hand before he could walk. Regardless of how inept he might actually be at betting the major sports of football, basketball, and baseball, he does so with a certain amount of blind confidence. However, in racing, the point of identity is not there and he begins to struggle with his first bet. The world of the horse is strange and confusing to him, as beautiful and exciting as it might be. Unfortunately, it usually remains that way all his betting life.

The horse bettor need not be confused if he understands but a few things. First of all, a horse is trained in exactly the same manner a great athlete trains. He exercises himself into shape for actual competition and then competes. If he is in good enough physical condition, and better than his opponents, he wins. If not, he loses. What could be simpler than that?

There are three basic wagers at thoroughbred tracks: win betting, place betting, and show betting. The minimum bet one can make at most tracks is $2. If he bets $2 to win, his horse must do just that—win. However, if he places $2 on a horse to place, he will be a winner if the horse runs first or second. If he wagers to show, he will be paid off if the horse runs first, second, or third.

There is a bigger risk in betting a horse to win, so the win payoff is bigger than the place or show payoffs 99 percent of the time. By the same token, the place payoff is riskier than the show bet, but not as chancy as the win bet. This means you will normally get less to place than to win, but more to place than you would on a show ticket. For instance, when Secretariat won the 1973 Kentucky Derby, he paid $5 to win, $3.20 to place, and $3 to show.

While the $2 bet is the smallest wager for you at a thoroughbred track, there usually are windows which sell $5, $10, $50, and $100 tickets. There also will be windows to which you can go and bet, for instance, a $6 combination ticket, which would give you $2 to win, $2 to place, and $2 to show. There are many other ways to bet at a racetrack, but there is no need to get involved in them yet. Bets such as daily doubles (which require you to pick the winners of the first and second races), exactas, perfectas, quinellas, etc., are gimmick bets at which you buck much greater odds. Few people win these gimmick bets, but when they do, the payoffs are generous.

A horse bettor should remember, too, that the racetrack has little interest in which horse wins or loses. State law requires that it return to the patrons approximately 83 cents of every dollar wagered. The rest goes for taxes, purses for the races, operating expenses, profit, etc. Thus it is basically immaterial to a track whether your horse, or mine, wins. It will have to give back the same amount of money—about 83 cents on every dollar. Many a bettor has psyched himself out because he thought the track itself was trying to put something over on him to keep him from getting his money back. It just doesn't work that way.

But before going any further, it might be well to define a few terms that you should know. For example:

What are combination and across-the-board bets? Are they the same thing? Across-the-board is a horse player's term meaning to bet the same amount on one horse to win, place, and show. Combination often is the name given to this bet. However, there can be distinctions between the two terms. For instance, at most tracks, a combination bet is a true across-the-board bet. As a rule these sell at $6 and $15. They break down this way: $6 = $2 place, $2 show, $2 win on the specified horse; $15 = $5 win, $5 place, $5 show on the specified horse.

At a few tracks, a $10 combination bet is sold that is a win-place combination; that is, the $10 breaks down to $5 win and $5 place on the specified horse.

Actually, if you hold a $6 combination bet, you hold three different bets on the same horse. You win, in effect, on all three bets if the horse wins, on two bets if the horse comes in second, and on one (your show bet) if the horse comes in third. Payoffs on a typical race might look something like this:

Horse	Win	Place	Show
A	$18.40	$8.60	$6.40
B		$4.20	$3.00
C			$3.20

If you had bought an across-the-board ticket on the A horse, you would have collected $33.40; on the B, you would collect $7.20; on the C, $3.20. Obviously, the C would have been a "loser," as it cost you $6 to buy.

What is an entry? An entry—properly termed *coupled entry*—is a group of horses (usually two) which are either owned or trained by the same person and, for betting purposes, are considered as a single betting interest. That is, if A and B horses are an entry and you bet on either horse, you will win if either A or B wins.

What is a field? A field—properly termed *mutuel field*—is a group of horses which, due to conditions at the track which limit the number of betting interests, are grouped together for betting purposes.

What is handicapping? Handicapping is the careful utilzation of that magic formula known to all horse players whereby they select winning horses. It has been known to involve every process from the careful scrutiny of past-performance charts dating back several years, to the study of breeding lines going back five or six generations, to incomprehensible mathematical formulas which defy description, to simple point systems, to the use of the occult sciences, to simply "liking the horse."

What is the morning line? There is no single morning line on any race. There is the track's morning line—the listing of "probable odds" which appears in the track program. There is the morning line in various newspapers—the "best guess" of probable odds by some members of the paper's staff. There are the morning lines in tout sheets of all descriptions.

A morning line is really nothing more than one man's best guess of what the odds should be when all betting is over and "they're off" sounds over the track PA system. It can be accurate or inaccurate and, though generally a fairly good guide, it's almost never 100 percent accurate.

What is an inquiry? An inquiry is the formal name for the process of adjudicating a claim or question of possible "foul" in the running of a race. Any jockey or driver in a race can initiate an inquiry into that race by claiming "foul" against any other jockey, driver, or betting interest.

In other cases the track stewards, the watchdogs of racing, can initiate the inquiry based on something that they perceived during the running of the race. During an inquiry, judges and stewards view the films of the race and determine whether or not a foul did occur.

What is a stakes race? Originally, a race in which the owners put up stakes—nominating fee, entry fee, starting fee—which all went to the winner of the race. Now, racetracks add money to these events; thus, one often hears: "Today, we will watch the fifty-seventh running of the Big Stakes race, purse $100,000 added." A large percentage of this added money goes to the winner (along with the owners' fees) and the remainder of the added money is divided among the second, third, and fourth horses.

Stakes races form the apex of the racing pyramid and generally attract only the finest horses. In many cases, such as the Kentucky Derby, a horse must be "nominated" to the stakes far in advance of its actual running.

What is an allowance race? An allowance race is usually an event in which the amount of weight carried is determined by the amount of money and/or the number of races won by a horse in a specified time. The following is an example of allowance conditions:

Three-year-olds and upward which have never won two races other than maiden or claiming. Weights for three-year-olds: 121 pounds; older: 124 pounds. Nonwinners of a race other than maiden or claiming since August 28 allowed 3 pounds; of such a race since July 31 allowed 5 pounds. Thus, a four-year-old who had won only in claiming races would be assigned a weight of 124 pounds, but if that horse had won these races before July 31, would have 5 pounds allowed and would run at 119 pounds. Some stakes races are run at allowance conditions.

What is a handicap race? A race in which the racing secretary of the track assigns the weight that each horse will carry is a handicap race. This assignment of weights is made according to the racing secretary's own evaluation of each horse's potential in the race to be run. The theory of a handicap race is that all horses will thus have an equal chance of winning. For example, if the distance of a race is to be 1 mile and horse A has come fifth, sixth, and seventh the last three times he ran at that distance, he might be assigned a weight of 112 pounds. If horse B has won his last three races at that distance, he might then be assigned a weight of 126 pounds, thus giving horse A a supposedly equal chance of winning the race. Several of the major stakes races are run under handicap conditions.

What is a claiming race? A claiming race is one in which any horse entered is subject to "being claimed" (purchased) for the amount for which the horse is entered. The only people who may claim/purchase a horse in such a race are owners who have started a horse at that particular race meeting. The claiming race is a method of classifying horses in order to produce races with horses of equal ability. Some claiming races have a range of claiming prices with weight allowances being made for horses entered at lower prices.

What is a maiden race? A race for horses that have never won a race. A *maiden claiming race*, of course, is a claiming race for maidens. A *maiden special weight* is a race for maidens that the owners or trainers feel are too good to be entered in claiming races. All horses in the race usually run at the same weight.

What are track conditions? The following are the terms used to describe the condition of the main track of a thoroughbred course:

FAST: At its best, dry and even.

SLOPPY: During or immediately after a heavy rain; may have puddles, but base is still firm and running time remains fast.

MUDDY: Soft and wet.

HEAVY: A drying track, between muddy and good.

SLOW: Still wet, between heavy and good.

GOOD: Rated between slow and fast.

OFF-TRACK: Refers to any condition other than fast.

What are the names, based on age and sex, given to thorough bred racers? These are common types called thoroughbreds:

COLT: An unaltered male less than five years old.

FILLY: A female less than five years old.

HORSE: An unaltered male five years or older.

MARE: A female five years or older.

GELDING: An unsexed male of any age.

RIDGLING: A male of any age with one or both organs of reproduction absent from the sac.

Never Bet a Lot to Win a Little

Before the bettor gets seriously involved in betting on thoroughbreds, he should promise to abide by the great commandment and one cardinal rule of wagering on horses: *Never bet a lot to win a little.* The bettors who insist on wagering on horses that look as if they cannot lose and, because of it, are sent off at very short odds are courting disaster. There is no simpler way to explain this than to review the story of the outstanding filly named Marian Bender.

A year or so ago, a well-known gambler, Mr. C., walked up to the $50 window at Pimlico to wager $20,000 to show on Marian Bender, who was going for her eighth consecutive win against the same kind of horses she had been beating with ease in the past. It never even crossed Mr. C.'s mind that he might lose. The mutuel clerk, who knew Mr. C. was Maryland's biggest bettor and didn't like to wait to collect his money, told the gambler that he would advise the cashier to get the money ready.

Mr. C. had actually gone to Pimlico to bet $10,000 on Marian Bender to win. However, she was such a short-priced favorite that there was the possibility that she would pay only $2.20 for each $2 bet. By the same token, the minimum payoff for a $2 bet is $2.10. Mr. C. could get approximately the same profit by doubling the amount of money and betting it to show. Now, he was really taking insurance. Marian Bender didn't even have to win. All she had to do was finish first, second, or third and he would collect his money.

There was a total of $199,423 bet on the race, the $30,500 Politely Stakes, and $152,633 of it was wagered on Marian Bender. She was the "sure thing" for which bettors wait. Of the latter figure, $41,642 was bet to win, $18,085 of it was in the place spot, and $92,908 of it was bet to show. Others besides Mr. C. knew a good thing when they saw it.

The show pool in the race totaled $100,852, which means that 92 percent of this money bet to show was wagered on Marian Bender. Under the financial structure of racing, a racetrack must guarantee a return of five cents for every dollar wagered on a race. This is known as the minimum payoff. State law, as previously mentioned, requires that the track deduct about 17 percent of the money wagered as a pari-mutuel tax and then return the rest to the public. If a condition exists, however, in which there is not enough money left to make the minimum payoff to the public after the 17 percent is deducted, the track must reach into its own pocket and pay off bettors. A condition such as this is known as a minus pool, which was exactly what Pimlico Race Course faced in this race. However, there was no need to worry about it, for not only did Marian Bender not win, she didn't finish second or third either. She was badly beaten fifth, sending people like Mr. C. and other known as "bridge-jumpers" heading for those bridges. They had lost thousands betting to win a little and they couldn't believe what they had witnessed.

For the record, the race produced total world record show payoffs when Marian Bender ran out of the money. Because the pari-mutuel system returns a proportionate amount of money for each ticket sold on each horse the show prices were staggering. Winsome Imp, which won the race, paid $67.20 to win, $25 to place, and $73 to show. Rambell, who was second, returned $42.60 to place and $159.40 to show. The third horse, Pegemina, rewarded her show backers with a payoff of $124 for a $2 ticket.

Marian Bender was the type of thoroughbred for which people look. She was the sure thing, the filly who could not lose, but she did. "You'll never find me at a racetrack again," Mr. C. said. "When horses like that start running out of the money, there's something wrong with the game."

Mr. C. is wrong on all counts. Horses like Marian Bender will run out of the money occasionally. Maybe she didn't feel well on that particular day; maybe she didn't like the cuppy footing at Pimlico on that day. These or dozens of other unknown factors beat Marian Bender that day, and these same hidden elements which defeated her will make other "sure thing" bite the dust.

The horse player who insists on wagering large amounts of

money on the sure things must live and die broke. He might collect five out of six bets and still lose tens of thousands of dollars. In the instance of Marian Bender, Mr. C. was going to collect $21,000 for his $20,000—a profit of $1,000 for his efforts. Thus, one does not have to be a math genius to understand the hazards of ignoring the great cardinal rule of horse racing: *Never, never bet a lot to win a little.*

With this one rule in mind, we are now ready to go into the basic elements of handicapping.

The Basics of Handicapping

You can read volumes and volumes of literature on how to bet on winners at the racetrack and end up so confused that what should be a quiet get-away-from-it-all afternoon becomes a horrifying nightmare, resulting in a violent headache and an empty wallet. Because for every handicapping rule one establishes with thoroughbred betting, there will be dozens of exceptions. There is no foolproof, get-rich plan for winning at the track. The only thing you can do is take every edge possible, hope to get a little lucky, and then bet on more winners than you do losers.

There are about one hundred so-called professional horse bettors in the New York area, and all of them are successful for one reason: they take the edge. It's the same edge available to everyone, but the average horse player is too ego-stricken and hungry for action even to see it.

The oldest saying connected with the Sport of Kings says: You can beat *a race*, but you cannot beat *the races*. That, in summary, is the edge and is what thoroughbred racing is all about. You have to pick your spots. You cannot bet every race. You have to know when to bet and when to watch. There are an average of nine races a day carded at almost every thoroughbred facility in the United States. Of the nine, fewer than three a day are worth playing. The rest will do nothing but drive the bettor to the poorhouse. If you're going to be successful you will have to learn to pass these bad races. If you're so hungry for action that you have to bet all of them, racing is not for you. It will whip you before they run the second half of the daily double. Thus, the first step in actually handicapping a race is to determine which races and which horses are *not* worthy of betting.

There are two types of races in which the unknown factors

are so great they are automatically unplayable. First of all, you should never bet races for maidens. A horse is known as a maiden until he wins his first race. Thus a maiden race is an event for horses that have never won a single race. The second unplayable race is one in which a high percentage of the field seem to have a legitimate chance to win.

Competition is a great thing, but not when you are betting your money. If you handicap a race and find that you cannot eliminate all but two or three of the horses as logical contenders, then pass the race. You are bucking odds which are too great and you would have to depend too much on luck to win. However, if you can narrow the contenders down to two or three horses, you have increased your chances for winning by a considerable percentage and luck will play a lesser role in your success.

On the negative side of things, you should never bet horses on anything but a fast racetrack, either. Depending on weather conditions, a track could be listed as fast, good, muddy, sloppy, etc. Anything but a fast track is a no-no. While some horses seem to step up drastically when they run in the slop, the average horse doesn't. A horse running on an off-track has at least twice as many chances to get into trouble as horses running on a fast track. Mud throws an unknown element into a race, once again handing the horse player odds that are too stiff to buck. If it's raining, stay home. Of course, if you must go to the track, see page 236.

In trying to select the horse upon which you will bet, there is no magic formula that will produce winners. You must study carefully and try to get as many factors as possible going in your favor. The most important of these, as we discussed earlier, are current form, class, and consistency. As you begin to study a race, eliminate any horses whose current form obviously is on the downgrade, those that are inconsistent, and those that appear to be competing at a class level at which they have not before been successful.

While it is hazardous to list rules by which one can eliminate horses, we are offering five here with a word of caution that there are exceptions to all of them, but not often. In trying to cut a field down to betting size, eliminate any horse which:

1. has not been first, second, or third in the past thirty days;

2. has not run in the last fifteen days;
3. has not won a race within the past sixty days;
4. is dropping down more than 25 percent in class;
5. is stepping up more than 25 percent in class.

The only exception to rule three would be if a horse has been rested for a period of over sixty days and has run at least once in the past fifteen days and was second or third in that race. After you have eliminated horses which don't qualify for betting, you are ready for the basics of handicapping.

Consistency and Betting

As you begin to handicap the *Daily Racing Form* is a a "must" tool. You will use it as your guiding light and the foundation upon which you build your judgments. However, you must keep in mind that what you read in the *Daily Racing Form* is but a small part of the actual picture of each horse. Regardless of how good he looks in black and white, he still can lose.

In looking at the *Daily Racing Form*, the first thing to determine is a horse's current form. How has it been running? Can you see steady improvement in its races, or does it seem to be running poorer each time it competes? Right above each horse's *past performances*, you will see, on the right-hand side, its total starts, firsts, seconds, thirds, and money won during each of the last two years. These figures are important to you.

It shouldn't take a great deal of study to determine if a horse is improving or falling apart. Its last three or four races should tell you its current form. If a horse looks as if it is in good physical condition, and improving, take a look at its total starts, in-the-money record, and money won for the current year. Is it consistent? Does it have a high percentage of firsts, seconds, and thirds, or has it been in the money only once in twenty starts? Look for horses that are consistent—horses that seem to finish in the money a good part of the time. A horse that has won one race in twenty is not as good a bet as a horse that has won three of fifteen, even if the former seems to have a small edge in class. A consistent horse is dangerous every time he faces the starter. So look for horses that are consistent.

While on this subject, it might be of interest to the racing fan to know that the one thing, above all else, that the outstanding claiming trainers in this country use as a guideline for good claims is consistency. When Buddy Delp, Jack Van Berg, W. P. King, King Leatherbury, John Campo, and Frank Martin claim horses they look for consistency. A horse that has started ten or eleven times and has been consistently in the money is the kind of horse they want. They would take a $5,000 plater with no breeding which has won three of twelve starts before they would take a well-bred $100,000 yearling purchase who is zero for twenty. Thus, handicapping in the manner of a trainer, you may find a reasonable yardstick for consistency in a horse's in-the-money record. Any horse that has a win percentage of 20 percent or that has been in the money in about 50 percent of his last dozen races is the kind of horses for which to look.

By using the consistency factor, we also can eliminate many horses in a race. A horse which has not won a race in his last dozen starts and has not been in the money is a poor betting risk, even if he is dropping down drastically in company. Horses that get beaten often for $7,500 will get beaten just as often for $5,000. Thus, when handicapping, go over a race very carefully, separating the consistent horses from the inconsistent. You'll find this one thing alone will step up your win percentage tremendously. And, for strange reasons, you will get big prices on some of your winners, even though they were the most consistent individuals in a race.

Determining True Class

The next step in your thoroughbred handicapping should be to determine a horse's class. Class is impossible to define in horses, as it is in men. Either you have it or you don't. In horses, every horse has a certain amount of class and this class determines at which level he can successfully compete in races.

An owner, of course, may be carried away by enthusiasm or the high price he paid and hold to the conviction that a certain horse in his barn has the making of a champ. He'll make his trainer keep racing this animal in top company under the belief the horse will sooner or later hit his stride and justify the confidence shown in it.

Often, though, it doesn't turn out that way and the owner is doomed to disappointment as his horse loses race after race while competing over its head. But when dropped down a bit to face somewhat inferior runners, the animal might find itself racing on the precise level where it belongs and turn into a winner. Or it could happen that the slight drop is not enough and the animal must be lowered some more—perhaps even a lot more—before reaching a point suitable for it as expressed by its ability to win.

As most players are aware, racing is a game in which only a fool thinks any horse can win on any level at any distance under any set of circumstances at any time at all. It is actually an intricate sport which involves considerable skill and knowledge and experience to gain even a modicum of success. But, of course, the average fan has no reason to realize this, being solely concerned with picking a winner or losing the bet. That the horsemen also win or lose, but on a vastly larger scale, becomes evident when one has an understanding of the huge sums of money they invest in an effort to obtain a stakes winner and then find themselves wrong. Note the words *stakes winner*. Of the 25,000 or so thoroughbred horses which appear in action during the course of the year, only a comparative handful attain that status—and that goes for horses racing at tracks all over the country, in minor competition as well as the major stakes of the Kentucky Derby, Belmont, Preakness, Garden State, Futurity, Santa Anita, and Oaks.

Yet, despite the relatively few horses which manage to get into the stakes-winning class, hopeful horsemen continue to expend large sums of money for untried stock at the yearling sales held in Kentucky and Saratoga each year—in amounts like $250,000 for a colt and $175,000 for a filly—and they do it with an awareness that many of the highest-priced acquisitions in past vendues and private sales failed not only to win stakes, but also proved flops to the extent that they never enabled owners to recoup their investments and maintenance costs. As a matter of fact, the turf world starts looking forward with curiosity after the spring and fall sales to the first starts of these expensive babies just to see what kind of runners they will be, knowing full well that most of them will wind up in the discard heap before long. Of course, it is the belief of buyers that their youngsters possess the class to become stakes winners that leads to the acquisition of these babies, regardless of the fact that, since they have never raced, there is no way of finding out for sure what kind of horses they might turn out to be.

The big gamble is made in each instance because of bloodlines and general appearance. The yearlings look good and the people who buy them evidently can afford the cash outlay. But, of course, the expenditure of a large sum for a horse does not make him a winner, nor will royal breeding necessarily get him to the winner's circle. And that's what smart bettors consider above all else: the level on which the horse in question has won or finished close up the most times.

Can there be any doubt that this is the best way of establishing a horse's basic class? For whenever a horse has won before in the recent past, he may be expected to win again—unless it is definitely known he has gone back in form or is being asked to race on a track whose conditions is not to his liking. A horse going back in form is another matter, of course. Under such circumstances, he could drop several grades and still be unable to get back on the winning path. However, the highest level on which he has won may be used as the basis with which to determine the horse's true class and, when lowered below it, the horse merits consideration for backing.

There is no simple formula for determining class. If a horse is running in a claiming race (a race from which other horsemen can claim, or buy, him for the price for which he is entered), it is fairly easy to decide if he is competing at his usual class level. The *Daily Racing Form*'s past performances will show you whether a horse entered in a $5,000 claiming race has been competing at that level, below it, or above it. Next to each of his previous races will be the actual claiming price for which the horse was entered. Thus, claiming horses are reasonably simple to classify.

However, the toughest races to handicap are allowance events, which are races for better grades of horses which are not competing for a claiming price. A horse cannot be claimed from an allowance race. If eight horses are in a race, it is almost impossible to tell at what allowance level they have been competing. Because of this, it is a complicated task trying to decide which horse gets the highest class figure. The easiest way to do it is to add up a horse's firsts, seconds, and thirds and divide them into his money won. For instance, if a horse has won one race, been second twice, and third twice—and has earned $15,000—we would give him a class rating of $3,000. By the same token, if there was another horse in the race with an identical 1–2–2 first, second, and third record and had won $10,000, we would give him a class rating of $2,000. A horse with the same record but with $5,000 in winnings would have a $1,000 rating. While this formula is not foolproof in determining actual class, it is reasonably accurate. Classier horses compete for better purses and have higher average earnings.

For example, a true stakes horse—as a victory or an in-the-money effort would establish him to be—should have no trouble whipping horses of lesser grade. And a good allowance horse can be ranked over the runners constantly appearing in claiming races, although this would depend to a large extent on the type of claimers in which the latter competed most often. But generally speaking, the higher the claim price, the better the horse—provided, of course, he's a winner or makes a strong showing in such company.

Sometimes it is difficult to split an allowance horse and one which gives a bang-up account of himself in a high-priced claimer, for when a horse proves capable of winning with a $25,000 or $30,000 claim tag (as featured at some of the better tracks), he could be good enough to hold his own with allowance performers. However, among the cheaper runners, it is not often that such difficulty is encountered. The difference in claiming price for which each has won usually serves as a fairly accurate guide to a forthcoming win when horses from different claim levels are brought together.

It is in this fashion that owners and trainers get a line on their horses and learn where to race them. From the beginning, it is an up-and-down process. A newcomer is first run where there is reason to believe he can win. The opinion may be formed on the basis of workouts or in trials against horses of a particular grade. If the horse wins first out and keeps winning, he is moved up a notch or two after each victory. But if he loses in his debut or continues to lose on the same level, he will be lowered gradually until he wins. In either case, the winning level will establish his true class.

The same rule applies to horses claimed recently and being sent into action by their new owners. Only here care should be exercised in making sure the claimed horse is not overmatched because of the claim rule which necessitates a step up of at least 25 percent in the next thirty days. For when a horse changes hands by claim or sale, the new stable often makes an effort to find out exactly what was obtained and also maneuvers the acquisition up and down the class ladder in an effort to determine his worth. Where he last won and finished close up to the leaders usually furnishes the best answer to this question.

The handicapping factors concerning a horse's current form, his consistency, and his class are things we can determine with a certain degree of accuracy just by studying the *Daily Racing Form*. After that, the nature of racing itself makes accurate handicapping extremely difficult.

The Value of the Trainer

The next most important factor in attempting to bet on winners is the quality and ability of the trainer. There is a small, select group of trainers in the country who saddle about 75 percent of the winners of all races run. They know what to do with a horse, how to bring him up to a race, and then how to win with him. They are as consistent as their horses. Trainers of this standout ability are few and far between, but the novice bettor would never know it. He would think he was getting just as good a break betting on John Doe as he would be betting on a horse saddled by someone like J. P. Conway. Nothing could be farther from the truth.

Racing is so backward in its publicity and promotional operations it has never taken the time to keep the bettors informed as to actual records of all trainers. Harness racing has its Universal Driver Ratings, while thoroughbred racing has nothing. If you can determine which trainers in your local area know what they are doing, you can step up your win percentage considerably. The story is the same for trainers, regardless of whether they race at Longacres Race Course in Seattle, Washington, Calder in Miami, or Saratoga in upstate New York; a few of them win 75 percent of all the races run. Because racing, like all other sports, is a game of percentages, one can take a tremendous bonus edge by following top trainers. None of them saddle 100 percent winners, but they get the money often enough to make it worth one's while.

A conversation overheard on the backstretch at Churchill Downs one sunny morning a few years ago brings home, with authority, the plight of the average trainer. Someone asked: "What do you think of so-and-so as a trainer?" Before the man could reply, an old and respected groom spoke up and stunned his audience with a profoundly philosophical statement: "He couldn't train a vulture to eat."

The statement stuck for years with those who heard it, for they knew, too well, it was the truth in its purest form and described many of those who operate today as trainers. They truly could not train a vulture to eat, much less condition something as fragile and complex as a thoroughbred. Nevertheless, the nation's racing commissions keep giving trainer's licenses to used-car salesmen, shoe peddlers, and fry cooks. As we have said, this is unfortunate for the bettor, because no person connected with a horse is more important to his development and success than his trainer. The man who supervises all his activities and is supposed to bring him up to his races in peak form will make all the difference to the bettor.

Any man who bets on horses should pull himself up and not make another wager until he has read *Training Thoroughbred Horses* by Preston M. Burch, one of the greatest trainers in history. This book is published by Blood-Horse, Lexington, Kentucky. The book is 130 pages long and is easy reading. If only 1/1000 of the information in the book rubbed off on the horse player, he would drastically increase his chances for betting on winners. The book was written as a guide for those interested in training horses, but it is so basic and clear in its facts that it is a must for horse players. The book will take one from darkness into light in just a few pages, exposing the intricate makeup of thought behind training methods, etc. One will get immediate insight into why horses are inconsistent in their performances.

There is no person connected with a horse who is more important to him than his trainer. This man supervises all his activities and is supposed to bring him to the races ready to run his best race. The simple fact that this doesn't always happen is an indication of the quality of training in this country.

To understand just a bit about how a trainer works, keep in mind he is influenced by the owner or owners of his horses. The owner may make him run a horse before he is ready or enter him in a sprint when he really should be going a long distance. These shortcomings cannot be held against trainers, but many horses get beaten because of overanxious owners. However, once past the owner, the trainer is on his own. He is responsible for the success or failure of his horses.

The biggest mistake most conditioners make is in spotting their horses. They might have a horse which had an excellent chance of winning in a $5,000 claiming race, but for reasons known only to their ids, they will keep running him for $6,000 and keep losing. Meantime the horse's form goes down and down. The smart trainers know where to place their horses.

One of the greatest trainers in the history of thoroughbred racing was the late Marian H. Van Berg. Allan W. Lavin, who was racing secretary at Oaklawn Park, once asked Van Berg to come up with a horse to fill a race for $8,000 claimers going six furlongs.

Van Berg told Lavin he didn't have a horse ready for that race, but Lavin, knowing every horse that Van Berg had, pressed him to put a particular horse in the race.

"He's already in," Van Berg said.

"He is not," Lavin replied. "I don't see any entry blank on him."

"Oh, you misunderstand me," Van Berg said. "He's in the third race for $5,000."

What Van Berg was saying was simply that his horse definitely would fit in the $8,000 race and might get a piece of the purse. However, he was almost a cinch to win at $5,000 and that was where Van Berg was going to run him. People who spot their horses in the right races win. Those who don't are strangers to the winner's circle.

There are no specific criteria for what makes a good trainer. The only thing that speaks is a man's record and this is available if a bettor wants to take the time to find out about it on his own. The only information available to the general public is a list of the six to twelve top trainers at a particular meet (usually published in the program). Unfortunately, the list seldom tells the public what percentage of races a trainer wins, or what percent of the time his horses are in the money. These two figures would take a lot of the guesswork out of handicapping and maybe one day thoroughbred racing will think enough of its fans to offer it.

It would be tremendously helpful if tracks would post, somewhere on the premises, on a day-by-day basis, the number of horses each trainer has started at a meeting and how many of them finished first, second, or third. We attempted to do this in modified form at Arlington Park some few years ago, just listing the wins a trainer had and the number of horses he had started at the meeting. Right off the bat, three trainers started beefing. Each had saddled five winners at the meeting, which was good. Of the three, one had started 56 horses, one 71, and the other 63. They felt it made them look bad to have saddled just five winners from that number of starters, and they were right. The lady in charge made us drop the number of starters column.

We would never tell you to follow any trainer, pressing your bet each time you lose, but, again, statistics tell us that your chances for success if you do this are extremely high. If the publicity office of your track can't provide this important data for you, start keeping it for yourself. You can start by finding out the top ten trainers from the number of wins at your track during the past five years. Then concentrate your efforts on these individuals. Remember that the professional horse bettors keep all of the trainer information for themselves and capitalize on it. The data is interesting in that the same names keep appearing among the winners year-in and year-out. The big boys follow these individuals, pressing when they lose and seldom failing to show a profit on a particular trainer every month.

Trainers' Tricks

Horse trainers are basically honest, generally speaking. There are a few, however, who have been known to manipulate their animals so that they do not win certain races. We do not imply that they resort to illegal practices, but merely employ clever maneuvers which, although legal, nevertheless deprive the bettor of a fair shake. If, however, you, the bettor, learn to recognize these tricks, you can perhaps turn them to your own advantage.

Some of the trainer maneuvers worth observing when handicapping a race follow.

The Drop in Class. This is a trainer manipulation that is apparent to anyone who can read racing past performances. Horses that fall into this category often go off as favorites. The drop in class may occur within a given type of race (example: last time out ran for a $10,000 allowance purse but today is running for a $6,500 allowance purse) or it may occur in the category of race itself (example: dropping a horse from stakes to allowance or from allowance to claiming competition). In any case, this maneuver is too apparent to be of any real value to the handicapper except to tell him that, under normal circumstances, the drop-down horse should outclass his competition and win.

Up and Down in Class. As mentioned earlier, another favorite trainer maneuver is the movement upward after the horse has won two or three straight or finished close up in his own class. When soundly beaten several times by better horses, the animal may be thrown into a race with horses of the same caliber. There are several reasons for this move. The trainer may merely want to try his horse in better company to see how good he is or just to improve the morale of the horse; on the other hand, he may be doing it for the purpose of deceiving the players so that the horse will pay a long price when dropped back in class.

Switch in Distance. Trainers frequently try to fool the public by switching their horses from one distance to another. They may enter a successful sprinter in a middle distance or even a route race where, almost invariably, it runs out of the money. They may race a horse at the longer distance until he has built up sufficient stamina to set or be near the pace at this longer distance, at which time they'll drop him back into a sprint and he'll win it. This maneuver can also have a twofold purpose: changing a sprinter into a distance horse or fooling the public. This tactic may also be worked in reverse by a trainer. He'll enter his distance horse in several sprints in which the speed horses will leave him in the dust. After several losses at 6 or 7 furlongs, he'll drop him in at $1\frac{1}{16}$ miles or $1\frac{1}{8}$ miles, where he'll win with ease, again knocking the form players for a loop and collecting a large mutuel payoff. A rule of thumb to remember: off class and current form you can safely bet a sprinter going in a middle-distance event (1 mile to $1\frac{1}{8}$ miles). Never, however, should a distance horse going in a sprint for the first or second time be even considered.

Change in Tracks. Here is a widely used trainer angle which involves running a horse on the grass or in steeplechase or hurdles events where he looks so bad that when he moves into the main dirt track, off his recent form his odds are usually sky high. He'll usually shine in this race since he is back in his proper element and many times comes through with a boxcar mutuel. Along these same lines, there is the "shipper"—a horse that is shipped into a minor track from a major one for just one or two races. The horse has usually been doing poorly at the large oval and, on paper, his form looks terrible. However, running with the cheaper animals in low-priced claiming events he will probably score the first or second time out at a good price. Conversely, during the last week or two of a major meeting most of the better horses have been shipped to the next major track on the circuit. The only horses left on the grounds are the "cheapies." A trainer may ship his charge in from a minor, obscure track, enter him in a minimum purse event at the major oval (which is usually much higher than the minimum purse at the small track where the horse had been campaigning), and "steal" one or two from the platers left behind at the major ovals.

A word to the wise: beware of shippers. Check them carefully before you either reject or bet on them.

Off Tracks. A trainer may have a very good horse who just cannot run on an off track (sloppy, muddy, etc.). If the trainer is smart enough to recognize this early enough, he will not let his horse run on a fast track until he is ready to "make a score." He'll enter him whenever possible but will scratch him if the track comes up fast. He will let him run only in the mud. After several races in the slop, his form will be so bad—on paper—that when he is allowed to go on a fast track, his odds will usually be sky high, at which time, to everyone's amazement, he'll run like a champion and pay a huge price. To combat this, when handicapping, pay attention not only to where the horse finished but also to what kind of footing he was running on. The track variant is given for this purpose. Use it in your handicapping.

Sacrifices to Get Lower Weight. The conditions of a race show that a horse that is entered for less than the top claiming price may carry less than top weight. An apprentice jockey aboard also means weight concession. Many trainers who know the ability of their animals as to how much weight they can carry and still be in contention will sacrifice the experience and know-how of a journeyman jockey for an apprentice, as well as taking the chance of losing their horse for a lower claiming price in order to win a purse. This manipulation, of course, is about as safe as playing Russian roulette, assuming, of course, a trainer wants to retain his horse. Some of them want their horses to be claimed so they will enter them for the lowest claiming price, get the maximum weight concession, and then hope for just two things: (1) that someone claims the horse and (2) that the low weight makes the horse a winner. If both occur, of course, the trainer comes out ahead in both departments.

Jockey Switches. We may as well face it, a trainer is not always aiming for the winner's circle every time he runs his horse. As a result, on the day (or days) when he's running his horse just so the animal can get some sun and air, he may go with a "bug boy" or mediocre journeyman jockey. However, on the day he's going for all the marbles, he'll usually engage (or attempt to) the best rider available at the track. So keep an eye out for this type of manipulation—a switch from an "also ran" to a top rider. The trainer could be telegraphing the message that "today is the day." Conversely, a trainer may step his charge down and engage the services of one of the poorest jockeys at the meeting. In this case, he knows he'll get a better price with a "nothing" rider aboard and is confident that the horse if good enough to win with a chimpanzee aboard. So he sacrifices ability (of the rider) for a better payoff.

Secret Workouts. Many trainers secretly work out their horses at a nearby or adjacent track rather than at the track at which they are campaigning, for the purpose of concealing the horse's actual form from the public. There is not much the average racing fan can do about this, but regarding published workouts, if a horse has a good workout on the day before he is scheduled to run and this is preceded by several not-too-good-workouts, this is a strong indication that his trainer is sending him out to win.

Heavy Weighted. There is no doubt that in your handicapping you have come across horses that are carrying so much weight that it's almost impossible for them to win and invariably they lose. Ever wonder why a trainer allows his charge to run hauling a ton of weight with little or no chance of winning rather than scratching him? The answer is simple. Under handicap conditions, the more often the horse wins the more weight he is required to haul in each succeeding race. He thus permits his horse to go with the heavy weight and lose. He may do this several times in order to get poundage off. When he is down to carrying a reasonable weight, he'll go out and win, beginning the circle anew.

These are some of the manipulations a trainer might use in order to get his horse across the wire first at long odds. Most average racing fans become incensed when they learn that trainers actually "play games" like these when they (the fans) have their money riding on the horse. They, of course, have all the right in the world to be angry. However, by training themselves to recognize these trainer maneuvers and searching for and finding them when handicapping a race, they will find that they can take advantage of these moves and let them work *for* them rather than against them.

The Value of the Jockey

If any facet of thoroughbred racing is overemphasized, it is the part a jockey plays in the performance of a horse. It is a proven fact that the average horse will run just as well for one average jockey as it will for another. A smart trainer once said no more than a nose separated the the best one hundred riders in the country. He probably was right.

Let's consider, for just a moment, the statistics of riding. There are approximately 1,500 jockeys who ride at least one horse in the United States each year. Of these, more than 500 do not win a single race. Of even more significance is the fact that fewer than 200 riders win more than one-half of all the races run in this country during any given year.

There are many professional handicappers who will bet on just six or seven riders at any particular racetrack, knowing that these riders will handle most of the winners. Almost without exception, they do not wager on a jockey who rides an occasional winner, even though he might be on a horse that looks the best.

In taking jockeys into consideration as a handicapping factor, it is important to know many things, of which the most important is how many winners the jockey has ridden at the meeting where he is now performing. This information should be available in the daily program. Live riders—those who are riding a lot of winners—are always good bets. A trainer knows when a rider is doing well and uses him on his best horses. There is no business in existence where success breeds success as it does in racing. Once a rider starts riding winners, he attracts live horses like a magnet. It goes without saying the bettor can take a little edge with him. However, as for riders, bettors should be forewarned that a jockey cannot make a horse run any faster than its ability permits. The best rider in the country is not going to make a good allowance horse beat a superstar like Kelso.

There are times, too, when a live horse can be determined by who is riding him. Seldom will you find a good rider on a horse that has no chance, unless that horse happens to be from a stable with which the rider has a contract to ride all its horses. It also is not unusual for a good jockey to ride a horse whose form looks bad, give him a race, and then go all out to win with him the second time he rides him.

As we have said before, there isn't any rule in racing to which there aren't exceptions. With jockeys, there are a few. For instance, Willie Shoemaker, who has won races whose purses totaled over $50 million, is a master at holding a tiring horse together in the stretch. Horses which quit for others seem to respond to his powerful hands, gaining confidence enough to hang on for those narrow wins. It is accepted among racing people that horses run well for Shoemaker because they like him. He steps those horses up.

At the other end of the spectrum is Ismael Valenzuela, who literally terrorizes horses. They run for him because they are afraid of him. Valenzuela is one of the strongest riders ever to compete in this country.

When the immortal Eddie Arcaro's eyes went bad and he decided to retire, it meant that Mrs. Richard C. Du Pont, who owned the great Kelso, had to find a new rider. With Arcaro gone, she went for Shoemaker, who rode Kelso four times, but was able to win with him only once.

Shoemaker sensed that the headstrong Kelso, who retired from racing with a record earnings of $1,977,896, needed a stronger rider and asked Mrs. Du Pont to take him off the grand old gelding. With the powerful Valenzuela in the irons, Kelso won fifteen of the first twenty races he ran after that. Kelso ran best for Valenzuela.

The world of apprentice riders, or "bug boys" as they are known around the track, is a spectrum all unto itself. The apprentice jockey rides with the eyes of many people—the foremost of which are the stewards—watching him. For this reason, he is trying on every mount, striving to get every ounce of strength from a horse and finish as close up with him as possible.

Around the racetrack, good apprentice riders are a license to steal. Because they will be trying hard with all their mounts, trainers like to ride competent bug boys. Because they are trying all the time, other jockeys like to bet on competent bug boys, and therein lies a situation of which the public is not aware.

Racing is basically an honest game, but it has those few who try to take an edge—legal and illegal. Unfortunately, some of these individuals have jockey licenses and ride daily at this nation's tracks. You show us a race meeting where an apprentice was the leading rider, and we'll show you some jocks who added a few more dollars to their retirement fund. Yes, journeymen jockeys bet on apprentice riders.

The apprentice is the biggest setup in the world in the eyes of the journeyman. He is trying hard because the stewards are watching him to see that he learns his trade; he has a weight allowance which helps get him live horses to ride, and he is most likely to be a frontrunner, hustling his mount to the lead right out of the gate. It's a natural situation. All the journeymen have to do is wage a hell of a battle for second place while they let the apprentice steal away to a lead which he can maintain throughout. We used to get angry about this situation but finally gave up and started betting on the hot apprentice riders when they were on speed horses. If you can't beat them, join them.

In conclusion, when trying to determine if a jockey will make a difference in a horse's performance, remember that a handful of riders at a particular meeting ride over half the winners. Try to stick to these riders and you'll cash a lot of tickets. This is not to say that a lesser light won't beat you occasionally, but you'll win a lot of bets by not betting on him. As for the apprentice riders, bet on them if they are among the leading riders at a meeting and pay double attention when you find one on a speed horse. You never can tell when half the guys in the race are betting on the bug boy.

The Importance of Weight

Enough weight can stop a freight train, and since a horse is not a common carrier any trainer worth his salt tries to spot an animal where his weight assignment is not in itself a defeat-causing factor. This does not mean that the trainer always strives for the lightest weight possible for his horse as it is fallacious to imagine that a horse will continue to improve more and more with each pound taken off his back from the previous race in which he appeared or the imposts he carried customarily in the past.

Some learned racetrack observer noted in the long ago: the detriment of lowered speed by weight increase is greater than the benefit of speed gained by lowered weight. And that observation has held true through the years. But there's simply a limit to the amount of improvement a horse will show while shedding poundage as the result of losing constantly and having no reason for the track handicapper to reverse the trend by penalizing the animal for a recent victory or because of the other causes which bring additional weight.

These are things such as allowances found in the conditions, choice of a journeyman jockey over an apprentice rider, the use of whom may reduce the weight burden by 3, 5, 7, or 10 pounds, depending on the degree of apprenticeship, or the very action of the trainer in exercising one of the wide range of options open to him, which vary according to the type of race it happens to be.

The very least weight that the horse in question may be permitted to carry under the circumstances is not the usual objective; what is sought is a comfortable package for the horse, one warranted not to hamper his progress and thereby let him be free to turn on the speed without reservation when it is needed in the final stages, where races most often are won or lost.

A heavily laden animal, persistently pressed through the stretch, frequently will sulk and shorten stride as the going continues to stay rough without letup. There are exceptions, of course. It could be that the horse is a real champ, possessing lots of heart and capable of conserving a measure of strength and stamina for the final drive, in which he'll prove his class by shaking off the lightly weighted contenders and bounding away for the win. More often than not, though, it will prove the other way around, with the horse getting none the best of it at the weights calling it a day after making a fair but futile attempt to lug the load successfully.

Examples of both may be found in the records of the leading stakes races run at major thoroughbred tracks in this country. The Santa Anita Handicap, for instance, provides several dramatic and illuminating illustrations of both lightweights beating home topweights and heavily weighted runners taking the measure of foes carrying considerably less. Stagehand won carrying only 100 pounds as his burden. Mark-Ye-Well, toting 130, defeated Trusting, with 112, and First Glance, with 113.

The year before Stagehand beat him, Seabiscuit carried 114 pounds in the same race but lost to Rosemont, shouldering 124; two years following the Stagehand setback, Seabiscuit won the Santa Anita with 130 pounds on his back, leading home Kayak II, his stablemate, which carried 129, and the relatively lightly weighted Whichcee, under 114 pounds, finished third.

The great Citation attempted to carry 132 against Noor, with 110, but could do no better than finish second, as the lightweight took the big money. On another occasion, Corn Husker, with 105, took the measure of Holandes II, with 121 as his allotment. The history of the Santa Anita Handicap is full of this kind of stuff and the same may be found in the case of other outstanding events run at tracks in all sections of the country.

Many people feel the best races on which one can bet are stakes and handicaps, and they probably are right. In these events, one has the opportunity to wager on a better, and usually more consistent, grade of horse. Is there any simple way to take an edge in handicaps?

The experts say there is, but we are not sure. First of all, weight is a factor in handicaps, while not necessarily so in stakes events. The racing secretary decides how much weight a horse will carry in a handicap, while predetermined conditions have been set down to decide what a horse carries in a stake.

In a handicap, we always look first for the horse carrying top weight. He is carrying it because the racing secretary thought he merited the honor and in most cases racing secretaries know what what they are doing and their judgment must be respected. However, there are some important things to keep in mind when considering a top-weighted horse:

1. The weight is based on what he has done and not on what he might do.

2. He is weighted in relation to the ability of every other horse in the race.

3. In theory, the racing secretary handicapped the race for every horse to hit the wire at the same time.

4. In theory, weight is supposed to do this, but it doesn't.

5. In handicaps, a horse is penalized for every one of his past successes.

6. Some trainers run in handicaps to get weight off. They figure if they win the race, it is an added bonus, but they expect to lose and know they will get weight off in the next trip.

7. Leading candidates for handicaps usually get beaten in prep races.

In trying to get a good line on the top-weighted horse in a handicap, we study his form very closely and try to determine if he is on the upside or the downside of a peak in his conditioning. Horses stay on edge for very short periods of time—usually two months at best. Thus, it is possible for a handicap horse which has won three important stakes in the last sixty days to be carrying top weight, although he obviously is not the horse he was a few weeks ago. Never forget, he is weighted in relation to what he has done and not what he might do. The unwritten rules of racing permit a racing secretary very little leverage to give a horse a pound or two because of his present condition. He handicaps only in relation to past performance.

In analyzing top-weighted horses in handicaps, we also try to guess what is on a trainer's mind. The trainer knows he can run his horse under top weight and that he might get lucky and win, despite the fact that the horse is not at his best. He also knows if he gets beaten, the racing secretary will take weight off the next time he runs. In certain respects, the trainer is a winner, regardless of the outcome of the race.

We have been burned so many times betting on preps for handicap races that we no longer wager on them. These preps are usually a week before the added-money race and are run at a distance of from one to two furlongs shorter than the coming event. They are put on by the racing secretary to give stakes candidates an opportunity to have a race over the track at a point in time that will put them at their best. If the prep is a race for a stake in which weight already has been determined, one can take a betting interest. However, if it is a prep for a handicap and the racing secretary is going to take its results into account when deciding on weights for the Big One, we'll pass, thank you.

If the prep is for an allowance condition stake, the winner will not be penalized for doing his number. But, if the prep is for a handicap, don't bet that the average trainer is doing his best to win. To win just means more weight when the big money is on the line. If you must bet preps for handicaps, bet on a horse which isn't even nominated for the big race. You can bet his connections are trying.

Condition of the Horses

Would you bet your money on a horse that had absolutely no chance of winning? Certainly not, you say, but unfortunately we do just this many times a week if we are daily patrons at a racetrack. We would never intentionally step up to a mutuel window and ask for tickets on a horse that could not win. We fall into this blind trap by unknowingly betting on sore horses that are 10 to 1 to finish, let alone to win.

It is difficult for the average eye of the betting fan to observe soreness in horses. Some trainers don't even know what to look for. If we were permitted in the paddock and allowed to examine the ankles, knees, etc., of each horse before a race we could find out if it had any temperature in those areas—a sure sign of trouble. If we could take a horse's temperature, we would then know if it had a fever. Because there is no way for thousands of racing fans to check closely on the physical well-being of an individual horse each day in each race, the man who bets on horses needs to know what to look for when he is visually trying to observe whether a horse is sound.

To begin with, 95 percent of the horses running in stakes races are sound at the time they run. We'd say that about 90 percent of all allowance horses are sound when they run. All of these horses may have physical impairments which, at one time or another, hamper their performances, but on racing days you can generally bet they are traveling sound. In claiming horses, it is an entirely different story, particularly at levels of $10,000 and below. While there are no figures to back this up, it is a safe assumption that soreness and unsoundness in horses increase in direct proportion to lower and lower claiming prices. This means that there are more unsound horses running for $3,000 than there are running for $15,000.

On a percentage basis, the highest number of sore horses at any racetrack appear in straight maiden, not claiming, races for three- and four-year-olds which have never won a race. We do not have any explanation for this, other than to say that the fact that these horses are maidens is at least an indication, not so much of lack of ability, but of lack of soundness. Any three-year-old which hasn't broken his maiden is a no-no, regardless of how much you like him.

Let's examine several ways the average bettor can get a better line on soreness and unsoundness in horses. First and foremost, you've got to keep your eyes open when horses are being brought to the paddock. Sore horses will go to the paddock heavily bandaged. Cold water bandages, which are soaked in ice water and medication, will be wrapped around a horse's front legs, almost to his knees. Any horse with cold water bandages is a bad betting proposition.

A horse that comes to the paddock with a blanket over his shoulders and appears to be sweaty in the shoulder area when the blanket comes off is a very bad betting proposition. This is a sure sign of soreness in a horse's shoulders.

If you look at a horse on the racetrack and can see that he obviously is not reaching out when he strides, you can bet he is sore. Even though he might warm up out of this, he's not a good betting proposition. Never forget, too, that a sore horse will never warm up in front of the stands. The jockey will walk him around to the backstretch before he lets him break off and run. The reasons for this are obvious. In front of the stands, the horse is in full view of three track veterinarians (in most states), the stewards, the racing press, and other horsemen. However, when he gets around to the backstretch, there usually is just one vet trying to keep his eyes on everything, and most soreness will slip by him. Also, almost all sore horses will go to the post with a pony. Racing officials, vets, etc., cannot detect soreness in a horse when he is with a pony. The pony's stride is much shorter than that of the thoroughbred; thus the latter's action always looks choppy with a pony galloping at his side.

The problem with the latter is that so few trainers know how to train a horse to go to the post by himself anymore that almost all of them have ponies. It makes it much more difficult to tell the sore horses from the sound ones. Actually, many horses will have muscular or arthritic pain in the hindquarters that makes their walking stride ungainly in the paddock. More often than not such horses have been thoroughly checked by the vet and will warm up out of their soreness and perform creditably. But, when a horse fails to step out fully with the front legs, or when stopping he takes weight off one or the other foreleg, that spells trouble. Don't risk a sou on that candidate for the ambulance.

Grass vs. Dirt

When interviewed about his champion grass runner Fort Marcy, Eliot Burch liked to slip in a remark about how his charge could also run well on the main track. He was right. Fort Marcy could run well on the dirt, but he was no champion. If forced to race on the main track throughout his career the game gelding would never have been the famous runner he was.

The fact of the matter is that grass and dirt racing are two distinctly different matters. That should be burned in your memory. You just can't transpose an animal's talents from one surface to another. It doesn't work. Sure, some horses such as Secretariat or Dr. Fager are shifty enough to do well over either course, but the majority of horses prefer one to the other and often the differences in performances are startling. For instance, Gun Bow and Kelso were the top handicap runners of their day and they had some memorable meetings. Both also tried the grass and were far from slouches on that surface. However, Mongo was able to handle Kelso over the green but couldn't do as well on the main course, while Gun Bow, also a tough one on grass, was beaten by the likes of Turbo Jet II. How many remember that grass ace? He couldn't touch Gun Bow on dirt but beat him over the greensward.

What it comes down to is that grass races are handicapped like any other race but you don't take efforts on the main track at face value. You go by grass performance only. So when each starter in the race has had a couple of shots over the green just study those races and forget the others.

Of course that doesn't help much when most, if not all, of the contestants have yet to try to grass. These races are mutuel murder. They're like two-year-old maiden races, only worse. For the most part you won't even have workouts to go on. The animal may show some morning trials in the record but if they aren't on the grass they won't be of much help.

When there is no established grass form you shouldn't be betting. If you insist on taking a shot you have nothing to lose but your money. And lose it you will. You are stabbing, not handicapping, and there's a world of difference between the two.

Off-Track Conditions

Does speed really stand up better on days when rain soaks a thoroughbred racetrack? Do frontrunners enjoy an edge when puddles form on a racing strip? Does a muddy surface hinder the horse that likes to come from off the pace? When track conditions are off, many bettors like to stick with frontrunners. They figure that the horses and jockeys in the front of the pack will avoid the flying mud that seems to discourage so many trailing animals.

The theory seems logical enough. But it's not necessarily true, as a survey we have made has shown. We checked 200 races at a mile or longer on off tracks (sloppy, slow, muddy, and heavy) to determine whether frontrunners did indeed fare better than closers. Then we compared these results with 200 races over fast tracks (we disregarded all races over surfaces classified as "good"). The survey encompassed 32 racetracks and took place in the middle of the summer in 1973. We checked no more than 15 races at each oval, so that the survey would not be overweighted by results at any one track.

When we found a route race on an off track, we recorded whether the winner was first or second at the half-mile call, or third or worse. If he was leading or racing second, we considered him a frontrunner. Otherwise, we rated him a closer. Then, we checked the track the next day that the surface was rated "fast." For each route race, we again noted the winner's position at the half-mile mark.

We studied the results of tracks from Ak-Sar-Ben to Woodbine. We analyzed racing at big tracks like Arlington Park and Belmont, and at minor ovals such as Coeur D'Alene and Prescott. The results surprised us. If frontrunners truly did have the edge over a wet surface, then they would have shown demonstrable superiority in our figures—but they didn't.

We found that the condition of the racing strip made virtually no difference when it came to picking frontrunners vs. closers. Frontrunners won just about the same percentage of races on both surfaces. They captured 84 of the 200 route races over rainy tracks (42 percent) and 78 of the 200 route races over fast strips (39 percent). After the first 100 races, the dry-track frontrunners actually had the edge over the off-track speed horses, but the rainy-day racers did better in the latter part of the survey.

While the samples at each track were relatively small, the overall findings seemed conclusive. Checking the results track by track, we found that frontrunners didn't seem to do any better on wet surfaces than they did on dry strips. For instance, frontrunners did well in the slop at Rockingham (they won 9 of our 15 races checked), but they did equally as well on fast surfaces (also winning 9 of 15). At Ak-Sar-Ben, frontrunners won only 3 of the 11 route races over a wet strip—and also won only 3 of the races over dry tracks.

Our survey shows that the horse to back on an off track may be either a frontrunner or a closer. It depends on the horse. An animal which has triumphed over an off track in the past is always one to be reckoned with if conditions today are sloppy or worse. Aging, sore-legged horses sometimes find that the softer footing eases their ailments, if only long enough to complete a race.

Stick with proven mudders when the rains fall on your racetrack and don't worry about whether the horse prefers to lead most of the way or would rather come from behind.

What Makes a Mudder?

There isn't a living soul who can tell any of us for sure what makes a horse a mudder, or why some top horses such as Riva Ridge absolutely lose their action on anything but a fast track. Some horses are natural mudders and can run on any kind of an off track. Others run well when a track is deep in watery slop, but with a firm bottom, and then refuse to extend themselves on a deep, soft, muddy track. Many trainers feel a horse like Riva Ridge refuses to extend himself in the mud because he is slipping and is actually afraid of falling.

It also is an accepted fact that any horse can learn to perform in the mud if he trains in it long enough. The bettor should keep this in mind, particularly in light of the fact that many areas of the country experience long periods of rain, which make a fast track the exception rather than the rule. If a horse has run poorly in the mud before, the chances are he will run poorly again. However, if he has trained in it for a couple of weeks, he might upset his past performances and still win.

The mud marks as carried in the *Daily Racing Form* are deceiving at best, although this is unintentional on the part of Triangle Publications, which publishes racing's bible. We have known many horses, the most recent of which was Mister Diz, who raced for two years without a mud mark by his name, when, in fact, he was an outstanding off-track runner and all of us cashed a big bet on him going flat mile in the mud at Laurel one fall. He was eight lengths in front all the way, loving the slop.

The mud marks are not reliable because the system by which the *Form* assigns them is totally unscientific, relying primarily on the opinions and judgments of people who have less expertise than you and I about a horse's ability to perform in the off going.

Mud always has introduced to racing an unknown factor of sizable proportions, but people still insist on betting when the track is off. There are at least 1,000 ways to lose a race on a fast track and at least 1,500 ways to lose on an off track. The odds are too great and the bettor should stay home when it's raining. Some horses perform well on the muddy tracks of the country. We've never known a bettor who was a true mudder.

Foreign Influence Confusing

As more and more horses are imported to this country to run, the bettor becomes more and more confused as to the capabilities of these horses. The average foreigner can be expected to perform far below the level of competence he established in his home country when he makes his first start here. However, there is no rule which says he won't be another Canonero II. Horses from South America have a better chance to run well here because they have trained over both dirt and grass courses in the southland. By the same token, horses from England, France, Ireland, and Italy have never felt a dirt track before, having been walking, galloping, and running over grass since birth.

Put a European horse on a dirt track in this country and you can expect him to get beaten. Not only will it mark his first trip around a dirt track, it will mean his first unnerving experience of having dirt kicked back in his face. It also is a fact that many horses from Europe seem to have low, flat heels, which hinder their ability to run well on the dirt. When their hooves come down they land hard and pound on the low heels. Our horses' heels are not low, not flat, and are accustomed to running on the dirt.

Don't Ask the Impossible

There are so many pitfalls in trying to handicap a winner at the racetrack that the bettor has no reason to go out of his way to find trouble. Unfortunately, rational bettors do just that every day, never seeming to grasp the overwhelming odds they are trying to beat.

When one analyzes a race and tries to pick the logical contender, he should think a dozen times before asking a horse to do something it has ever done before. For instance, heavy thought is required before asking a sprinter with established 6-furlong form to stretch out and go 1⅛ miles.

Regardless of how many sprint races a horse has run—and won—he is a risky proposition when asked to go a route. He will be facing a completely different set of racing circumstances, and every one of them will most likely have a negative effect on his performance.

With the exception of half-mile racetracks, a sprinter races around only one turn, with the race starting on a straightaway on the backstretch. Going a route of ground, he will most likely be asked to race around two turns, which is confusing to a horse who is not used to it.

A sprinter has been drilled for speed and will run as hard as it can for as far as it can. It will spend all of its energy in a very short period of time. Can a horse that has been drilled for speed be asked to control it when going a distance? Only a horse of unusual ability can make this adjustment, and few of these are found in the claiming races which make up eight out of every nine races on the average racing card.

By the same token, a router that is asked to sprint will be at a distinct disadvantage for just the opposite reasons. He has not been drilled for speed, even if he is a router who usually sets the pace in distance races, and will find the seasoned hell-bent-for-leather sprinters hard to handle.

In other situations, the bettor asks for trouble when he bets on a seasoned dirt runner, of any quality, to beat seasoned turf horses on the grass. The percentages of racing tell us that, again, only an unusual horse can run as well on the grass as on the dirt, and vice versa.

A horse with outstanding form on a fast track may be 4 to 5 in the betting when he tries the mud, when in reality he should be 20 to 1. Again, the bettor is asking for trouble when he expects a horse to do something he is not accustomed to doing.

Every bettor should simply adopt one rule: *Never ask a horse to do something he has not done before*. The unusual horse will beat you, but so seldom that over the long run you'll be hundreds of dollars ahead of the game.

Managing Your Money

Now that you understand the basics of handicapping, there will be one more lecture before we actually wade into the *Daily Racing Form* and try to pick a winner. You can be the greatest handicapper in the world and live broke if you do not learn to manage your money at the racetrack.

There is another old saying around the racetrack that "a fool and his money are soon parted, usually before they run the second half of the daily double." You cannot go to the racetrack and carelessly throw your money around and expect to beat the races. It is difficult to understand the lack of respect a man has for his money once he pays the price of admission and enters the sacred domain of a track known as the mutuel area, in the betting lines.

A man will cry and moan about having to pay to get into a racetrack ("everybody else has a pass"), curse the quarter he lays out for the program, and absolutely die a dozen deaths over the $1 he must spend for the *Daily Racing Form*. Then, he will put his brain into neutral and step into the betting line and wager, literally, 95 percent of his bankroll on horses running in races that he had no business touching.

The player knows he had no business betting them, too. You can hear him crying about it to all of his friends—after the race is over. He plays the red board like an expert because his stupid wagers make him a real pro at it. His concept of money management is to get rid of it as fast as possible. He had a horse named for him which ran in the East for years—Money Destroyer. This kind of bettor is racing's biggest sucker, but he need not be.

A reality of betting, unfortunately, is that at least 50 percent of the horse players are in so deep financially after the first two races on the program they spend the rest of the day just trying to get even. The basic problem with the average horse bettor lies in his lack of respect for his money. He gets to the track and just can't wait to get rid of it. He gives strong backing to that segment of psychology which says a bettor is a man bent of self-destruction.

After you have developed respect for your money and learned to treat it as if it were a loved one, you have a chance to be a successful gambler. The next step in the world of money management is to decide what you want your money to do for you. If you are betting for fun and relaxation, you take any approach you want, However, if you're betting to make money, it's an entirely different matter.

Chances are the average horse player has never stopped to think about his goals. His ego demands that he attempt to bet on as many winners as possible, so he makes from nine to sixteen attempts a day, depending on the number of races and the additional gimmick bets such as daily doubles that are offered. Because there is little scientific data concerning the average horse player, no one has ever been permitted to peek into the bettor's ego. But this drive to bet on winners is there.

"I caught a $60 horse in the last race today," a bettor says. "It was wonderful." Then, when someone suggests this big winner buy a round of drinks to celebrate, he breaks down and explains that he still lost money—that the $10 he bet to win on the $60 horse brought him back $300, but he was a $314 loser before he cashed that bet.

Forget about betting on winners and design your betting program to make money. Never forget that there is a tremendous different between betting on winners and making money. You can bet on hundreds of winners and still lose money—if you also bet on thousands of losers. If you can learn to respect your money and then accept the fact that your bankroll is more important than your ego—and that you want to make money more than you just want to bet on winners—you have increased your chances for making money at the track.

Now you are ready to think about betting on a horse or two. On the matter of money management, there is no acceptable way for a good bettor to bet any way other than win, place, or show. Every gimmick bet is out, including daily doubles, exactas, quinellas, triperfectas, superfectas, and pick sixes, just to name a few. The problem with gimmick betting is twofold: (1) it is difficult enough to pick one horse to finish in a particular fashion, let alone trying to pick at least two, which you must do in a gimmick bet; and (2) the outlay of cash in relation to your chances for winning by playing varying combinations in gimmick wagers is so out of proportion to the return that there is no rational way to bet them. Forget them, forever.

The Ten Commandments of Thoroughbred Handicapping

As was stated at the beginning of the chapter, there are approximately 20 million people in this country who, at least occasionally, attempt to cash a bet on a horse race. Their task appears easy in the beginning and the second guessing doesn't start until the horses are midway through the stretch and the equine wonder on which they have wagered is obviously and hopelessly beaten. What went astray? Why didn't the horse win?

All of us have asked the same questions and have come up with many answers—most of which make little sense when objectively analyzed. Why can't we let it be sufficient that the horse just got beaten? We don't need to give him an excuse.

In every race run in the world every day there are hundreds of ways to get beaten. The factors—most of them unknown—that make winners and losers are as numerous as the cars in front of us on the freeway going home each night. It is very difficult to pin them down and try to come up with reasons why we can't seem to bet on more winners—or even *a winner*.

There is no way one can get an absolute guarantee that the horse he likes will win, but there certainly are things a bettor can do to increase substantially his chances for winning—maybe by more than 50 percent. The edges available to the horse player are numerous and obvious. Frequently he seems to ignore them, which seems to indicate that the guy who bets regularly has a psychological problem which has its basis in a deep-seated desire to destroy himself.

We don't happen to believe this, but the way many bettors behave, they do give the critics ammunition. If betting edges are available, and the bettor refuses to take them, isn't something wrong with him? Without taking sides in the argument, we would but like to point out ten betting edges that every horse player can take and drastically step up his chances for showing a profit at the racetrack. Let's call them the Ten Commandments of Handicapping.

1. Thou shall bet only on trainers who saddle a high percentage of winners. The first commandment is of the utmost importance. The same group of trainers at any given racetrack saddle a high percentage of all the winners. The smart bettor takes time to find out who these individuals are and follows them. By finding out who actually saddles winners, the bettor also finds out who doesn't saddle winners. The winning percentage of every bettor would take a big jump if he concentrated his dollars on this select group of trainers, even if it meant betting only one or two races a day at the most. If your money means anything to you, find out which trainers are the live ones and which are in a state of rigor mortis.

2. Thou shall bet only on jockeys who ride winners almost every day. While there is a certain limited group of trainers who saddle almost all the winners at any racetrack, there is an even smaller group of jockeys who ride these horses. Without reflecting on the respective merits of riders, never forget that 80 percent of the races at your track are won by the same fifteen or twenty riders. Stick with this group and forget the guys who only occasionally get a mount. They may be as good as the fifteen or twenty, but the horses they ride are usually second-stringers. Up your winning percentage by sticking with the good riders.

3. Thou shall never bet a horse on anything but a fast track. There is not one successful gambler today who ever made a living betting horses in the mud. Anyone who claims he has is suffering from bad memory or is stretching the truth. The hazards of handicapping are so great to start with that only a fool risks his money on anything but a fast racetrack. Why go out of your way looking for trouble? When the track is off, stay at home. You'll save a lot of money.

4. Thou shall never take less than even money on any horse. Any bettor who goes for horses that are less than even money is paying too high a price for a chance to win. Other than the apparent risks involved in any horse race, the guy who wagers on odds-on horses is asking to get his throat cut by the sharpies around the racetrack. The thieves work hard to tie up the odds-on horses, knowing if they are out of the money, they have to make a fortune, regardless of who wins.

5. Thou shall never bet a lot to win a little. This commandment ties in with the one above. Anytime you have to bet $100 to make a $20 to $30 profit, you're playing the wrong game. Many a bridge-jumper has been killed laying out thousands to pick up a few hundred. Again, the risks are just too great. Heaven only knows how many bookmakers have paid trainers and jockeys to make sure an odds-on horse didn't win. The bookmaker held a lot of money on the horse and didn't want to lay it off. If he knew the horse, which the public thought looked unbeatable, wouldn't win, the fortune was his.

6. *Thou shall never bet a race in which more than three or four horses have a chance of winning.* Again, the percentages should be our guide. A certain number of trainers and jockeys send out most of the winners and we can improve our percentage by sticking with them. By the same token, we can improve our winning percentage by leaving alone races in which several horses appear to have a legitimate chance of winning. A race is a tough thing to beat to start with and we only look for trouble if we bet in races in which every starter has a chance. If you can narrow the contenders down to three or four, and then can find a reason to bet on one, two, or even three of them, the race is playable. If not, then pass the race and wait for a better chance.

7. *Thou shall never make a bet during the first week of a new meeting.* It is only natural to want to get into action as soon as the horses arrive in town, but that should not be the game of the guy who really wants to beat the races. Give the horses, the trainers, and the jockeys a chance to get familiar with the racetrack and their new surroundings before betting your money. If you'll just sit back a week and watch trends develop, you will greatly improve your chances for winning. Always remember that many trainers give every horse a race over a track before cracking with him.

8. *Thou shall never bet until you have looked at the horses.* Most racing fans are lost when it comes to judging the physical appearance of horses. When they look at a horse to see if it is sore or lame, they don't quite know what they are looking for. Again, if your money means anything to you, try to learn something about horses. Lameness is fairly easy to detect and certainly is not beyond the eye of the average horse player. You can learn to spot a sore horse and should. Many a 6 to 5 shot went to the post so sore he had no chance of winning, and the smart bettors got their load. Go to the pub-

licity office of your racetrack and ask a member of the staff to put you in touch with a trainer who can tell you what to look for in trying to determine the physical condition of a horse. The publicity office may growl at you, but the trainer will be glad to explain what he can.

9. *Thou shall never bet on gimmicks such as exactas.* As attractive as gimmick wagering has become in this country, racing associations should ban it as a favor to the bettor. Gimmick wagering, such as exactas and perfectas, breaks more horse players than anything else. The investments in gimmicks cost a horse player too much of his bankroll and the odds against winning are so great that he has little chance of cashing. Add to this the fact that the thieves try to tie up the gimmick races in order to win a lot betting a little and the chances of cashing in such events are just short of impossible.

10. *Thou shall never bet more than you can afford to lose.* This may be the last commandment, but it is the greatest. Betting on horses is a risky business and a man should never wager more than he can afford to lose. As soon as the average bettor gets in the hole, he panics, forgets everything he knows about handicapping, and struggles to get even again. But he just gets in deeper. Set yourself a reasonable limit and never go over it. If you find yourself in a long losing streak, quit betting for two or three weeks. You'll see things in better perspective when you return to action. Never chase your money. You can't catch it.

There is nothing earth-shaking about the Ten Commandments of Handicapping. They are all facts of which most horse players are aware but choose to ignore. Remember that there is no such thing as easy money around the racetrack. Those who do well follow a strong financial program and have worked many hours at being successful. You will have to do the same if you are to be elevated to the same plane.

Chapter 8

The Trotters and
Other Forms of Racing

It's a well-known fact today that hundreds of million of dollars are bet every year at flat and harness tracks around the country and that horse racing is far and away the largest spectator sport in the world. The dollars that are wagered provide a large source of revenue for both state and local governments, the racing industry, and in some instances the astute bettor.

But where does the bettor have his best shot? Is one game easier than the other? Can you make more money at the flats than you can at the trots?

Trots and Flats Not So Far Apart

In some parts of the United States, two of the more popular forms of betting involve horses—the thoroughbreds and the harness horses. Although there are some people who swing for both sorts of horse action, generally speaking, a thoroughbred player likes the runners while the harness bug goes only for the jugheads, as the trotters are often called.

While they appeal to different elements of horse players, thoroughbred (flats) and harness (trots) racing have a number of striking similarities. For instance, both sports breed for speed and the object is the same—to win the race. But thoroughbreds run or gallop and are ridden by a jockey in a saddle. Harness horses are guided by a driver seated on a sulky and during the race must maintain a specified gait.

Gait refers to trotting or pacing, two specific methods of locomotion peculiar to the standardbred, or harness horse. While the tendency to trot or pace is inbred in most standardbred horses, the ability to maintain gait at high speeds and over a distance of ground is acquired only through long months of intensive training. A trotter, for example, is a standardbred that races with a diagonally-gaited motion. His left

245

front and right rear legs move forward almost simultaneously, then the right front and left rear. Often noticeable is high knee action and a left-right nodding of the head. A pacer, on the other hand, moves both left legs swinging forward in unison, then both right legs. It's a pistonlike movement often called a lateral gait and most pacers seem to sway from side to side. About 19 out of 20 will wear hobbles, leather or plastic straps worn connecting front and rear legs on the same side, to encourage the legs to move forward and back together. Here's your chance to impress the wife or girl friend. If the horse you see doesn't have these straps, say knowingly, "That's a trotter." The odds are roughly 20 to 1 you'll be right.

Occasionally in qualifying races, scheduled to test a horse's ability to show enough speed to meet a track's minimum standard, the two gaits are in the same field. Otherwise, trotters race against trotters and pacers against pacers.

Of course, the harness horses race at one distance, mainly—a mile. This automatically gives the followers of the sulky set a built-in advantage. The betting man or woman doesn't have to worry about the significance of times for six furlongs, a mile and a sixteenth, a mile and a furlong, a mile and a quarter, etc. Harness racing track times don't vary more than two to three seconds, depending on whether the track is five-eights, a half-mile, or a mile. The runners have certain tracks where horses go to four to five seconds faster.

The standardbred, like the thoroughbred, traces his lineage to those of Byerly Turk, Darby Arabian, and Godolphin Barb. This means that the modern standardbred horse is a thoroughly pedigreed animal. With but few exceptions, to claim standardbred status for a horse, his ancestry must have been standard and registered for generations. The chances are, those horses you see on the track can be traced back through more generations than you can. In harness racing the top sires have been Adios, Tar Heel, Star's Pride, and, of late, Meadow Skipper. All had high turns of speed and all could carry it over eight furlongs.

The differences between thoroughbred and standardbred horses are obvious. Standardbred horses possess longer bodies, less height, and heavier legs, and their appearance is less attractive than that of their thoroughbred cousins. While thoroughbreds go farther in a race on any given program, they are inferior by far to the harness horses in stamina.

Harness horses often are called upon to go two and three heats of a mile each in one day. That would mean two and three miles, something the thoroughbred is unable to accomplish on a staggered basis. Harness horses usually race about once a week, and a trainer tries to give a minimum of four days' rest between starts. The number of horses present in a particular class also affects the number of opportunities a horse may have.

The thoroughbred travels the mile faster than the standardbred. Harness races are contested at speeds averaging 25 to 30 miles per hour for the mile distance. When leaving the starting point and when in the homestretch, speeds of close to 35 miles per hour are attained by the best horses. A good thoroughbred covers the mile at speeds of about 38 to 40 miles per hour. As to the difference between trotters and pacers, little more than a second separates the world trotting and pacing records (the pacing record is faster). A pacer, generally, is considered slightly faster within a specific race classification, and a pacer can get away faster at the start.

Running time has some bearing on the figures of thoroughbred horses but in reality weight and class carry the most importance. Class is of almost equal value in the sulky world. But weight isn't supposed to mean too much in the harness set. There have been occasional innuendoes that flat fans almost always ignore the gate position of a horse because it has no particualr bearing on the outcome of races over three furlongs.

Many people like to get a break—but not a harness horseman! A break occurs when a horse leaves its required gait and "breaks" into a gallop. As horses are creatures of habit drivers try to be particularly careful to avoid allowing a horse to go into a break, thus undoing the work of months of intensive training. Breaks are caused in several ways. A break coming up to the starting gate could be caused by a speed—either fast or slow—that is uncomfortable for the horse, but it usually can be brought under control before the start is reached. Other common causes are tired breaks, those occurring when a horse has been raced beyond its ability, and breaks caused by interference or by a hoof hitting against a leg. A thoughtless spectator throwing paper on the track can frighten a horse into breaking. Where clearance exists, a driver must bring a breaking horse to the outside away from traffic and pull him into his proper stride. A breaking horse must lose ground while galloping. When back on gait, he will and must try to get back into contention. He is not disqualified for a break if the driver restrains him properly. However, if another horse is "lapped on" a breaking horse at the finish line, the breaker automatically is set back in official standing behind the horse or horses which are "lapped on," providing those horses are on gait. A horse is said to be "lapped on" another at the wire when its nose is at least opposite the hindquarters of the horse ahead. Lapped-on positions can be determined by examining the photo-finish pictures displayed after each race at designated points in the stands.

Training Methods:

Thoroughbreds vs. Standardbreds

Both thoroughbred and harness-horse conditioners believe in sharp, fast workouts for their horses before a start. While thoroughbreds have one stiff workout a week, harness horses might get two or three because of the nature of their constitutions.

Let's clear up one thing right now. In the trotters (this is, of course, a misnomer because most of the events are paces) there is a difference between a workout and qualifying races. Many fans think they're the same thing. As a matter of fact, a great deal of money is shot through the mutuel machines annually based solely upon how fast a harness horse ran in his qualifier or whom he beat. It's a mistake to base your betting on such an inaccurate source of information. Harness qualifers are run for a multitude of reasons—the least of which is to tip off a horse's good current condition. In the first place there's usually something wrong with an animal that has to qualify. The judges require horses to run qualifying miles for a myriad of reasons—most of which are bad:

1. If an animal has broken in his last two starts, he's usually asked to qualify. Breaking is a sign of bad manners or just plain tiredness. Not the kind of activity you'd expect from a winner.

2. If a horse had been scratched by the judges for lameness he must run a qualifying race before the officials. No matter how game they are, lame horses are losers.

3. If a horse had been out of action for more than a month

(sometimes it's two months) then that animal must qualify. How sharp is a horse after a layoff? Only the trainer knows for sure and he's not telling.

These three rules are usually the primary guidelines when looking for reasons that horses run qualifying races. There are other reasons. Australian horses, and other foreign side-wheelers, are asked to run in qualifiers so the judges get an idea of in what sort of company they belong. Trainers and drivers don't show off too much in these events—who wants a horse to start in A company when he can work his way up the class ladder picking up paychecks all the way?

With all these factors going against qualifiers, what importance can they have for the horse fan and horseman? Qualifying races are tighteners for horses rounding back into condition after something has gone wrong. Whether an animal has been injured or overworked it has shown in his recent form by bad races or long layoffs. But now the horse is ready for competition—almost.

Some horses are never ready for competition. Take the case of bad-gaited trotters that have weak drivers. Time after time these horses, no matter how talented they are, will be breaking because their regular reinsmen can't handle them. If they break twice in a row they must qualify. So what do these second-rate reinsmen do? They get one of the better drivers on the grounds to handle the horse for the judges. The horse runs like a champion, breezing past the competition and qualifying in record time. Even the regular driver thinks he's ready.

Next time the horse runs, he's 8 to 5 with "Old Stonefingers" back in the bike and the "superstar" jumps before they reach the clubhouse turn. Don't be misled. If a horse is finicky enough to need an exceptional driver to make him qualify, then he's certainly no bet back with his regular reinsman.

A much better sign is the use of an average driver, or even some unknown, to drive the horse in the qualifying event. What this means is that there's little doubt the horse will pass the test and he's simply being prepped for actual competition.

It's easy to be misled by qualifying races. Oftentimes a handicapper will look at a horse's qualifer and see that his horse beat some pretty good competition in the workout. He's impressed. Naturally so, but hopefully not enough to bet his money on the strength of this news. Qualifying fields are mixed batches of horses in borderline classifications that are entered for various reasons. You could have B-3 horses running against C-2 stock and not be trying. What if the better horses had provisional drivers up who were trying to qualify? What if the better horse was simply out to meet the qualifying time set by the judges? Don't assume a horse was good because he won—the other horses were probably looking to get beaten.

Times in qualifers are another monkey wrench to the handicapper. Opinions differ as to how accurate and honest they are. Since most races are run at night and the qualifers are run in the daytime there is a discrepancy. There are no lights to bother the horses and no crowds to excite them. Conditions are ideal for racing—even though the horses aren't pushing themselves too hard. Your best bet is to disregard the times of qualifers and wait until a horse has his first race back in competition under his belt before you start pace or speed handicapping.

Don't put too much stock in the charts either. Often the qualifying charts are inaccurate since they're put together by amateur chart makers. Outside moves often aren't recorded and the lengths between horses can be way off if the visibility is poor due to rain, snow, or fog. Take these charts as gospel and you'll find yourself heading for the poorhouse. The public is usually welcome to attend the qualifers, which are held on Saturday mornings. This way you'll be able to judge for yourself which horses are trying and which are exercising. Take advantage of the opportunity—you'll be a smarter bettor for it.

Jockeys vs. Drivers

The purpose of both is to steer the horse home a winner. But it seems true that the driver in the harness game contributes far more to the winning of a race, especially on the smaller half-mile tracks, than the jockey. At the flats, the best horses will usually prevail.

In thoroughbred racing, trainers spend hours with their noses buried in condition books looking for races in which their horses will be getting favorable weight concessions. Trainers of stakes horses withdraw their charges when track handicappers saddle their stars with too much weight for feature events.

The thoroughbred obsession with "weight on and weight off" has not made its way into the sulky sport. Most harness horsemen feel sulky racing begins after a certain amount of momentum has built up because the effect of a driver's weight is neutralized. If a standardbred had to get moving from a dead stop—as a thoroughbred must out of the gate— then a horse would certainly feel the weight of a 175-pound reinsman over a 125-pound chauffeur. But once momentum has been achieved, a driver who weighs 175 pounds will create hardly more drag on the wheels than a 125-pound sulkysmith.

Weight is conceded by almost all harness horsemen to be an important factor when a track turns up muddy. As the sulky wheels plow deep furrows in the sloppy going a lighter driver has much more maneuverability than his heavy adversary. But don't overrate a driver because he's light and don't underrate a reinsman because he's heavy. Check his records and see what his winning percentage over the years, instead of his weight, says about his ability. If he's won his share over the years then he'll usually manage to get a piece of the pie this time too. But it doesn't hurt to look for special situations. Here are a couple that favor lightweight sulkysmiths:

1. Off tracks favor light drivers.
2. Good light drivers that are catch driving for heavier handlers will usually improve a horse.
3. Favor lightweight drivers on wire-to-wire (start to finish) horses over heavier drivers.

These three situations are areas in which a competent lightweight driver will have some advantage over a heavier reinsman. Other factors being equal, including the position of the driver's weight with respect to the wheels, you can bet a hefty reinsman with little fear of giving away any advantage.

As we just stated, a driver is very important to the success of a trotter. In fact, experts in the field of harness racing scale the importance of a top driver with a low of 20 percent to a high of 35 percent in the degree of contribution to the picking of a winner. As you can readily see by these statistics, having a top driver in the bike is an absolute necessity if you expect a high return on your investment. This is not to say that the less talented drivers don't have their paydays, but they're too few and far between. Therefore, when a horse is ready, a trainer will seek out the best driver he can, but more important, one that "fits" his horse.

If a trainer has a horse in top shape that does his best racing up front, he would be looking for someone like Chapman, Willie Myer, or Filion. If his horse makes a middle move for the lead best, he would want a Webster or a Gilmour. But off the pace, he would look for a Sholty, a Phalen, or a Carmine Abbatiello. Yes, some horses go best for different drivers. A horse does his best racing when he is allowed to play his own game, whatever that may be.

Many drivers contract with reinsmen of lesser ability to handle their mounts when on vacation or driving better stock out of town. Avoid these moves to inferior drivers—they may build better relations between the harness set but can only lead to bankruptcy for the bettor. If the horse was a winner his own driver would be here to handle him.

There is a difference between half-mile and five-eights-mile ovals or the once-around-the-park mile tracks. The reason is simple enough to understand. Five-eighths-mile and one-mile ovals are more "honest" in nature, leaving more room for driver mistakes. The four sharp turns of the half-mile ovals are testing on both horses and drivers, and it is here the ability of competent catch drivers can turn a certain defeat into possible victory. With only two and three turns, as is the case with the five-eights- and one-mile ovals, the tendency most drivers have is to allow their horse to coast on the outside from the half-mile pole, hoping they have the most pace through the home lane.

There is also a difference in half-mile tracks. For instance, Roosevelt and Yonkers, although both half-mile tracks, are vastly different racing ovals. The horses start and finish in the same position at the two tracks and make the full circuit twice, but there the similarity ends. The distance from the top of the stretch to the finish line is 440 feet at Yonkers. At Roosevelt, it's 560 feet. All factors being equal, the best horse will win most of the time at the Long Island plant, while at Yonkers, racing luck plays a big role in deciding eventual winners. At the Westchester oval one must select sidewheelers which can gain position quickly, prompt or set a realistic pace, and yet retain enough energy for that final sprint from the top of the stretch to the finish wire. That is, the short stretch at Yonkers makes speed horses tough to beat, while at

Roosevelt, where the stretch is 120 feet longer, "closers" have the edge.

Roosevelt is noted for its inordinately high percentage of winning favorites every meeting—sometimes running as high as 41 percent. This, unfortunately, leads to a steady stream of odds-on favorites (who win about 60 percent of the time) and small mutuels. Yonkers, on the other hand, is known as the "graveyard" of favorites. Early speed horses seldom do well at Roosevelt, with the exception of very wet and sloppy nights. Cold weather and high winds almost always take a toll on frontrunners in that vital last eighth of a mile at the Westbury track. By the way, the United States Trotting Association makes comparison performances at all major tracks and a speed rating is compiled which would approximate "par" in golf. By construction, design, texture, and other factors, some tracks obviously rate faster than others of equal circumference. Racing programs carry these comparative track ratings. Then if you find that a horse has trotted in 2:08 on a track that is rated a 2:06 oval, you could reasonably expect the horse to go a second faster (in 2:07) on a track rated at 2:05.

Because driving requires extreme skill and split-second decisions it takes great training and experience before a driver is considered competent to drive at a pari-mutuel track. Most drivers serve long apprenticeships as assistants to established trainers and get their preliminary driving experience at matinee meetings where purses and wagering are not involved, and then are licensed to drive at county fairs. After a driver has the necessary preliminary experience, he is issued a provisional license which he carries for at least a year and also until he has twenty-five starts at a pari-mutuel track. Such a driver is designated by a (P) after his name on the program. This compares to the (*) designating an apprentice jockey at the running races.

Incidentally, the colors worn by drivers are registered by the United States Trotting Association and the particular pattern and combination chosen by a driver can be used only by him. A driver may ask for a change during his career, and, if available, new colors may be registered for him. These changes rarely are requested and a driver may be identified readily, year after year, by the colors of his jacket and cap.

Other Similarities Between the Thoroughbreds and Standardbreds

Track condition also has similar meaning to horsemen in both sports. The off track bring out the best in horses of both sports who have the mud-loving family tree. Piet, who was owned by J. Graham Brown, a Michigan hotel man, loved the goo when he was racing and so did Mr. Brown's Seven Hearts. They passed along this trait to their sons and daughters, and most knowledgeable horse players are alert to those points. Another mud-running fool in his heyday was On-and-On, who was owned by Calumet Farm. His sons and daughters have shown sharp improvement in soft going.

In harness racing Tar Heel, who has now become number one sire with the death of Adios, always reveled in off going. He has passed this along to a majority of his offspring, and the sharp harness-racing devotee keeps his eye peeled for the opportunities to make this knowledge pay off.

As a rule, we have found that temperature has little or no bearing on form. This is not to say, though, that there is no difference between winter and summer racing. Extremes in temperature will make a vast difference. A horse suffering, maybe, from a bit of arthritis will do much better in the warmer weather, but you'll see maybe ten or twenty horses on the grounds who will perform extremely well in November, December, and March, doing the bulk of their money earning in those cold months. These, of course, are your "cold-weather" horses. But more important than weather is wind. At New York's Aqueduct (which is laid out from north to south) when that southeasterly wind comes off Jamaica Bay, frontrunners will definitely win the majority of the sprints on that day. If northerly winds prevail, look for closing horses to be blown right down the stretch. Circular winds, by the way, make for a "dead" track and closers again would be the order of the day. This gives one a definite edge.

At the trots, there definitely are horses who will perform better in different kinds of weather—real hot- or cold-weather horses. But, unlike the flats, there is no wind factor to make the game gimmick-oriented. You see, anytime you go around more than two turns, no wind factor prevails. As a matter of fact, when extremely high winds prevail, the tendency some drivers have is to wait, as no one wants to be first over the top, and the horse on the lead sometimes is allowed to loaf to some ridiculous fractions and win easily. But these are only extreme cases.

Though most horse players don't realize it, post position also plays a part in each sport's thinking. The rail is highly advantageous in harness racing as it is with the thoroughbreds. No jockey likes to send his horse three- or four-wide throughout a race because in the end the strength-sapping effort will be enough to poop out the horse.

It's the rare horse that can go the whole mile on the outside and accomplish the job. Of course, in the flats, it's the rare horse that can hook up in a speed duel that staying at another horse's throatlatch requires and come away with the victory. Here are examples that come to mind in each sport. Some years ago Jaipur and Ridan rushed from the gate in the Travers at Saratoga and slugged it out the entire mile and a quarter before Jaipur stuck his snoot in front in the final stride. A similar though not as tightly contested finish took place in the 1971 Preakness when Canonero II pushed Easter Fleet all the way until about 100 yards from the end when the Venezuelan visitor put him away.

In harness racing, Une de Mai, the French mare, pulled the same tactics on Nevele Pride, the superhorse of the United States, and hounded the American trotter for most of the mile-and-a-quarter Roosevelt International. Then Une de Mai, when everyone had given up on her, came again and overpowered Nevele Pride. A Dutch invader, Hairos II, won an early running of the International when he went the entire mile and a quarter far off the rail and with a 270-pound driver in his sulky.

By the way, the post position is determined by the luck of a draw. A numbered ball is placed in a shaker for each entrant in the race. A person designated by the presiding judge, and in the presence of the presiding judge, draws or rolls out one ball (sometimes called a pill) as each entrant's name is read. The number drawn becomes that horse's post position. A representative of the horsemen must be present and no owner or trainer with a horse in the race can be denied the opportunity to witness the drawing.

Understanding Trotting's Classification System

Harness racing has a system to match horses to provide exciting contests. The network includes three main types of events—conditioned, classified, and claiming races. Unravel their elements—learn the strong and weak points of each—and you may whip the system.

At most raceways the events presented each night will fall into one of five categories: Conditioned; Claiming; Early or Late Closing; Stake or Futurity; and Open, sometimes called invitationals or Free-for-Alls. By and large the great majority of races fall into the first two classes. A few tracks use classified racing, where the racing secretary places horses in letter classification groups.

Conditioned races, as the name implies, are events in which certain specified standards must be met in order to acquire eligibility. One of the major tasks of a race secretary is to present evenly matched fields. In order to do this, he writes conditions to exclude horses with too much ability from the race in question. By use of conditions for each race in this category, the race secretary makes it possible for all horses to have both equal racing opportunity and the chance to compete against horses of similar capabilities. Claiming races are another avenue to the same accomplishment. Here the owner risks the loss of his horse at a prespecified price and races against horses of approximately the same monetary value. Early or Late Closing events, and Stakes or Futurities require nomination a specified period before the event, and usually require one or more payments, often added to the purse, before the event is raced. Open races are reserved for the best horses on the grounds. The fields are most often filled by invitation, extended only to horses that have demonstrated the ability to go with the best.

At each track a Condition Book, listing all events to be raced for at least a week prior to the entry date for the first program, is issued. Owners and trainers enter, at the specified daily time, horses for the events for which they are eligible, either according to conditions, or if desired, by claiming price. In actual practice many events are so conditioned that two or more divisions will develop, thus allowing, by a process of seeding, an even closer matching of abilities within a field. If more than the permitted number of starters are entered, horses with the greater lapse of time since their most recent start have preference.

We have frequently seen over the years such things as a C–2 pacing winner at 4 to 5 who came back the next week —in the same class—to finish unplaced at 43 to 1. The point is that up or down movements in harness racing cannot be determined solely by the purse value (conditioned races), lettered class (classified races), or claiming price (claiming races). Check the 1–2–3 finishers in each of your contender's races before deciding which ones are moving up in class and which are dropping. Now, let's look further into each of these types of races, concentrating on horses shuttling among the various grades—such as from conditioned to claimer, or from claimer to classified—rather than within the category.

Conditioned racing matches groups of horses by restricting entry eligibility. In the utopian conditioned race, only eight horses in the world would be eligible—and they'd each stand a fine chance of winning. To bring a field like that together, the United States Trotting Association permits a secretary to use as qualifying standards age, sex, money earnings, number of starts, and finishing positions. The more requirements used in a race, the narrower the entry list, and the closer the contest. At least that's the theory. For example, a race with the mild condition of "winners of more than $2,000 this year" could attract both a $1,250 claimer and Albatross, who is a $1,250,000 claimer. However, a race with the more stringent requirements of "mares, four years and older, who have averaged less than $100 per start in last six starts, and who have not finished third or better" will probably bring together a more evenly matched group of contenders.

As described previously, it's easy for ringers to slip into conditioned races. An event for "nonwinners of $2,000 or two races this year" may well attract a classy animal who's making only his fourth start of the season. For this reason, a conditioned race for a certain purse normally attracts a better grade of horse than a claiming race for the same purse. Thus, a horse who competed for a $1,500 purse as a claimer, who is now moving into a $1,500 conditioned race, should be regarded as stepping up in company—even though the purses are equal. Beware of animals jumping into conditioned races from the claimers. Often it's a case of wishful thinking by a trainer who's afraid to lose his horse.

Classified races are used by only four tracks—Brandywine in Delaware, and Monticello, Roosevelt, and Yonkers in New York. Under this method, the racing secretary alone determines class levels. Classes are designated by letter, from C–3 all the way up through A–1, AA, JFA, and the highest rank, FFA, or free-for-all. The secretary assigns each horse to a class at the start of the meeting and then moves them up or down based on their performances. Like conditioned racing, classified racing gives the edge to younger, lightly raced animals. New York's rule is that three-year-olds must start in Class C, unless they were big money earners as two-year-olds. Even stakes competitors often receive breaks when they are entered in a classified race in mid-season. And, again, as with conditioned races, classified races must be scanned to insure that a ringer—such as a New Zealand newcomer or a three-year-old future star—is not entered. The metropolitan New York tracks try to eliminate Down Under cinches by forcing all horses aged seven and up to compete in A–3 or higher— very tough competition—or enter the claimers. Not so at the other tracks. A few seasons ago at Monticello, Don Hayes entered five New Zealand first-time starters in classified races in a single week. All were bet down, and all breezed to victories in their American bows.

Lately, the metropolitan New York secretaries have tried to solve the more difficult problem of cutting down on the three-year-old standouts. Now these youngsters are often segregated. C–2 older horses at Roosevelt compete for $2,-750 while C–2 three-year-olds are offered $3,000. Also scheduled are handicap races for three-year-olds, putting B–1 pacers on the outside against B–3 pacers on the rail. The B–1 horses get no free rides, because their B–3 opponents might well be future A horses.

A classified field racing for a certain purse usually attracts faster horses than a claiming price for the same purse—just as in conditioned racing. By offering higher purses for cheaper claimers, secretaries encourage horsemen to enter their steeds in claiming races. Although the purses vary, Brandywine, Roosevelt, and Yonkers classified standardbreds are considered to be equal in class. The Monticello racer, who competes for far lower purses, is rated at least two or three classes below his counterparts at the other tracks. In other words, a C–2 pacer at the three major-league tracks might race in B–3 or higher at Monticello. You can imagine the fields in the Catskill track's C–3 contests.

There are five types of claiming races:

1. In the *straight claimer*, all horses are eligible to be claimed for a single price.

2. The *claiming allowance* equalizes the difference in value between old geldings who have little racing life left and younger animals with years of earning power remaining by allowing higher-priced younger competitors to face cheaper veterans.

3. The *optional claimer* allows claimers to battle conditioned or classified animals, with the claimers getting the better posts on a handicap basis.

4. The *claiming handicap* or *claiming allowance handicap* offers a range of claiming prices, with the animals with the higher base claiming prices getting placed in the worst posts.

5. The *conditioned claimer* restricts its eligible contenders by placing a condition on the race—such as three-year-olds only, or nonwinners of a race this meeting—to further insure tight fields.

Horsemen enter their horses in claiming races—where they risk losing them—because they feel the conditioned or classified opposition their horses may have to face is too strong. (In metropolitan New York, as mentioned earlier, trainers of horses seven years of age and older have no choice—unless the horses are fast enough for A–3, they must compete in claimers.)

Some bettors have expressed confusion about comparing horse racing in the various numerical classifications at tracks such as Yonkers with horses racing for a claiming tag. If you're in doubt, use the following breakdown for comparing the two:

Class	
FFA	B-1 & $15,000 Clm.
JFA	B-2 & $12,500 Clm.
AA	B-3 & $10,000 Clm.
A-1	C-1 & $7,500 Clm.
A-2	C-2 & $6,000 Clm.
A-3 & $20,000 Clm.	C-3 & $4,500 Clm.

It's easy for pacers who are superior to their opposition to find their way into conditioned fields, and a horseman may get tired of finding an odds-on standout entered against his horse each week. In classified racing, a racing secretary may feel a man's horse is B–1 material, while the trainer insists the horse shouldn't have to race higher than B–3. By entering their horses in claimers, the trainers themselves get to determine who the opposition will be.

The most successful trainers of claiming animals—men like Herve Filion, Bob Farrington, and Carmine Abbatiello—run their horses at as low a level as possible and risk losing them. These men are among the most realistic in appraising the true worth of their animals.

When a horse is being dropped from a conditioned or classified race to a claimer, check the trainer. Is he dropping the horse to a competitive level, or is he merely giving him a shot at this company before dropping him to where he can win? If the horse is being trained by a man who's not especially skilled at placing his horses, take care.

Claiming horses are considered equal in class. If you're playing at Suffolk Downs, for instance, don't think a Liberty Bell $4,000 claimer can annihilate your local competitors in that class. And if you're at a big metropolitan oval, don't overlook the newcomers from smaller tracks.

Put yourself in the boots of the trainer. Then you'll be able to analyze the significance of movements from conditioned races to claimers to the classifieds, and everything in between.

Reading a Harness Racing Program

The bettor's first look at a harness racing program might send him into shock, but relax, for it's not as difficult to read as it appears. Every symbol, letter, and number has a meaning.

The horse's head number, saddle cloth number, program number, mutuel number, and post position are the same except where there is an entry (more than two horses running for the same betting interest) in the race. The initials immediately following the horse's name represent color and sex, while the figures denote age. The names following are the horse's sire, dam, and sire of the dam in that order.

Under the horse's name are his lifetime earnings and lifetime record, preceded by his age when the record was made up to January 1 of the current year. Following the lifetime earnings is the name of the driver, his age, weight, and colors. Next is the horse's best winning time on a half-mile, five-eighths, or mile track for the last year and this racing season. This is followed by his starts, the number of wins, seconds, and thirds in purse races and his money winnings.

Beneath the horse's name are records of his most recent races. They read from bottom to top, the top line being the horse's last race. The date of the race is followed by the name of the track. All tracks are half-mile unless they are followed by the figure (1) which means that it is a mile track or (¾) which is a three-quarter-mile track, and so on. Condition of the track on the day of the race, the conditions of the race, or, if a claiming race, the claiming price are then given. Race distance, time of the leading horse after ¼ mile, ½ mile, and ¾ mile follow, then comes the winner's time. The figures that follow in order show the post position of the horse, his position at the ¼, the ½, ¾, and the stretch, with lengths behind, except for the leading horse, whose number denotes the lengths ahead, and finish with beaten lengths.

If the horse was a winner, it shows how far it was ahead of the second horse, and the losers show how far they were behind the winning horse. The next figure shows the horse's actual time in that race. Whenever a small ° appears after the calls, it denotes that the horse raced on the outside at least one-quarter of a mile. In some instances these figures will not appear because the track at which the horse raced did not have its races charted. Then follows the closing odds to the dollar, the horse's driver, and order of finish, giving the names of the first three horses.

A thoroughbred performance record reads in much the same way, with very few exceptions. The past-performance line as published in the *Daily Racing Form* will list the date of the horse's race, the track at which he ran, the condition of the track, the distance of the race, fractional times and the winning time, the conditions of the race, post position, position and lengths back at each of the calls, rider odds, speed rating, and the first three finishers in the race.

Following is a key to abbreviations found in most of the country's harness racing programs (most of the terms and abbreviations are also used for thoroughbreds):

KEY TO ABBREVIATIONS

Horses Color
b—bay
blk—black
br—brown
ch—chestnut
gr—grey
ro—roan

Horses Sex
g—gelding
h—horse
m—mare
f—filly
c—colt

Track Conditions
ft—fast
gd—good
sy—sloppy
sl—slow
my—muddy
hy—heavy
wt—wet

Wagering Information
e—entry
f—field
*—favorite
NB—no betting
NR—not reported

Finish Information
ns—nose
hd—head
nk—neck
dh—dead heat
dis—distanced (over 25 lengths behind winner)
p—placed

Race Classes
+—up in class
-—down in class
=—same class
cd—condition race
clm3000—actual claiming price on this horse
nw—non-winners
w—winners
pref—preferred
inv—invitational
hcp—handicap race
mdn—maiden race
qua—qualifying race
ec—early closing event
lc—late closing event
stk—stake race
mat—matinee race
fA—free-for-all
FFA—junior free-for-all

Track Lengths
(1)—mile track
($\frac{1}{2}$)—$\frac{1}{2}$-mile track
($\frac{5}{8}$)—$\frac{5}{8}$-mile track
($\frac{7}{8}$)—$\frac{7}{8}$-mile track

Racing Information
o—raced on outside for at least $\frac{1}{2}$ mile
x—horse broke at this point
‡—races without hopples
†—races with trotting hopples
C—horse claimed
lx—break caused by interference

General Information
be—broken equipment
hn—head number
acc—accident
ex—equipment break
dnf—did not finish
ps—per start
TDis—time disallowed
*—win on off track this year

(P) after name of driver indicates driver holds a Provisional License issued to those of limited experience and subject to approval of the judges.

Qualifying Races are not competitive and are not included in the starts of a horse but are merely used to determine the manners of a horse and its ability to complete the course within the time standards set by the Judges for the class in which the horse will compete.

| Class Comparison | PROGRAM and HEAD NUMBER | Date of Race | Track Raced On | Track Condition | Type of Race | Class Comparison | Condition or Claiming price | Mud Mark | Free Legged | Distance of Race | Time at ¼ | Time at ½ | Time at ¾ | Time of Winner | Post Position | Position at ¼ | Position at ½ | Position at ¾ | Stretch Position and Lengths | Finish Position and Lengths | Horse's Actual Time | Speed Rating | Equivalent Odds to $1.00 | Driver | Best Win Time of Year | Name of Winner | Name of Second Horse | Name of Third Horse |

ASK FOR HORSE BY PROGRAM NUMBER

LEADER'S TIME — ORDER OF FINISH

4   ALBATROSS*
1:54³—1—3—741,549
10:21 Fhld ft FA=

b.h.4, MeadowSkipper-VoodooHanover-DancerHanover
Amicable Stable, Hanover, Pa.
STANLEY DANCER 45, 135   Blue, Gold

m:28 :57 1:26³1:57³ 4 1 1 1¹ 1¹¹ 1¹⁷ 1:57³ 135-04 * .30 $ Dan

1:54³ Spk‡ 1972 23 17 4 1 373,421
1:54⁴ Lex¹ 1971 28 25 2 1 558,009
Trainer—S. Dancer
Albatross Nansemond SundancerD

Harness Racing Golden Rules

The harness handicapper must keep several important factors in mind during his search for a winner, while discounting the myriad tips, rumors, and hot info prevalent at every track, in every state, in every corner of America—or England, or Australia, for that matter. If the handicapper decides to concentrate on the more important variables that go into the makeup of a race, his winning percentage has to improve. Herewith you'll find a number of matters that appear, to us at least, to be the finalizing factors that determine a race winner. Our suggestion to you is this: use the following data as a checklist. If your concentrations have tentatively arrived at a race selection, check the horse against these factors. The more "stumbling blocks" it is able to pass, the better its chances of winning.

1. *Post Position.* One of the most—if not the most—important factors in determining the outcome of a harness race is post position. This is especially so at the half-mile ovals but holds true at the larger tracks as well. The reason for this observation should be obvious to most "trot" fans: the horses breaking from the outside posts (seven and eight) have a definite disadvantage over those breaking from the inside "holes." This disadvantage is brought about by the fact that the farther a horse is away from the rail, the farther he has to travel in relation to those breaking from the inside posts (one, two, three). On a half-mile track, unless the outside horse is "tons" better than the rest of the field, logic and ability dictate to his driver that instead of going into the first turn—which comes almost immediately after the break—trying for the lead on the extreme outside and losing much ground, he go to the rail and await his chance to park out and make a run for the leader. Very seldom, however, does this chance ever come due to the four sharp turns and very short straightaways. Thus, the outside horses must travel approximately 63 feet farther than those breaking from the inside. Converting this extra distance into time, we can see that the unfortunate horses in seven and eight positions must be up to three seconds faster than the inside horses. Since the advent of conditioned racing, all horses in any given race are supposedly equal in speed. Theoretically, if all eight horses lined up, broke, and ran a straight mile down a turnpike, the race

should wind up a dead heat among all eight runners. However, when traveling the same mile on a half-mile track with its four sharp turns, position is all important. Burdened, therefore, by their poor post positions the "seven" and "eight" horses are very bad bets and should be avoided.

To bear out this theory, a breakdown of winners from each post position was recently made at six of the nation's largest half-mile tracks for an entire meeting. The results follow:

Post	Percentage Wins
1	21%
2	18%
3	15%
4	11%
5	11%
6	10%
7	8%
8	6%

These figures graphically prove the disadvantage a horse breaking from the outside post has going against him. Regardless of odds, we can see that the "one" horse wins nearly four times more races than the "eight" horse. Odds such as these are too much to buck.

It seems logical, then, that one should bet only horses breaking from the one, two, or (sometimes) three holes. Unfortunately, it's not always that easy. These horses should be given first consideration but if the "four" or "five" horse looks particularly good (considering other handicapping factors such as past performance, driver, speed, etc.) one should not be hesitant about betting one of these. Especially if the odds are right. One thing must be emphasized, however; under no conditions should the "seven" or "eight" horse be bet at short odds. We have seen that a total of 14 percent winners break from those two positions, an average of 7 percent. If the total races checked numbered 1,000, the figures point out that the "seven" horse won just 80 times and the "eight" horse took just 60 of the 1,000 events. Breaking this down into an "odds" situation, the odds against the "seven" horse winning are 15 to 1 while those on the "eight" are even longer at 17 to 1. If one of the better horses in the race is breaking from one of these two outside posts, most uninformed bettors will chose him off his past performances and today's odds—disregarding his post position odds. He may even go off at odds as low as 2 to 1 or 3 to 1. The horse looks like a winner on paper but when the 17 to 1 post position odds going against him are considered, he is not really a good bet at all. And, of course, if one of the longer priced horses is breaking from an outside post, his chances of winning are even more remote. Further evidence of the importance of post position can be seen here. The figures were compiled at five major tracks for one entire meeting:

Order of Winning Post Positions 5 Meetings

	A	B	C	D	E
PP1	2	1	1	1	1
PP2	1	2	2	2	2
PP3	4	4	3	3	4
PP4	5	3	6	4	3
PP5	3	6	4	5	6
PP6	6	5	5	6	5
PP7	7	7	7	7	7
PP8	8	8	8	8	8

As can be seen, post position one is extremely consistent in number of wins, scoring four of five times with just one lapse to second place. Position two is even more consistent since it moved up one notch with no lapses. The middle posts (three, four, five, and six) are too erratic. Three, for instance, lapses often enough to keep us from grouping it with one and two as an inside post. It should therefore be grouped with four, five, and six as a middle position and, unfortunately, due to the inconsistency of these middle positions, no definite rules can be laid down regarding them. Finally, the figures show conclusively that the two outside positions should never be played.

Post position is just as significant at the larger five-eighths-mile tracks. However, due to the fact that there are just three turns which are not as sharp as those of the half-milers, and that there is a longer stretch for the faster closer, the "seven" and "eight" horses win just a bit more often; the "seven" has a 10 percent win percentage and the "eight" 7 percent—still not nearly good enough to make them bettable. How should one go about utilizing this all-important information when handicapping a race? The things that post position tells us are the horses to avoid, which to consider, and which to concentrate on. Coupled with the available past-performance information, this can be enough to make you a consistent winner.

2. *Class.* As was stated earlier, while there are five categories of races, there are three basic types of races harness horsemen can choose from when spotting their stock. They are (1) claiming races, (2) classified races—the A, B, C system, and, (3) conditioned races. Under the classification system, drivers and trainers are at the mercy of racing secretaries as to what class levels their stock may run at (maybe).

Where they run is usually based upon the type of races a horse has been running his last few starts. If he destroys his opposition, then there is a great likelihood that he will meet tougher horses in his next outing. But if he just manages to be around the money, finishing second or third, beaten by a couple of lengths, then there is little reason for a horse to be moved up.

This is done for two reasons. The first is that not moving a horse over his head is extremely beneficial to the animal, physically and mentally. By running against harness horses he can beat an animal builds up confidence and can even improve his own ability. Should he be forced to meet better stock it may be completely detrimental to his ability to win anything—in any classification.

The second reason that some horses don't make it to the winner's circle is often financial. The simple mathematics of harness racing's purse structure system make it possible for a trainer to be content to finish second and third regularly in a lower claim and rake in as much, if not more, money than a horse winning only occasionally in a higher class.

Our feelings are so strong on the class factor that they can be summarized in one sentence: Never bet a harness horse unless he has won against tonight's class of competition in the past, or has raced within a length of the winner considering tonight's class. To put it another way: Never, but never, bet a horse moving *up* in class unless the animal shows a previous win or close-up finish somewhere in its record. Enough said about class.

3. *Drivers.* Since we all understand that good drivers win more races than do inferior reinsmen, we can further assume that the majority of bettors fully realize this fact and, as a

result, the drivers with the highest winning percentages will return rather low mutuels. Seldom will you see a horse reined by Insko, Filion, Dancer, or Chapman return a toteboard rattling mutuel. Seldom? Probably never. The average harness fan is so attuned to the driver factor that some of the fans do nothing more than bet on drivers. Usually, due to handicapping inexpertise, they are forced into this foolhardy escapade. We can benefit from their ineptitude.

We handle the driver factor like this: If our selection is to be driven by a reinsman who has a winning record of 12 percent or who has won with the horse in the past, it qualifies for play. If the driver has been unable to amass the 12 percent, or has never won with the horse, we either search for another selection or pass the race. You'd be well advised to do the same.

4. *Condition.* Unlike in the thoroughbred sport, harness racing officals apparently feel the listing of public workouts is relatively unimportant. If someone can offer us a more substantial reason for the lack of workout information, we'd be happy to listen. Actually, as was stated previously, we suspect that since a harness horse is not asked to produce a high burst of speed on days prior to the running of its race, such information would be quite useless. This is untrue. For one thing, thoroughbred fans often misinterpret the workout information available to them. When handicapping the flats, we usually use a workout only as evidence of relative fitness. The time of the workout means little to us since, obviously enough, no trainer in the world wishes to see his charge leave his race on the training track. Published harness race workouts would be extremely beneficial to the harness fan on that basis. An animal's working out could (and should) be interpreted as a sign of relative fitness. Since this information is unavailable, the only solid information concerning a horse's condition can be found by checking the date of his last outing. We use that information in this manner: the magic number, to us, is seven. The maximum number of days we will allow a harness horse to remain inactive is nine, and the closer it gets to seven and below, the stronger our betting inclinations become. A horse, all other things being equal, that has raced within seven days becomes a definite play. If the animal's last race occurred less than seven days ago, the higher our bet and our winning expectations become. Try to use that same logic while handicapping.

5. *Track Condition.* If the track is listed as anything other than fast, the race is a pass unless the entrant has recorded a victory over an identical (not similar) surface, or is an obvious frontrunner. You'll note that we stated the horse must be racing over a fast track unless it has previously exhibited a talent for racing on a surface considered something other than fast. We stated, and will repeat, that the trotter or pacer must have turned in a winning effort on an identical, not similar, surface. In explanation let us say that if the horse has won on a "good" track, tonight's surface must be labeled "good." Not "sloppy" or "muddy" or "heavy," but "good." Likewise, if the horse won over a "sloppy" track, tonight's surface must be labeled "sloppy." No other designation will do. Too many losers fail to recognize that a vast difference exists between a "good" and a "heavy" track. Most of them determine that a horse able to win on a track containing a particular amount of moisture can repeat its winning effort on another moist surface. Some can, but others become merely also-rans.

6. *Consistency.* "Consistency" and "money earned" are two important factors in anybody's ball park. Look all over the world and this is the name of the game. Most people judge others by their reliability and their financial status. Ever see an older, cheaper model car with M.D. plates? Think of how many people would comment to themselves, "Boy, I'd never let him operate on me!" That has become the American way. Judgment of ability is based upon earning power in most cases. This doctor could be the greatest brain in the world, but they figure that if he's driving an older car, he's not with it. Put an incompetent into a high-powered $20,000 sports model and he has the respect of almost everyone.

There is something else here: People figure that what someone gets he must have earned. If someone is good, he should be able to earn big. And if someone is consistently good, he will become the best. This is the idea in applying these factors to harness race handicapping. First, consistency must be there. Then, the money must be there to say that whatever was achieved was done in good company.

The story of an animal's racing consistency is told in his record. If you are concerned mainly with "win," and you should be, then you are interested in a horse's winning average. You want to know how many times a horse has won in how many starts. That is his win percentage and his record to date. Look at a horse's line and you will see the number of races and the number of wins he has had. Forget about the seconds and thirds for a moment. Divide the number of starts into the number of wins and you have the animal's win percentage.

All season long baseball players are judged on their batting averages. They might go from season to season being paid according to the batting average they maintain. We are concerned with the horse's win percentage in almost the same way. We are trying to predict his potential based upon his record of consistency in the past. And you would be amazed at how many big-priced horses you can catch in this way. A horse with a consistent record might have a couple of bad races and wind up high in price. Then his consistency may be maintained by a victory and the public is fooled one more time.

An adage we use concerning the matter of consistency is: the more frequently a horse has won, the better his chances. For this reason, we always insist that a contender must have won at least 20 percent of his races this season. Otherwise— no play! Some readers, the ones with less patience, may say, "Hey, wait a minute. That'll eliminate a lot of races." To them we reply, "It sure will. It will eliminate races like maidens, cheap claimers, dashes involving chronic 'breakers' and the like." We avoid these regattas as we do the measles. You have no right betting them in the first place. Remember—and if you get nothing else out of this chapter than this, we'll be quite pleased—*never bet a horse with a winning percentage of less than 20 percent this season*. Your winning percentage will automatically increase, for you will automatically avoid unplayable situations.

But this is not all the story. A horse's win percentage is only so good in relation to his money earned. We do not mean a horse who might have finished second in a big stakes event and earned a pile. But, in general, one can use earnings to determine classification.

We often see horses shipping into Yonkers and Roosevelt from out-of-town tracks. You may see a horse who has started 25 times with 14 wins, 6 seconds, and 2 thirds. Then you look to see the animal's money earned and note $4,500. One might be compelled to pass judgment upon the grade of competition this animal has faced in putting together that impressive win record. The lack of money takes away from the respect that record might have gained. When one of this type of horse wins, it could be likened to the brilliant doctor in the cheaper model car. The doctor was good but just didn't care too much that he wasn't soaking his patients.

With horses we must be guided in the right direction. A horse does not determine his competition except by his ability. If he is good and worthwhile he will show this by a high win percentage and the money will start to roll in. Just remember that the money belongs to the horse and not to you, so play with caution. This is the record of what it has attained and is only a hint at what it can be expected to do in the future. Nothing is absolute but this does serve as an excellent guide in aiding one's final decision.

You have been offered a half-dozen rules that we consider to be the most important when it comes to handicapping harness races. By adding these to your handicapping repertoire, we're quite sure your winning percentages will dramatically increase.

One thing most professional bettors—either at trots or at the flats—have is patience. They realize that no matter how skillful they may be, they cannot come up with a good selection in every race. And rather than stab just for the sake of a bet, they leave the guessing to others. This attitude helps them stay ahead in several ways.

First, the experts have a more controlled outlook than the average bettor. Like harried executives who feel refreshed after a coffee break, they come back to their handicapping tasks feeling alert and invigorated. They can more easily concentrate fully on the race—noting the final workouts on their selections to insure that the horse doesn't look lame; unusual tote action on any of the contenders; and finally, the race itself. If an expert has no bet, so much the better—he can watch the race objectively, rather than viewing his selection alone.

Second, the pros make fewer bad bets—wagers made only to have something riding. They never feel the desperation of the man who's wagered against the 1–2 shot hoping he'll break stride. They don't have to worry about an incompetent driver. They don't fear first-time starters. When in doubt they do not bet, and consequently their records are superior to those of the average bettor.

Third, they can afford to make bigger bets on their solid choices. Rare is the bettor who has not, at least once, blown half his stake in the early races when the only horse for the day that he liked was in the eighth. Then, when the standout pick won, the bettor had a much smaller wager than he should have had. If a professional bettor likes only two horses for the day, he can make far more sizable wagers than the guy who's betting nine races and daily doubles, exactas, and superfectas.

The attitude that you must bet every race is the greatest stumbling block to financial success at the racetrack. Many veteran players wouldn't think to skip a race. It's there, they reason, and somebody's going to win, so why not take a shot?

What would happen if the play-every-race bettor carried this type of thinking into his everyday life? He'd order every item in a mail-order catalog. He'd eat everything on the lunch menu. He'd go into a shoe store and buy every pair in the window. Naturally, few people run their lives this way. The smart shopper looks for items that are on sale. The gourmet plans to eat a meal only if it promises to be nutritious and delicious. And nobody would buy a shoe that wouldn't fit. But at the racetrack, such care is often lost in the emotionalism that surrounds a race. Remember that you don't have to bet a race. You can just as easily pass it up. Let the rest of the crowd struggle with the problems.

If it takes you more than an hour to come up with all your selections—and your minimum odds requirement for each—it's time to revamp your handicapping procedures. You're probably trying to figure every detail for all nine races and you're probably wasting a lot of time. If you haven't got all your picks for the card by the time the third race is over, you've got to look again at what you're doing. Let's look at some of the kinds of harness races that rarely deserve more than five minutes of your time—at most:

1. Free-for-all races, open events, stakes, and early closing and late closing races usually attract classy—but often mismatched—fields. The top contenders might rank close to each other, with two or three entrants completely outclassed. Rank outsiders rarely win these events, and the outstanding competitors hardly ever go off at worthwhile odds. Too many bettors try to knock down the favorites and second choices, and throw their money away.

2. Races that appear to be so closely contested that it's difficult to figure what's going to happen. If you can't get a reasonable mental picture of how the race is going to be run—

which horses figure to be in the contending positions at the half-mile mark—skip the race.

3. Races where the chances of several entrants are difficult to analyze. A shipper, a drop-down, and a first-time starter are typical unknown quantities. So is a horse coming off a qualifying race or off a layoff—is he ready for an all-out try today? So is a horse going from a poor driver to a top reinsman—will the star make a big enough difference? Any time that an unknown factor looks to be a point of contention, you've got problems. The fewer the factors you have to worry about, the more easily you can make good selections.

4. Some younger trotters and pacers perform with marked success at five-eighths, three-quarter, and one-mile ovals. When these tracks are shut down, the up-and-coming performers are often sent to half-mile layouts such as Roosevelt and Yonkers, where they are usually bet down to favoritism, with poor results. They either break, go wide on the turns, or the like. Never play a horse which has been performing on other than the same size track as today's until the horse shows that he can handle the different size merry-go-round. Actually, it is wise to count all "green" horses as losers. The reports from the stable have been glowing but the one thing the youngster needs before anything else is seasoning. There's no way that these horses can make it the first or second time around a half-mile track in one piece. There are a thousand things wrong with these animals—not used to racing with lights on at night, can't pace with other horses because they've been working alone, and the crowd noise scares the hell out of them. Be scared yourself, stay away from the phenoms until they've proved themselves.

5. Races that have attracted only inconsistent performers. A $1,500 claiming race with five consistent horses might be much easier to handicap than a $10,000 claimer featuring eight horses that have forgotten how to win. Usually the form horses will go off the favorites, leaving you with the choice of taking low odds on an inconsistent horse, or shooting for a big price on an inconsistent, out-of-form horse. Avoid races carded to attract only performers with poor records—such as "nonwinners of a race this year," "nonwinners of $500 in their last six starts," etc.

6. Horses that either break or win are worse than a poor investment—they're suicide. There are certain animals which

go to the post as the betting choice time after time, and either win or break. If you want to take a less than 50–50 chance of taking all or blowing your roll it's up to you. If you do you're a sucker, and you've got to wind up with a case of the "shorts."

7. Most horse players are sentimental, but don't let it affect your betting. That is, horses that have been great and are known to the public start to lose their luster but they keep getting betting action. People bet on past great achievements and memories while the horse's current condition doesn't matter a plug nickel. You've all heard the statement "He's only got to run back to his form last year when he beat. . . ." Start to face it—when a horse goes bad he can go rotten. Don't start flipping through the history of racing to remember *when* your horse was good. If he's not good off his current form, then he's no good at all. A drop in class doesn't make a winner—the shape he's in today does.

8. One last point on how to avoid sure trot losers regards newspaper choices. If you're too lazy to do your own handicapping, why not let your local newspaper selector do the work for you? It sounds easy, but you're going to get slaughtered by sticking to the sportswriters. If your horse has a real shot he's going to be underlaid completely out of whack to what he's worth. If you want to get shortchanged, then it's your hangup. You'll get nailed by the thumbs for it.

A final note about the newspaper choices. Often, when the flat season closes the thoroughbred boys move to the trotters for action and have no line on what's happening. They follow the newspaper selectors religiously and you can make yourself a good penny betting *against* these selections if they can be beaten. You'll bet a good price on any other selection. This is the key point with all of these unwarranted underlays—bet into them. Once you see one of these money burners going to the post you've got yourself a great shot to get an overlay on a horse that has a good chance to win the race. Don't be sucked in by dead chalk—you'll only get choked—turn it to your advantage.

Naturally, there are a great many dissimilarities between the two horse racing sports. But obviously the one great driving goal of each player is to cash a bet. From that standpoint there is a mutual understanding among horse players. But, where does the bettor have his best shot? Is one game easier than the other? Can you make more money at the flats than you can at the trots? You decide for yourself ... and good luck!

Don't Give Your Bookmaker the Edge

Up to this point we've been concerning ourselves primarily with betting on the thoroughbreds or trotters at the track. But a lot of people can't make it out to their favorite oval all the time so, naturally, they figure, "I'll give the book a call and put in my action with him." If you think the odds are against you at the track, you'd better think twice before you start phoning in those chains, reverses, and other betting devices that one can make with the "friendly" bookie.

When you bet with a bookie, you have at best half a dozen more alluring and complicated ways of betting than you do at the track. All are intriguing and all appeal to the small bettor who is looking to make the big score ... and on credit, yet!

Take the parlay. In this bet, a player couples two or more horses to finish as stipulated. If horse A (at 3 to 1) is parlayed to win with horse B (at 6 to 1), and both win, then each dollar wagered becomes 28. One dollar at 3 to 1 on A becomes $4 when A wins and the $4 goes automatically on B at 6 to 1, becoming $28 if B wins. When you select two horses it is a two-horse parlay; three, a three-horse parlay; four, a four-horse parlay.

Parlay payoffs can be juicy (within the limits established by the bookie) and it is the possibility of real money coming back from a lonesome buck or two that snares the bettor. Bookmakers in many cities refuse parlay action because they are afraid of getting hit badly. A few bookies permit the so-called round robin bet, which involves the playing of all possible two-horse parlays on three or more horses. That is, a three-horse round robin is three two-horse parlays.

Another interesting wager that is taken by most bookies is the "if" bet. When making an "if" bet, you wager whatever amount you want on the first horse and then stipulate that a certain amount of your winnings be bet on a second horse. The "if" bet differs from a parlay in that you specify the exact amount you want bet back on the second horse if the first one wins. In parlay betting, the entire amount won on the first bet is parlayed back on the second horse.

Another popular bet is the back-to-back wager. One dollar

is put on horse A to win and another on horse B to win, both "back-to-back." This merely means that if A wins, a dollar of the stake and winnings goes on B to win in addition to the dollar already bet unconditionally on B. If B wins, a dollar of the stake and winnings goes on A to win in addition to the dollar already bet unconditionally on A. The wager, involving a double and automatic "if," is in the nature of a timid parlay. This is an attempt to be conservative if one horse loses and to increase winnings if both horses score.

There is yet another stellar attraction which the bookie offers you—the "reverse" play. This involves an automatic if-money bet, like the back-to-back wager also a reversal of the positions on which given amounts are hazarded. Thus if horse A is bet $2 to place and horse B $2 to win, back-to-back and reverse, and if A does place, run second or better, $2 automatically goes also on B to place, a bet not unconditionally made; and if B wins, $2 automatically goes on A to win, another bet not unconditionally made.

Of course, we haven't discussed another big difference in betting with a book. The payoff! If you're at the track and are fortunate enough to catch a long-priced winner, you get it all—every cent that's coming to you. Not so with the bookie. He has certain "limits" which he has established (and which vary among bookies) and before you place any bet at all with him you should know what his limits are. Naturally there are no admission, parking fees, etc., when you play with a book, so you are ahead in that regard. But let's assume that at the track you hit a daily double which pays $437.80 for $2. You merely walk up to the cashier's window, plunk down the pasteboard, and he counts out $437.80. Let's further assume that you had placed this same bet with your local bookmaker. When he receives the payoff figure, he hands you $150. Why? Because his limit on daily doubles is 75 to 1. Since this was a "limit" double, that's exactly what you receive: $75 for $1, or $150 total for your $2 bet. Betting through a bookie, therefore, and not at the track has cost you $287.80 (the difference between the actual double and the bookie's limit).

The same holds true on a flat bet. The usual bookie limit is 20 to 1, so if you have your $2 riding on a horse that happens to win and pays off more than $40, you're again "shortchanged." It can become mighty frustrating to pick a horse at long odds, see him win and pay off better than $100 and get back just $40. But then again, if you bet with a book, these are the hazards you must live with.

Some other fancy restrictions most bookmakers have set up to protect themselves are "overall limits," "front money," etc. A book may have an overall limit of $750 to 1. This is to protect him from the lucky one who might hit him for a long-priced parlay or chain. No matter how much a parlay or chain pays, you will never get back more than $1,500! As for "front money," most bookies will not take a place or show bet on a horse or a combination of horses unless you bet them all to win, also. For example, if you want to bet $20 to place or show on a certain horse, you must bet something, usually an equal amount, to win also.

With the advent of the superfecta in New York, Pennsylvania, New Hampshire, and elsewhere, bookies are not "letting" their customers play the wild bet in which the first four finishers must be selected in their proper order of finish. The odds are 1,680 to 1 in an eight-horse field, but most bookies have a payoff limit of $200. And you expect to win by bucking odds like that? The only solution, if you must bet horses with a bookmaker, is not to play any of his gimmicks.

Quarter Horse Racing

Quarter horse racing is one of the fastest growing sports in the United States and is slowly making its way east. For years quarter horse racing was centered in the Southwest, the Rocky Mountains, and California, and it was primarily a cowboys' game. It was a "my horse can beat your horse" sport. But the quarter horse industry has become big business. It offers the biggest purse in all of racing—some $600,000— in its great Futurity at Ruidoso Downs (New Mexico) in the late summer each year. Quarter horse mares and stallions now bring prices equal to those commanded by their thoroughbred counterparts.

Quarter horse races are conducted at various distances, ranging from 350 yards to 870 yards and are usually held on a straight cource. The race is over shortly after it starts, so don't blink your eyes. Quarter horse racing is strictly a speed game. Bet the horse that is quickest out of the gate and one that shows he was either in front or near the lead in almost all his races.

There are many great debates as to the importance of post

position in quarter horse racing, but no one can make a case as to which is really the most important. When betting on quarter horses, however, don't bet on horses on the inside two or three post positions if the horses breaking right next to them have enough speed to get in front of them creating an immediate traffic jam.

The only edge you can take as a quarter horse bettor is to concentrate on horses which are consistently first or second out of the gate and which remain close to the lead all the way.

The jockey is more important in quarter horse racing than in the thoroughbred sport and you should try to stick with those riders who handle a high percentage of winners. There is an art to riding the "hell bent for leather horses" and there is little doubt a good, alert quarter horse jockey can step up your winning percentages.

Just remember, speed, speed, and more speed is the name of the game, regardless of whether the race is at 100 yards, or 800 yards.

Greyhound Racing

Greyhound dog racing is a billion-dollar-a-year affair and is one of the fastest growing pari-mutuel sports in the land. In 1973, there were fifteen dog tracks in Florida, three in Massachusetts, one in Arkansas, four in Colorado, two in South Dakota, seven in Arizona, and one in Oregon. Greyhound racing is extremely popular in all of these states and, in many cases, attracts more people and betting money than does either thoroughbred or harness racing. In Florida recently, for example, the tax revenue from the greyhounds exceeded that from all horse tracks and jai alai frontons—the other two legal betting sports—combined. Because of this, several other states are now considering legalizing the sport.

For the unindoctrinated, the dog races are similar to their equine cousins, lacking only the direction of a jockey or driver. The greyhounds are placed in starting boxes at post around a track about one-quarter mile in circumference chasing a mechanical lure or rabbit. There are frontrunners, closers, sprinters, routers, rail huggers, and plodders just as with the horses but on a much smaller scale. For harness racing buffs accustomed to "breakers," we can substitute "bumpers," as the dogs will often bump each other right out of contention. There's an accurate form chart, similar to a trotting program, composed of past-performance lines, times, previous odds, weights, and a chart caller's commentary similar to that on the *Daily Racing Form*.

At the dogs, the name of the game is quinella, and quinellas are offered in all races including daily double events. There are also perfectas, trifectas, and numerous other gimmick wagers. But much as in harness or thoroughbred racing, the real professional bettor, realizing the number of races— usually twelve at most tracks—a speculator must contend with each night, concentrates on spot-play wagering angles, which are the players' best avenue of approach. A superior spot-play system is one that is simple to use. Once a system becomes too involved it's almost always quickly discarded by anyone using it—especially after a few successive losers. Systems that call for progressive wagering are usually bad unless the progression is on a predetermined basis to keep betting to the lowest possible amount. As form can sometimes go haywire for several races in a row at the dogs, due to accidents or other reasons, a "doubled amount" wagering system can be very costly and will seldom recoup all previous losses. You're smarter to stick to a sound method of play and bet something like this: 2–2–4–4–6–6, etc.

While greyhounds are breathtakingly fast they lack stamina—consequently they race at much shorter distances than do horses. Most distances range from sprints at about $5/16$ mile, medium distances at about ⅜ mile, marathons at about $7/16$ mile, and an occasional supermarathon at about $9/16$ mile. The sprints are usually covered in about 31 to 33 seconds, medium distances in 37 to 39 seconds, marathons in 44 to 46 seconds, stretching out to almost one minute for the supermarathon.

With races this short, there's little room for error, and dogs bumped at the start will have little time in which to catch up, and rarely do. As there is no jockey or driver to do the steering there is considerable colliding, but the wayward dogs are almost never disqualified and placing results will stand official. Judges may disqualify if they deem an infraction to be particularly severe but it must have a disastrous effect on the race before a dog is taken down. Fighting dogs and chronic bad actors are ordered into nonbetting schooling races until such habits are eliminated.

Greyhounds race every three or four days and can be quite

formful within a two- or three-week period. The races are graded on an A-B-C classification system with victorious dogs being rewarded with class upgrades. Chronic losers are dropped down in accordance with race secretary guidelines. Time is rounded off to the nearest 100th of a second and a finish margin of 15 lengths will amount to about one-second time differential. In handicapping the greyhounds it is important to note that a few lengths' victory margin will amount to just fractions of a second in actual time.

Greyhound handicapping shares similarities with thoroughbred and harness handicapping as the three major points of speed, class, and current form must be stressed. Superior class A dogs will generally beat class C dogs at the preferred distance for each, but a sharp, in-form, lower-class dog could beat a dull, off-form, high-class dog.

Post position is important to a degree, with the inside boxes enjoying a slight edge, but not nearly so much as at the harness races. For example, at Flagler Kennel Club in Florida over a designated span at the ⅜ distance, the one box produced 155 winners, the two box 156 winners, with 120 and 134 respectively for boxes seven and eight. The ability to break fast from the box will offset most position handicaps but a dog leaving from a middle or outside box is more likely to get bumped than one breaking from the pole. As the tracks are about one-quarter mile in circumference, the turns are sharp and many dogs have a tendency to veer or race wide on the bends.

Basically, speed is the name of the game, for despite the variety of distances they're actually just sprinting. The frontrunners run as fast as they can for as long as they can, and most closers are merely slower-starting frontrunners. A frontrunner that has been tiring at marathon distances may do better in sprints, but then again it may not, for the percentage of pure speedsters will increase in the shorter races. At most distances you're better off with the frontrunners or the ones closest to the pace as possible. In most races those that break first will stay throughout, as they're less likely to encounter traffic problems and other impediments and the lone speed dog in any race is a worthwhile mutuel play.

In addition to pure speed, one must also seek out class drop-downs and obvious class mismatches. On-the-improve, younger dogs are often good plays, as are races in which sharp dogs are pitted against dull ones. There's no such thing as a weaker sex in dog racing, and even the topstake races will contain both male dogs and bitches. Weight is important as a loss or gain of too much can be a tipoff as to the animal's physical condition, and the past-performance charts will disclose how a greyhound may race at a given weight.

As in the thoroughbred or harness race, one must try to chart out the greyhound race beforehand. Try to determine which dogs will break first, which will trail, and which slow starters may be likely to encounter traffic problems. Perhaps there is one dog who is simply faster than the others as shown by comparative times, or perhaps there is one whose true form is clouded by a series of mishaps. Races in which dogs were bumped or impeded must be tossed out from a handicapping scheme and you must always attempt to discern if a winner's impressive victory margin was due to his superior speed or merely the result of benefiting from racing luck. The appearance of two speed dogs in a given race may suggest an intriguing quinella, as they're just as likely to race one-two as opposed to head to head. The chart caller's commentary is of particular significance when trying to forecast what is likely to happen, and, as at the horse races, you may try to select a winner via a methodical weeding out of potential losers. That is, greyhounds should be bet because they are breakers, possess late speed, have a class edge, have post position advantage, or conditions of the race are favorable. "Green" dogs on their way up or formerly high-grade dogs rounding into form again are chancy.

For the first fourteen days of a new meeting, you'll be wise to bet animals off their recorded histories. After the first two weeks, play a greyhound according to its normal racing pattern and according to the conditions of tonight's race. A big advantage that "pro" dog bettors enjoy is that in meets of one hundred days or more, no new dogs are accepted the last twenty days. In meets of less than ninety days, no new greyhounds are accepted in the last fifteen days of the meets. This gives a bettor fewer dogs to keep track of.

All things considered, frontrunners get the best of it, especially when the closers encounter trouble back in the pack. What often happens is that the buzzsaw that isn't pressured in the early going can go all the way at good odds. But, in order to be playable, a frontrunner must be leaving from an inside box and must be the type that always gets the lead immediately after the start of the contest. If it gets out, it will probably go all the way or at least be a money finisher; but if it has to fight a while to get to the wood, the chances are poor for an on-the-board finish.

In handicapping, when you find a greyhound frontrunner that was second at the one-eighth call in either of its two previous races, and it fell back out of the race, you have a solid play. But, as the threat of collision and interference is ever constant, it's difficult for even the swiftest of dogs to be considered sure things. Consequently, payoffs are good, especially the exotic type, and your favorite win ratio should average in the vicinity of 31 percent. The favorite in the quinella should average about 50 percent, which may lend hope to chalk players.

Chapter 9

The Whys and Hows
of Legalized Sports Betting

For the most part sports betting in this country is illegal. It is a multi-billion-dollar business which operates from the dimly lit doorways of the back alleys of the land. It also may be the biggest industry in the United States. In 1970, this country's biggest corporation, General Motors, had total revenues of over $25 billion. Many officials in the Department of Justice, the Internal Revenue Service, and other governmental agencies believe illegal sports betting in the United States is a $40 billion-a-year-plus business.

The sports betting industry operates almost completely outside the law, and with little government control or regulation. It is still illegal in most states, but operates with few problems because law enforcement agencies have difficulty policing something the public wants and demands.

In cities where moralists force action against bookmakers, the police agencies offer token cooperation. In the mid-1960s, for instance, anti-gambling interests in Louisville were complaining that bookmakers were operating openly and that the police were doing nothing about these illegal betting offices. The police wanted to satisfy these people but the manner in which they handled the entire matter tells us how hypocritically some people look at gambling.

It was a bright, sunny day in Louisville—a perfect day to be on the golf course, and that is just where one of the city's biggest bookmakers happened to be. We shall refer to him just as "Joe," which wasn't his name.

Joe was about to putt on the par 4 hole three when the golf pro rolled up in a golf cart and told him he had an important telephone call. Upon arrival back in the clubhouse, Joe picked up the phone and the conversation went something like this: "Joe, this is Sergeant so-and-so. We're going to have to lock you up for an hour or two. Lotsa people screaming. You know...."

Joe said he would be glad to go directly to the police station, but that he had left three friends on the golf course and he wanted to finish at least nine with them. The sergeant told him to go ahead and finish the nine and that he would have a police car waiting to drive him downtown at that time.

When Joe finished nine, he excused himself, walked to the waiting police car in the parking lot, dutifully got into the back seat, and relaxed for the fifteen-mile ride to downtown Louisville. He was booked, locked up for thirty minutes, released on his own recognizance, returned to the country club, and spent the evening eating and drinking with his friends. The next morning he appeared in court, paid a $100 fine, and went back to work in his bookmaking office.

"This happens twice a year," he confided. "All of us cooperate. There's no trouble, no problems, and it keeps the do-gooders off the police department's back."

We have no way of knowing whether the situation in Louisville in the mid-1960s was representative of the rest of the country, but we have a strange suspicion it was and still is. The police have absolutely no enthusiasm for enforcing anti-gambling laws. They know the biggest and best-known businessmen in town bet on horses and sports with the corner bookmaker. It's their money, they want to bet, so why bother them or the bookmaker?

Officials at Churchill Downs always insisted that the police department close up Louisville's bookmakers whenever the track was running, and they did. Anytime Churchill Downs was open, the police sent word to all bookmakers to close their doors until the horses left town. Churchill Downs was important to the economy of Louisville and no one, including the city fathers, wanted any of that betting money drained off by bookmakers. If you wanted to bet on the horses when Churchill Downs was in action, you had to go to the track to do it. Again, we have a feeling that arrangements such as this exist all over the country.

The biggest critics of legal sports betting contend that legal wagering on sports such as football, basketball, baseball, and hockey would corrupt sports in this country. The argument has absolutely no depth and less substance. Sports betting already is a multi-billion-dollar-a-year business. It is already here.

As Howard Samuels, the first head of New York City's Off-Track Betting Corporation, has said many times: "Those who take this line of thought are completely unrealistic in their thinking. If I were them, I would be much more nervous about illegal gambling which had no governmental controls than I would be with legal gambling under government control."

Samuels, the nation's foremost advocate of legalized sports betting, notes that the nature of the sports gambling business is such now that it remains, basically, a property of the so-called underworld crime families. The revenue derived from illegal sports gambling in major cities is used by the underworld to finance its infamous dealings in such things as narcotics, loan sharking, prostitution, and to buy into legitimate businesses. Thus, ironically, about the only thing the traditional penal law approach to gambling has served to accomplish has been not to extinguish gambling, but to channel it underground into the hands of organized crime syndicates. Organized crime has grown like a cancer in the last few decades primarily because of the penal law approach to gambling. As of 1967, when the President's Commission on Law Enforcement and Administration of Justice issued its *Task Force Report on Organized Crime,* gambling income was thought to constitute about 70 percent of organized crime's total income. The *Task Force Report* estimated that organized crime's annual gross revenue from gambling ran somewhere between $20 to $50 billion, with profits to organized crime of approximately $7 billion a year. There is no reason to believe that such illegal gambling revenues to organized crime have not substantially increased since 1967.

Traditional law enforcement of the penal laws on gambling is resulting in increased waste of public funds and corruption in this country. To illustrate, in New York City alone in 1973 it cost in excess of $7 million in police manpower costs, not counting the costs of equipment, court processing, and prosecution, to investigate gambling offenses. The New York City Police Department categorized the results of this enforcement effort as "picayune," inasmuch as it was able to obtain from this effort only a few gambling convictions and even fewer fines. The Department said that these results were looked upon by the illegal gambling fraternity as a "minor license to engage in gambling." These New York City figures are probably a fair reflection of gambling law enforcement costs on a nationwide basis.

On top of this, special hearings conducted in New York

City a few years ago by the Knapp Commission revealed that bribery arising out of illegal gambling is one of the major causes of police corruption in New York. We have no doubt that this is probably true of most other jurisdictions in the United States as well. That is, it is traditional that bookmakers pay off a certain amount of money each week to police officials, policemen on the beat, and politicians just to stay in operation. The payoffs in New York City run into the hundreds of thousands of dollars—maybe even millions— each month.

For the payoff, the bookmaker is permitted to operate without too much worry of anyone cracking down on him and putting him out of business. The world's noted gambling authority, John Scarne, reported that New York bookmakers currently are paying about $1,500 per week for each telephone that they have and that the money is usually collected by a member of the vice squad.

In Chicago the figure is about $1,000 per week, while the tab in St. Louis is about $800, Scarne said. When the heat is on, as it was during the Knapp Commission hearings, a New York bookmaker may pay as much as $5,000 per week per telephone to stay in operation. That we permit this condition to exist stuns the imagination and goes far beyond hypocrisy. It is the opinion of Samuels and others like him that we are a nation which continually kids itself into believing what isn't so.

"In my opinion," Samuels has said, "legalized gambling on sports will, at worst, only create another minor pressure which the participants in these events will grow to ignore. We should recognize the fact that the participants in sporting events today know that people throughout the country are presently betting heavily on the outcomes of the games in which they are playing. From my observance of these sports spectaculars, I have not seen that this knowledge on the part of the players has in any way affected their performance. I would call attention, for example, to the jockey in the sport of horse racing. All the jockeys know, before the race is about to start, what people attending the race think of their chances of winning. Up-to-the-minute pari-mutuel odds are constantly flashed before the eyes of every person present at the racetrack. With all this vigorous and out-in-the-open wagering I do not think that the performance of the jockeys has been seriously affected. Could the jockey's performance conceivably be better if the only betting on the race was done illegally?"

Gambling, as we stated in Chapter 1, is one of the timeless pastimes of man. We gamble on bingo. We gamble on horses. We gamble on poker. We gamble on the stock market. This is not to say that gambling does not lend itself to abuses. Of course it does. There have always been, and probably will always be, a small percentage of the population who will be unable to refrain from gambling to excess (many of whom are presently gambling through illegal channels). We must always bear in mind, however, that this is an imperfect world, a world composed of individuals of wide-ranging faults. Today in the United States the simple facts are that people *are* gambling prolifically, primarily illegally, and in the face of quite rigid penal laws on the books of almost every state in the United States. In addition, many Americans are increasingly traveling to foreign countries to spend their tourist dollars gambling.

People today do not view gambling as a moral issue, but primarily as a source of entertainment. The people of New York City, for example, in a referendum in 1963, voted three to one in favor of off-track betting. Perhaps one of the reasons why New Yorkers, and probably the great majority of Americans today, view gambling as an entertainment is because of increasing affluence in this country. In past times, when the standard of living was considerably lower, there was obviously more justification for being concerned about how the average individual spent his money. In the past, it is true, far fewer people could afford the luxury of gambling. In fact, almost all entertainment in the past was a luxury!

Today this is no longer so. We would illustrate this point by noting that a customer survey done for New York City's OTB by the firm of Daniel Yankelovich Inc., showed that wagering with OTB was largely a middle-income activity and that the people wagering with OTB were quite selective and moderate in their wagering. The study also showed that most of the bettors with OTB were seasoned bettors who had a great deal of prior betting experience.

Recognizing the basic fact that the people of this country are intent upon gambling, even in violation of the law and even with the consequence of aiding organized crime, we cannot be so foolhardy as to continue to illegalize something which people no longer consider to be immoral and illegal.

Before the House Select Committee on Crime, Howard Samuels said, "I believe it is more 'moral' for the government to legalize gambling than it is to force people to gamble in the unregulated and ruthless domain of organized crime. What we should do, and what OTB is attempting to do in New York, is to recognize the dangers inherent in gambling and to attempt to bring gambling within the control of legalized governmental wagering systems where it can be carefully regulated and where the wagered dollar will ultimately be returned to the people.

"This is not to say that I don't respect the moral convictions of those who view gambling as an evil. I would be the last one to cast any aspersions upon such a time-honored belief. However, I believe legalized gambling is the lesser of two evils.

"I would also stress that the movement of the law from a prohibitory to a regulatory approach to gambling would in no way violate the firmly held beliefs of those who think that gambling is immoral. Such people would in no way be forced to gamble in violation of their principles. But such a movement of the law would do justice to the principles and freedom of those who are in favor of partaking of governmentally regulated systems of gambling."

To legalize all types of sports betting in every state would be the first step toward cutting off underworld revenues. No one is any longer naïve enough to believe that there is no such thing as organized crime. It is very real. It is very rich, and it is very powerful. State and national police agencies can conduct all the investigations they want, arrest all the underworld figures they want, but organized crime will never die until its money is cut off. Legalize gambling and the battle is half won.

The underworld now controls sports betting in major cities because it is the only organization with the manpower, the know-how, and the money to operate such a gigantic business. The underworld, whatever it really is, runs the illegal gambling business in the country with complete efficiency and authority. Its expertise is respected in all legitimate sports offices, including those of the National Football League, the National Basketball Association, and major-league baseball. The underworld is more concerned about the "fix" than any other group connected with sports. Being the nation's bookmaker, it doesn't care to get hit hard by anyone who might have tampered with the outcome of a game, hoping to make millions betting.

The National Football League office has been tipped off more than once by a suspicious bookmaker who became nervous about heavy money showing on a team for no particular reason. Bookmakers want the game to be played on the level. They make money without cheating. There have been times in recent years when the National Football League conducted investigations because bookmakers were not releasing a pointspread line and taking bets on certain teams. For instance, in the 1960s, the bookmakers took the Kansas City Chiefs off the board, believing someone on the team was doing business to help others win bets. The NFL conducted an extensive investigation, which turned up nothing. But the bookmakers still believe they were right and to this day pay very close attention to everything that happens in Kansas City.

Howard Samuels believes legalized sports betting would all but put the so-called organized crime out of business in the United States. He points to the success of New York's Off-Track Betting Corporation to illustrate his point.

"There isn't any question that OTB [which has over 115 offices throughout New York City which take bets on area thoroughbred and harness tracks] has put most of New York's horse bookmakers out of business. People can walk right into an OTB office and bet. Why would they want to sneak down an alley to bet with a bookie?"

In late 1972, the Fund for the City of New York published a report on gambling that was based on a survey of bettors made by the Oliver Quayle organization. (The Fund for the City of New York is a nonprofit organization established in 1968 by the Ford Foundation to do research on social issues affecting the city.) Among the many conclusions it drew was this one: "Three times as many horse players say they bet with OTB as say they bet with bookmakers. OTB would appear then to be cutting substantially into illegal bookmaking operations."

The Quayle survey also analyzed the betting habits of gamblers. In one series of questions, sports bettors who also bet on horses were asked how they placed their action on the ponies. The question is significant, for it offers insight into how a bettor who must bet sports with a bookmaker reacted to legalized off-track betting on horses.

First of all, 41 percent of those who bet sports illegally with their bookmakers had transferred their horse action to the city's OTB offices. The report concluded that "while bookmaking is still a thriving business, betting with OTB has taken a very substantial sum of [the bookmaker's] former business away."

When off-track betting was implemented in New York, many of its opponents said that it would bring about the moral collapse of the city, serving to whet the appetites of bettors to wager more with bookmakers. The Quayle report noted, however, that of those surveyed, 29 percent said they were betting with bookmakers "much less" than before, and about 30 percent said somewhat less. Thirty-four percent said they were betting with bookmakers as before the advent of OTB, 5 percent said they were uncertain, and 2 percent said they were betting more. The Quayle report continued, "All the foregoing data make it clear that OTB, with all its teething problems, and occasional computer breakdowns, has taken a great deal of betting money out of illegal channels. Those who fear that the advent of OTB has whetted an appetite for betting that can only be satisfied by wagering with bookmakers can put their fear to rest. Our data show that, of those still betting with bookmakers now, only a handful say they are wagering more with bookies now than they did in the past. Such data also demonstrates rather conclusively, in our judgment, that while legalizing sports betting will not do away with bookmaking on sports like football, basketball, and baseball, most of the money now bet with bookies on these sports (which is also most of the total money now bet on sports) would flow into a legal operation."

There is really little question among New York City officials that OTB has taken the small bettor away from the bookmaker. William Kahn, district attorney for neighboring Nassau County, disclosed in an indictment of an organized crime bookmaking ring that his wiretaps had produced interesting information. Their tapes showed, Kahn said, that bookies were turning down horse bets of under $100. Those wishing to bet smaller amounts were told to "go to OTB."

The advent of OTB in New York also forced the big betting layoff centers in the New York area to close. Now if a bookmaker gets too much money bet on a horse and wants to "off" some of it, he just sends a messenger to OTB to bet it. It's insurance for him and his business, and he loves it.

While OTB is excited about the over $2 million a day it handles on New York harness and thoroughbred racing, it is anxious to get into the sports business. "Every study we have undertaken has proven, beyond a doubt, that the horse business is about five percent of the gambling market," said Samuels. "The rest is bet primarily on sports, although a small percentage of it flows through casinos in Nevada."

The figures are stunning, but they offer insight into the tremendous size of the sports gambling business in the country. Samuels says it is safe to say that at least $90 of every $100 bet in this country is bet on sports such as football, basketball, baseball, and hockey.

The interest in sports betting goes back to something we discussed earlier in the book—the familiarity of the gambler with sports and his basic ignorance of horse racing. He has been raised with football, basketball, and baseball—and probably hockey—but finds the world of horses strange and alien. He is uncomfortable around horses but feels quite relaxed and knowledgeable about betting on sporting events. He can't argue with authority and conviction about why he likes a particular horse in a race, but he knows, beyond any doubt, why he likes the Rams over the Packers. When sports betting becomes legal reality in this country, the nation will be amazed at the amount of money that is wagered each week.

The reluctance of most states to legalize sports betting has its roots in a rather hypocritical morality. State legislators know that sports betting exists and that it exists as a gigantic business. However, they have been reluctant to speak out in its behalf for fear of offending the straight-laced voters in their districts. Gambling is an emotional issue to some people and politicians do not want to get trapped into fighting emotion unless they can use it in their behalf. However, most legislators are now looking at sports betting more realistically, and their primary concerns are with the amount of tax monies it will raise.

Many states also have taken a "wait and see" attitude. Few states want to be the pioneers in this field. The start-up problems of legalized sports betting would be almost as big as the business itself and it would be an expensive proposition for any state to get started. The only state at which other states can now look for a past-performance record is Nevada, where sports betting is legal. But sports betting is a minor gambling activity in Nevada because of unfair taxes (the bettor must pay 10 percent on every bet) and most states feel it does not offer an accurate guide as to how sports betting should be conducted. State A is waiting for state B to legalize sports betting, make all the mistakes, and iron out all the wrinkles before it gets involved.

Before going into how a state or the federal government could go into sports betting, let's take a look at Nevada's legal bookmakers and how they operate.

Nevada's Legal Bookmakers

Along the Las Vegas Strip and in Downtown Casino Center are a group of establishments known as the "sports books." Their function is to permit customers to place legal wagers on various sports events that are occurring about the nation.

The sports books go by names like Churchill Downs, Santa Anita, Saratoga Club, and other horsey titles. A good portion of the action at these betting mills is on horse racing. But one can make other wagers too. And according to those close to the operation, most of the "big money" is bet on contests like football, baseball, and others involving only two sets of possibilities.

In contrast to the plush, carpeted atmosphere at the large casinos, the sports book establishments are, for the most part, completely functional, consisting generally of wooden benches, a few betting windows, a payoff window, and walls lined with racing forms and blackboards containing changing statistics. But make no mistake, the action here is every bit as tense as a high-rollers crap game at The Dunes, and often the stakes are even greater than those that cross the green felt at a Caesar's Palace baccarat game.

Most of the big money these days is being bet on either football or baseball, depending on the season and the degree of interest in an individual contest. It is interesting to note that the odds on this type of action are set by local oddsmakers who are employed by the establishment. For some idea of the responsibility involved in this type of handicapping, consider the fact that the odds posted at Las Vegas sports books are used by illegal operators all over the country.

At the Churchill Downs sports book on a sample day, the Los Angeles Dodgers, with John pitching, were quoted at +130 against the Chicago Cubs with Hooton pitching. The Cubs were quoted at −140. Freely translated, this means that if you were to bet $100 on the Dodgers you'd win $130 (assuming the team won, of course). On the other hand, if you wished to bet on the Cubs you'd have to put up $140 to win $100.

The same day the San Diego Padres with Arlen pitching were quoted at +11/5 against the Pittsburgh Pirates. The Pirates were —5/13, meaning that if you bet on the Pirates you'd have to lay $13 to win $5. In this contest the Pirates won 11 to 0, thereby surprising no one. However, in another contest the San Francisco Giants with Willoughby pitching were quoted at +165 against the St. Louis Cardinals, who were the favorites, at —175. In this instance the underdog Giants won 3 to 2.

The spread between the odds, in each case, is the percentage which the bookmaker grinds out—providing he is successful in laying off enough of the action to equalize his bets, which doesn't always happen.

As was described in Chapter 5, to determine the odds the professional oddsmakers take a number of things into consideration including the starting pitchers, team batting average, and a number of other factors. Hopefully, from the standpoint of the bookmakers, the official oddsmakers have a better insight into the action than the customers who bet against their reasoning. But it doesn't always happen that way. With the play available to everyone in the country, including people on the inside, plus the fact that the oddsmakers must handicap numerous sports events while the customers can concentrate on a single contest, sometimes the "experts" get outhandicapped. The operators at Nevada's legal sports books recognize this fact yet apparently manage to survive in spite of it. Almost every day supposedly inside information crops up, much of which is pure unadulterated humbug. The trouble lies in separating the facts from the rumors.

There's a story concerning a local bookmaker who was deluged with bets on a horse entered in a maiden race at a California racetrack. On the morning line the horse was 30 to 1 and showed absolutely nothing. However, when even the so-called smart players began to plunge on the horse the bookmaker began frantically to lay off the action, but had little success because every other bookmaker in town was being similarly deluged with the same type of bet. Apparently, the inside information, whatever it was, was also being circulated in other areas, or a wad of the off-track money was being diverted to the track. In any event when the horse finally went to post the track bettors had hammered the odds down from 30 to 1, to 11 to 10. The race was run and the horse ran a bad ninth in a field of ten.

No one knows where the rumor started but it's whispered about in local horse circles that a well-known plunger had, just prior to post time, placed a number of whopping bets on the original favorite in the race—who incidentally won by eight lengths, and due to the action on the bad tip had been jacked up in payoff odds from a 3 to 2 morning line favorite to a 4 to 1 second choice.

At some of Nevada's legal books bets of $10,000 are frequently received on a single contest, particularly during the football season. On horse racing, however, a $500 limit seems to be the official rule of thumb.

There's action for the smaller player, too, ranging from a minimum of $2 on horse racing events to $5 to $10 on other sports. And for the player who wishes to press his luck a bit there's also parlay action available. For example, one of the strip sports books has a sign posted over the betting window that basketball parlays pay off at a rate of 13 to 5 for two teams, 6 to 1 for three teams, and 10 to 1 for four teams.

One of the biggest problem areas for Nevada's legal bookmakers is the 10 percent federal tax which must be colleted on all wagers. The tax is bitterly resented by both the sports book operators and the customers they serve, with good reason. In the case of horse race betting the tax represents an almost prohibitive lug, since the pari-mutuel odds on which most bookmakers pay off have already been subjected to a massive watering down by local authorities in areas where the various tracks are located.

Because of this it's no secret that the federal tax drives many of the bigger bettors to the illegal operators who thumb their noses at the government's efforts to collect. On the other hand, the legal bookmakers still get a fair share of the business from people who enjoy gambling within the framework of the law and tourists who have no connections with an illegal operator. Also, there's the undeniable fact that in the case of a really big hit illegal bookies have been known to split the scene rather than settle their scores.

One concession to Nevada's legal bookmakers is a recently

passed law which makes it permissible for them to accept telephone bets which originate within the state. Interstate calls, however, are still prohibited. The chief opposition to the practice in the past has been from Federal authorities who have been worried about Nevada becoming a clearing house for illegal betting if the green light was given to telephone wagering.

In the meantime the employees at Las Vegas's legal sports books continue to function with a seeming air of bored indifference, serving both the local residents and the 18 million tourists who visit the town each year.

New York City's Off-Track Betting Corporation

The term "off-track betting" in general, of course, refers to bets made on a horse race away from the racetrack where the race is run. The term "off-course wagering" is also applied to bets made away from the track. More specifically, "off-track betting" refers to legalized betting on horse races away from the track. Although legal off-course wagering has existed in other countries for many years, New York is the first state in the country to operate legalized pari-mutuel betting on horses away from the track. Nevada has legalized wagering, but it is not pari-mutuel.

The City of New York had been requesting the state legislature to pass an off-track betting bill for many years, and the bill which gave us the New York City Off-Track Betting Corporation, better known as OTB, was finally passed in April of 1970. Actually, OTB is a public benefit corporation, operating under New York State statutes which allow the City to run off-track betting. A public benefit corporation is run more like a private corporation than like a government agency. The major difference between a public benefit and a private corporation is that all the corporation's profits are returned directly to the government rather than only a portion of the profits going to government through taxation.

The current legislation provides that OTB give to the horsemen and racetracks in New York State on which it takes bets up to 4 percent of the total OTB handle on each track's races. OTB's contribution to the tracks is actually based on a sliding scale of from 4 percent down to 1 percent, averaging approximately 2.5 percent over the year. Also under the OTB statute, as amended, the Corporation's gross revenues are to be 17 percent of the total amount of wagers handled less the commission to be paid to participating tracks within the state. Of the first $200 million of net revenues of the Corporation (as defined), New York State is to receive the greater of (a) 20 percent of such revenues, or (b) as tax, ½ of 1 percent of the gross amount wagered; the City of New York is to receive the remainder. Net revenues in excess of $200 million are to be divided equally between New York City and New York State.

As to how the money taken in is distributed, let's suppose that OTB handled $700 million in bets in one year. Here's approximately how it would be distributed:

$570 million (83 percent less .6 percent for breakage and 1 percent for uncashed tickets) would go back to the bettors in the form of winnings,

$14 million (2 percent) would be paid to the operators of the tracks on which OTB accepts bets,

$12.5 million (.5 percent tax: .3 percent breakage and 1 percent uncashed tickets) would be paid to the state as tax, breakage, and unclaimed winning or refund tickets,

$56 million (8 percent) would be used for OTB's operating expenses, and

$40 million (80 percent of $51 million) would be New York City's share of OTB's profit.

$7.5 million (20 percent of $51 million less $3.5 million tax) would represent New York State's additional distribution out of OTB's profits.

Branch offices of OTB are located throughout New York City. As a general rule, OTB betting closes approximately one hour before the track's post time for each race. Closing times for each track handled by OTB are posted in every OTB office. The smallest current bet denomination is $2. By the way, rather than creating confusion by having horses carry both a "track number" and an "OTB number," OTB designates its horses by letter. If OTB assigned a horse the number 4 and the track assigned the same horse the number 5, you would be very confused upon learning results. With the lettering system, there is less chance of confusion. In addition to win, place, and show betting, at present OTB offers the daily double and the lottery bets—exacta and triple betting.

At the current time, OTB regularly handles the NYRA (New York Racing Association) tracks—Aqueduct, Belmont Park, and Saratoga. These tracks run on a rotating schedule and OTB handles that single NYRA track which is open at any given time throughout the year. OTB also handles New York harness racing at Roosevelt, Monticello, and Yonkers raceways. Additionally, OTB handles bets on tracks in other states, such as Maryland, and it schedules special events such as the Kentucky Derby, the Preakness, the Washington, D.C., International, the Colonial Cup, and others. These special events are determined at the discretion of the Corporation. If OTB were permitted by the federal government to combine its pools with out-of-state tracks it is likely that it would always handle racing at one out-of-state track at least in addition to the tracks it now handles. These tracks could be in Florida, Maryland, New England, Pennsylvania, California, or virtually anywhere.

Of course, whenever OTB takes bets on an in-state race it attempts to combine its pools with those of the track. In the event that technical breakdowns result in a failure to combine pools, OTB has the option of paying at track prices, refunding all bets, or creating its own pool at a separate payoff rate. In the past, OTB has always paid at track prices, with the exception of the Belmont Stakes, which is usually run as a "separate pool" event. Incidentally, winning tickets can be cashed in at any OTB branch office.

One of the unique features of OTB is telephone betting. In order to bet by telephone with OTB you must be a resident of New York State, be over eighteen years of age, and be an account holder with the Telephone Deposit Betting Center of OTB. Once you are an account holder, you may bet any amount of money up to the total you have on deposit with OTB. You might think of this as something like a special checking account with a bank. There is no minimum or maximum deposit, but *no* credit is given.

When a telephone account is opened, you are asked to pick a "secret code word." This code is known only to you and the telephone betting agent (through the computer). The agent doesn't know your name, and the code word appears in writing only once, on your application. Thus, it should be very difficult for someone to use your telephone account. If, however, someone should discover your account number, the

OTB betting phone number, and your secret code and place bets against your account, then, yes, you are liable. OTB will assist you, however, if such an event occurs. OTB maintains a recording facility which tapes every call to the OTB Telephone Betting Center. This system of telephone recordings is for the customer's protection and is available to him in cases such as this. The recordings are admissible as court evidence if this is ever desired. But telephoning from outside New York State to place a bet with OTB is specifically prohibited by federal law.

How to Legalize Sports Betting

There are dozens of ways for states, or the federal government, to get into legalized sports betting with a minimum of problems and expense, but we will discuss only the most practical ways here.

First of all, the simplest manner for governing bodies to get into legalized sports betting would be to pass legislation that would leave the industry in the hands of its current bookmakers. However, each of these bookmakers would have to purchase an original license for a tremendous sum of money—let's say $100,000 to $250,000 just for the sake of argument. The license would have to be renewed each year for a lesser fee and the bookmaker would be required to pay a percentage of his gross handle in taxes. Any legalized betting system which taxes the bettor (as in Nevada) never will work and will serve only to keep the sports bettor in the hands of the illegal bookmaker. Thus, the bookmaker must have the responsibility of taxes.

If governing agencies decided to license bookmakers, strict regulations and requirements would have to be established as to the moral character and financial stability of any individual attempting to get a license. Under such a system, laws would have to be passed that were so strict and tough that they would drive any and all illegal bookmakers out of the business. If money is to be bet, it must be bet through legal channels.

If bookmakers were licensed, sports betting undoubtedly would be conducted pretty much as it is now. Bettors would still lay 6 to 5 or 11 to 10 on their sports bets and buck the tremendous odds against beating the football cards.

While on the surface, it appears that state governments would reap less revenue by licensing bookmakers than by operating the businesses themselves, no one really knows. It is an indisputable fact, however, that states could avoid the tremendous start-up costs of legalizing sports betting by leaving it in the hands of those who already control it. States also could buy time to study sports betting and determine if it was actually worthwhile for them to get into the business.

Such a system also would eliminate the situation that many legislators cannot justify in their minds—that of the state being a bookmaker. If sports betting were conducted in the manner it is conducted today, with bettors wagering on individual teams, there would be the chance that the state could lose money, although it is highly unlikely. But, it still remains a fact it could lose. Legislators do not like the idea of a state bookmaking shop having to reach into tax monies to pay off bets.

However, the state could get into the sports booking business without any risk by offering wagering on a pari-mutuel basis in the same manner it is now conducted on horse racing. For instance, the average horse buff who patronizes the off-track betting offices in New York plays in the $2 to $5 range. This same bettor on sports would be betting $20 to $50 per game. If the bettor were wagering on the pari-mutuel system, he would be getting the best odds of all time, which would knock out the corner bookmaker.

For the sake of argument, let's look at the baseball bettor. Right now, he must bet into the 10 percent line (10-cent line) or the 20 percent line (20-cent line). With legalized sports betting, he would have to cope only with a 5 percent takeout. Every big baseball bettor, of which there are thousands and thousands, would go strong for this and the volume handled on games would be tremendous.

Each game would have its own separate pool, and the money wagered on each team would determine the payoff. A 5 percent tax, plus the breakage, would add millions to tax coffers, and all of this would be painlessly extracted from the money bet.

Let's say the Mets are to play the Cardinals in a game at Shea Stadium (imagine a betting parlor right next to the stadium) and as the day dawns the probable pitchers are listed as Seaver for the Mets and Gibson for the Cardinals. No odds are posted until the betting is under way, then the money makes the line as it does at the racetrack. After the first half-hour, let's say there is $130,000 bet on Seaver and $100,000 on Gibson. After taking the 5 percent right off the top, the amount left in the pool would make Seaver the 6 to 5 choice. Betting would continue until game time and the odds would change as the money comes in. Bettors would be paid off on the final odds, as in horse racing, and not on what they were when the bet was placed.

This is the only way governments can operate sports betting without taking any risk. In basketball and football the bettor would get even a better break. Today he lays 11 to 10 on either team he plays. With legalized sports betting, he could easily end up getting a bit of odds. How? First of all, he will not lay 11 to 10, but even money.

Games that figure close are listed at half-points. The half-point could be used to make certain there are no ties. The line would never change, and by not changing the line, legal bookmaking parlors have insurance they would not lose. In Las Vegas, for instance, a game can open at two points and change as the money comes in. When the favorite wins, the books get hurt.

Under the pari-mutuel system, the line would never change, but the odds would. It is possible for the player to lay the points and win only $7 for each $10 bet. On the other hand, it is possible for the bettor to take the underdog and win $13 for each $10 he bets. Today, under the present system, he would get even money.

Actually it is possible for a bettor to lay the points and if the money shows strongly for the underdog, he too is receiving odds even though betting on the favorite.

The pari-mutuel betting system definitely would work for sports betting. The fact that is has a past performance in horse racing makes it attractive for states that want to control the entire operation, including the actual booking. The same pari-mutuel systems that handle millions of dollars daily at the nation's racetracks could easily be adapted to handle sports bets.

There also is the possibility that states could utilize for sports betting parlor offices they already maintain for other businesses. This, of course, would cut down operating expenses. But regardless of how a state wanted to handle a pari-mutuel sports betting operation, there is little doubt in the minds of the authors, or anyone else, that it would be a financial success within a short period of time. The volume of business would guarantee huge tax windfalls for states.

A third system by which states could legalize sports betting would be through a weekly lottery. The lottery would be tremendously attractive to both the state and the bettor. It could offer huge payoffs for a small bet—say $1 per entry—and would be reasonably easy to start.

The lottery could use both college and professional football games of varying combinations. For instance, a lottery card could offer ten college games and ten professional games. Those selecting all twenty games correctly would have their cards placed into a container from which would be drawn a winner, a second, third, and fourth place finisher. The first prize could easily be $100,000 per week and might run as high as $1 million per week.

For those who objected to fighting the tremendous odds of picking twenty winners, a lottery with smaller prizes could be offered to those who tried to pick twelve or fifteen winners, etc. A state football lottery would be a cinch to make money, whether it was conducted in New York, Florida, Texas, Kansas, Montana, or California. Its public acceptance would be immediate. It also would be extremely attractive to those states which have weekly lotteries, for they have agents throughout their areas who are already doing business. Thus, start-up expenses for them would be minimal.

The lottery would also satisfy critics within the sports industry itself who feel that gambling is bad for the game and that it opens the door to attempted fixes. It would be impossible for anyone to fix twenty games to insure a winner.

While the lottery would be attractive to state governments, it also has a certain fascination for the national government. A national football lottery would be a multi-billion-dollar revenue raiser for the government. Lotteries similar to the football lottery also could be conducted on basketball, baseball, and hockey.

A fourth system which state governments might want to consider would be one which utilized the country's fascination with football cards. The odds are stacked heavily in favor of the house on the football cards and there is little chance that any agency would ever lose money on them. Tax revenues would be tremendous, for the cards have the advantage of being priced within the range of everyone who wants to have a little action riding for him or her during the weekend.

As we have said, there are dozens of ways in which states, or the federal government, could get involved in legalized sports booking. The above four proposals are presented in oversimplified form, but they are the most practical ways for any agency to begin. Costs could be controlled in all of the systems and all could be started with comparative ease.

The one thing which all states must work to prevent is overtaxation of the bettor. Anytime the tax bite becomes so great that it cuts down the bettor's chances for financial success, he is going to go underground again and do business with a bookmaker who operates completely outside the law and pays no taxes.

The pari-mutuel system has the most tax advantages for both the booking office and the bettor. The money is painlessly extracted from the total bet, with a set amount returned to the winners. If states install other systems which are not conducted on a pari-mutuel basis, and tax the bettor heavily, they will doom legalized sports betting.

As we have said before, sports betting in Las Vegas is reasonably unsuccessful because of the 10 percent tax the bookmakers must charge bettors. It's a big bite and the bettors don't like it. Thus, they stay underground.

The question of taxes will be a key issue when sports betting becomes a reality and it deserves the careful, judicious thought of this nation's politicians. To get too greedy, and ask too much from the bettor, is to kill a program before it starts. Legislators should make up their minds to treat the bettor with kindness and collect the millions of dollars a token tax will bring in on a volume business. This is the only way to take the sports bettor away from the bookmaker. The sports bettor would much rather do business with a responsible betting agency which is regulated by the government than with a back-alley bookmaker, regardless of how respected the latter might be. But, tax him heavily, and he'll go down that back alley to make his bets.

In summary, there can be little doubt that sports betting is a multi-billion-dollar business in the United States, and possibly is our biggest business. It is, indeed, scandalous that this giant operates almost completely outside government control and regulation. It is even more scandalous that the revenues from sports betting go to finance the heinous drug traffic and loan sharking of the underworld, when this money could be going to the public in the form of tax revenues.

The time has come for this nation's legislators to take a realistic look at sports betting, accept the fact that the public wants it and is going to have it, and that the interests of the country can best be served by legalization and complete government control and regulation.

It is an inescapable fact that the citizens of the United States want legalized sports betting. This country is one of the few in the civilized free world that doesn't have it. It is time for our lawmakers to act and get the good citizens of the country out of the dimly lit doorways of back alleys. We're betting they will.

Sports Gambling and the Tax Problem

One of the more bewildering topics in legal gaming circles today is the procedure which governs collection of federal income tax on a player's gambling winnings—particularly for the casual player who is lucky enough to make a relatively large score. From a purely technical standpoint, IRS regulations state, "Your total gambling winnings must be included in your income. If you itemize your deductions on Schedule A (Form 1040) you may deduct your gambling losses incurred during the year, but only to the extent of your winnings." That's the law. But implementing that law is something that would probably make Elliot Ness turn in his badge and take up bootlegging!

To begin with, few casual gamblers keep a record of every bet they make. So even assuming that along about Thanksgiving Day, in any given year, a fellow gets lucky and manages to beat the dice tables for a modest sum, who's to say whether this puts him ahead, or behind, or approximately even for the past eleven months? To complicate the issue still further, there are usually no records kept by a casino of an individual player's gambling transactions—especially those which are on a cash basis. Therefore, the matter of what to report is usually up to a player's conscience. We say usually, because there have been reports of IRS officials tapping big winners on the shoulder and requesting Uncle's share of the loot. They have also, reportedly, told players that it would be necessary for them to prove any reported losses which a player attempted to apply against the gambling winnings—a feat which would, for the average player, be roughly comparable to figuring out the exact amount of loose change that is brought into Churchill Downs on Derby Day.

To get the answers on gambling and the tax problem we went to the ultimate authority on tax law as it relates to gambling: Warren A Bates, District Director of the Reno, Nevada, office of the Internal Revenue Service. The question asked was: "Since a casual gambler does not normally keep any records and the casinos or racetracks do not keep track of bets with individual customers, is a taxpayer required to document losses applied against gambling winnings, and if so, what form of documentation would be acceptable?" Mr. Bates's reply is as follows: "The question of documentation is quite complex and involves a long line of court decisions. However, we can come to some general conclusions regarding the documentation problem. Section 6001 of the 1954 Internal Revenue Code requires that every person liable for any tax imposed by this title, or for the collection thereof, shall keep such records, render such statements, make such returns, and comply with such rules and regulations as the Secretary or his delegate may from time to time prescribe.

"Regulation 1.6001-1 states in part that any person subject to tax under Subtitle A of the Code (said title relating to income tax), or any person required to file a return of information with respect to income, shall keep such permanent books of account or records, including inventories, as are sufficient to establish the amount of gross income, deductions, credits, or other matters required to be shown by such a person in any return of such tax or information."

With the formal quotes out of the way, Mr. Bates then went on to say that while the regulations do not require any particular form for keeping records, it is required that they be kept accurately. It is therefore the taxpayer's burden in proving any deduction claimed for these gambling losses. He pointed out that various courts insist on documentation of offsetting losses. Although the type of documentation is not clearly defined, the following have been used with varying degrees of success to show gaming losses:

1. Statements from the casino management that an individual lost significant amounts on specified dates.

2. Cancelled checks to casinos.

3. Evidence of wagers: i.e., Keno tickets played, racebook tickets on horses, and athletic games bet.

4. Taxpayer's informal records supported by evidence of his net worth and changes thereto.

Mr. Bates readily admits that it is a dufficult area of enforcement and each case must be decided on its own merit, weighing all the facts and circumstances. In an attempt to clarify the procedure used we were then clued in on the details of several court decisions involving the matter of application of gambling losses as applied against gambling winnings.

In the first of these cases a taxpayer was not allowed to offset claimed gambling losses against gambling gains where the losses recorded in his records were shown, on the testimony of a handwriting expert, to have been entered at one time and not contemporaneously with the losses. The tax court in this case determined a reasonable amount which could be offset as losses.

In another instance, an individual had his gambling losses denied for lack of proof since the taxpayer failed to maintain adequate records reflecting his gains and losses from gambling.

In still another case a taxpayer was not allowed to deduct gaming losses arising from horse race betting where there was no way to estimate the taxpayer's winnings over a period of time. He kept no records; and the amount he reported was won on a single race.

Of considerable interest was a direct quote from an actual court ruling involving a taxpayer, which stated that "a taxpayer has an incentive to overstate his loss figures to reduce taxes and the Commissioner could reasonably reject these figures in the absence of any data which would provide a basis for testing their reasonableness."

On the basis of the information noted above, we have to conclude that anyone who intends to apply gambling losses against gaming winnings reported to the IRS had better start keeping some records. And the more comprehensive the records are, the better, because based on past experience your word probably won't carry much weight in the legal department of the IRS. Everyone involved admits that it's a sticky sort of problem. But on the brighter side there are probably 10 million casual gamblers in this country who, just for once, would like to be faced with this interesting problem, regardless of whether or not they were permitted to deduct their losses for the same calendar year.

Glossary

Across-the-board. Horse race term for placing win, place, and show bets on the same horse in the same race. Same as *combination bet*.

Action. The opportunity to bet.

Added money. Money that the track adds to the purse.

Allowance race. A race in which the weight to be carried by each horse is determined by the condition-book rules.

Also eligible. Horses that are eligible to run in a race if other entrants are scratched.

Also-ran. A horse that has run out of the money.

Backstretch. The straight portion of a racetrack parallel to homestretch.

Back-to-back bet. A bet with a bookie which involves more than one "if" bet.

Bet. A wager placed by a person on a sporting event or horse race.

Betting edge of winning. Any advantage which improves the bettor's chances. Same as *edge in betting*.

Blinkers. Equipment that limits a horse's side vision. Same as *blinders*.

Bloodline. A horse's pedigree.

Bookmaker. A person who takes race and sports bets. Same as a *bookie* or *book*.

Breakage. Odd change left after paying off each winning bet. This is usually taken by the track or bookmaker.

Breaking stride. When, in harness racing, a horse runs, canters, or gallops. Trotters and pacers must pace or trot only.

Breeding. In horse racing, production of fine strains of thoroughbreds and standardbreds.

Bug boy. Apprentice jockey.

Bull ring. A name given to a small track with sharp turns. It may be either a half-mile or five-eighths mile track.

306

Calcutta. A pool in which players are auctioned off to the highest bidder.

Chalk Horse. A horse favored by bettors. Usually the horse with the lowest odds.

Claiming Race. Each horse is entered at a certain claiming price and any horseman may claim (buy) the horse, provided he has deposited an amount equal to the claiming price with the racing secretary's office in advance. If two or more horsemen put a claim on the same horse, they draw lots to decide the claim.

Colt. An unaltered male less than five years old.

Condition. A horse's form.

Condition book. The publication of the conditions of a given race.

Conditions. The requirements for race: age, sex, weight, purse size, and so forth.

Daily Double. A separate totalisator pool produced by single-ticket bets on two horses running in different races (usually first and second). Both horses must win to produce a payoff. *Twin daily doubles* involve four horses in an extension of the daily double.

Daily Racing Form. A publication that contains complete information of all horses in the race, as well as data on the race itself.

Dam. A horse's mother.

Dash. Sprint race of six furlongs or less.

Declare. To scratch a horse from a race.

Disqualify. To disallow a horse's finish because of some infringement of rules during running of race.

Division. Situation resulting when there are too many entries for one race so two races are run.

Driver. The person who rides in a sulky during a harness race.

Drop-down. A horse racing in a lower class or classification than in its previous race.

Dutch. Betting two or more horses in the same race in a manner that, hopefully, will produce a profit.

Easy pigeon. An ignorant bettor.

Entry. When two or more horses owned or trained by the same person are entered in the same race, becoming a unit for betting purposes. That is, they are covered by the same mutuel ticket. Same as a *coupled entry*.

Even money. Odds of 1 to 1; a wager in which neither side gets odds.

Exacta. Betting situation in which bettor must pick the horses who finish first and second in one race. One mutuel ticket covers both choices.

Exotic bet. A wager involving more than one team or horse in all sports that offers big odds, but that should be avoided because of the difficulty to win. Same as *gimmick bets* or *oddball bets*.

Fast track. Even, hard, dry track that allows for the best racing conditions.

Favorite. The team, player, or animal picked by the majority of bettors and handicappers to win a sporting event.

Field. Several horses grouped as one contestant in a race. Same as a *mutuel field*.

Field bet. A bet placed on horses entered and racing beyond the twelve post positions, running "in the field."

Filly. A female horse less than five years old.

Flat. Normal racing dirt strip, as opposed to turf (grass) or jump course.

Football pools. A form of betting on football games, usually with odds against the bettor.

Form. A horse's general physical condition.

Form player. A race player who before placing a bet on a horse takes into consideration the past performance of each horse entered in the race.

Forty-cent line. A bookie's baseball or sports line that has a differential of two points between his lay and take odds.

Front money. Money that has already been won.

Front Runner. A horse that has fast early speed and who likes to take the lead.

Furlong. Measure of distance; one eighth of a mile or 220 yards.

Future Book. Bookmakers sometimes list all horses nominated for a stakes race well in advance of the actual running and accept wagers at stipulated odds. Payoffs to winners are made according to those odds, regardless of the eventual totalisator prices. If a horse fails to start for any reason, all bets on that horse are forfeit to the book.

Gait. The foot movement of a horse. The principal gaits are the canter, pace, gallop, and trot.

Gelding. An unsexed (castrated) male of any age.

Goal spread. In hockey, the goal differential given in the betting line.

Good gamble. A good bet, an almost-sure win.

Good track. A track that is rated between slow and fast.

Grass races. Horse racing events held on a grass surface.

Hand. Measure of height for a horse, approximately four inches.

Handicap. An advantage given or disadvantage imposed against a horse in a race.

Handicapper. A person who tries to select the probable winner of a sports event or race. Also a race track official who assigns a handicap (weight) to certain horses in a race.

Handicapping. The assigning of a handicap in consideration of all entries with reference to relative chances of winning.

Handicap race. A race in which the weights to be carried by each horse are assigned by the track's racing secretary.

Handle. Amount of money bet on a race.

Harness racing. Sport featuring standardbred horses pulling two-wheeled sulkies in trotting and pacing races.

Head. Measure of distance; the length of a horse's head.

Headed. When a horse losses by a head.

Head of the stretch. The start of the homestretch.

Heat. One leg of a race in which the winner is decided by winning two or more trials or heats.

Heavy track. When surface of the track is in process of drying after a rain; a condition between muddy and good.

Horse. An unaltered male five years or older.

Horseman. An official owner or trainer of a thoroughbred race horse.

Horse player. One who bets on horse races. Same as a *chalk player*.

Horse room. A race-betting room with all the necessary betting equipment and latest racing information.

Horse's class. Level of a horse's performance.

Hot-dog team. An over-rated team; a team that is not as good as record shows.

Hunches. Bets placed on impulse rather than studied knowledge of odds.

Hustler. One who seeks advantage through the ignorance of his victims. Same as *shark* or *cheat*.

If money bet. A wager made with a bookie in which a fixed amount is bet on a horse with the stipulation that if this horse wins, another fixed amount will be wagered on another horse or horses.

Inquiry. The process of adjudicating a claim or question of possible foul in the running of a race. The track officials view the video of race to determine whether the claim of foul is valid.

Interfere. To block a horse's progress during race. To cause a horse to change course. It is usually a foul.

In-the-money. To finish a race in first, second, or third place for which there is a mutuel payoff. But since a horse receives purse money for a fourth-place finish, owners consider a fourth place as an in-the-money finish, too.

Jockey. The person who rides a horse in a thoroughbred horse race.

Jockey Club, The. The organization set up to regulate and implement rigid rules for racing at a given track or tracks.

Journeyman. An experienced, professional jockey.

Juvenile. A two-year-old race horse.

Lay. To bet a greater amount of money against a lesser amount. Same as *laying the odds*.

Laying points. To give points in a sporting bet.

Lay off. Not to bet.

Line. A sports bookie's lay-and-take odds on a sports event. Same as *betting line* or *price line*.

Lineage. In horse racing, a sequence of direct ancestors.

Linemaker. The person who sets or makes the price line or odds. Same as *oddsmaker* or *pricemaker*.

Long-shots. A bet in which the chances of winning are slight.

Maiden. Horse that has never won a race.

Maiden claiming race. Claiming race for nonwinners.

Maiden race. A race for horses who have never won a race.

Mare. A female horse five years or older.

Match game. The deciding game in any sports series contest.

Match race. A race between only two horses.

Maturity. A race for horses who are entered before their birth.

Meet. The entire race meeting of one race track.

Minus pool. A betting situation in which so much money is bet on one horse that the odds return a pay-off of less than ten cents on the dollar. The track is responsible for making up the difference between the amount in the mutuel pool and the required pay-off.

Morning line. Track handicapper's estimate of the odds of each horse at posttime. This forecast of odds is published in the track program and listed on the tote board before each race.

Mount. A race horse.

Mudder. A horse that runs well on a muddy track.

Muddy track. A track's surface that is very wet and slow.

Mutuel pool. The total amount of money bet on all horses in a race.

Mutuel ticket. The ticket purchased at the mutuel window on a horse in a specific race. Same as tote ticket.

Newspaper line. The pointspread listed in a newspaper. This is not an official betting line.

Objection. A claim of foul during the running of the race. Objection is lodged by either the jockey or a steward of the race.

Odds. The way in which a team's, player's, or horse's probability of win is stated, as estimated by the handicappers, linemakers, and the betting public. Correct odds are really the ratio of the unfavorable chances to the favorable chances.

Odds making. The business that gives odds on various sports events, and so forth.

Odds on. A horse whose final odds are less than even money. Same as *odds-on-favorite.*

Office pool. Employees of a business put up money and draw a number. Number usually based on total points, points by running team, or period when winning score was made.

Off pace. Situation in which a horse runs behind the leaders of the race.

Off-the-Board. A bookie's term for not taking any bets on a given sporting event. Same as *no-bet.*

Off track. Refers to any track condition other than fast.

On-the nose. To bet that a horse will win, as opposed to a place or show bet.

Optional claiming race. A claiming race in which the owner can enter a horse not to be claimed, thus preventing other horsemen from claiming his horse.

Overlay. To make an odds-to-one bet which is greater than the event warrants.

Pace. Speed of the race.

Pacer. Horse whose right fore leg and right hind leg move in tandem; same with left side.

Paddock. The area where horses are saddled and paraded before their entry onto the track.

Pari-mutuel. The system of betting in which winners receive all the money wagered on race after the government's and track's shares have been deducted.

Parlay. A bet in which the bettor couples two or more teams or horses to win, and both must win to collect.

Parlay Cards. Betting cards with numbers on them representing number of runs scored by five or six teams in baseball. Similar cards are available for football and basketball.

Past performance. The record of a horse's activity.

Payoff. The collection of a bet. Same as *pay*.

Payoff odds. The odds at which a bet is paid off.

Perfecta. The bettor collects when the two horses he wagered on in one race finish exactly in the manner he selected.

Photo finish. A race finish so close that the photo of the finish determines which horses are in the money.

Pick sixes. Exotic wager in which you must pick the winners of six races or events to win. Pays off at high odds.

Pipeline. Channels through which betting information moves.

Place. A second position in the finish. Same as *second place*.

Points. Numerical figures used to equalize a sporting event for the bettor by making one team a certain number of points better than the other.

Point shaving. A deliberate attempt by players in a sporting event to hold the scoring below predicted pointspread of the two teams.

Pointspread. The points given to or taken from a team in hopes of equalizing the contest for betting purposes.

Pool. The total amount bet on one race. Same as *money pool*.

Post position. Order of horses at starting gate before a race.

Progression betting. Increasing the size of the bets by a set formula.

Qualifying race. Practice race for trotters and pacers in which they perform before stewards to show their fitness to race.

Quinella. A form of betting in which the bettor tries to pick the first two finishers in any order.

Racing form. Information sheet giving pertinent data about horse races.

Racing secretary. The official at race track who is responsible for planning the racing meet and establishing the conditions for each race. At most tracks, the racing secretary also serves as the track handicapper.

Rail bird. Horse-racing addict who likes to watch a race from a rail position.

Reverse bet. A bet made with a bookie which involves more than one "if" bet.

Ridgling. A male horse of any age with one or both organs of reproduction absent from the sac.

Round robin. A race or sports bet placed with bookie which involves the playing of all possible two- or three-race or sports parlays on three or more horses or teams.

Router. A horse that prefers to run in long races.

Route race. A long race, generally one longer than seven furlongs.

Rundown. A sports bookie's line on the day's betting events.

Run out. For bettors, a race finish other than first, second, or third. For owners, a race finish other than the first four positions.

Saliva test. A test administered to horses that finish in the money to determine whether illegal drugs or pain-killers have been used.

Score. To win at sports gambling.

Scratch. To remove or withdraw a horse from a race.

Shipper. A horse that is moved readily from one track to another.

Short end. The lesser amount risk in any bet that is not at even money.

Short price. A horse whose final odds are extremely low, paying a low price.

Show bet. Betting on horse to at least take third place.

Silks. The jockey's colors or outfit.

Sire. A horse's father.

Sloppy track. The condition of a track during or immediately after a heavy rain; may have puddles, but base is still firm and running time remains fast.

Slow track. A track which still may be wet; condition between heavy and good.

Smart money. Player who knows his percentages and odds. Also money bet by persons who supposedly have "inside" information not available to the betting public.

Soccer pool. A form of betting on soccer games.

Speculator. Another name for a sports bettor.

Sports bet. A wager placed on a sporting event.

Sports bettor. A person who bets on sporting events.

Sports line. Information kept on sports teams.

Sprint. A short race, seven furlongs or less.

Sprinter. A horse that competes at short distances.

Stake race. A type of race in which the owners put up part of the purse money. Added money usually is contributed by the track.

Standardbred. In harness racing, a purebred trotting or pacing horse.

Standoff. A tie, no decision. Some as *deadlock*.

Steeplechase. A horse race of two to four miles with ten to twenty hurdles (jumps).

Stewards. The officials at the race track who are responsible for judging all aspects of racing conduct, such as investigating claims of fouls during the running of a race.

Straightaway. The straight portion of the racetrack, as the homestretch.

Straight bet. A single bet on a single team or horse to win.

Stretch. Either of the straight sides on a racetrack.

Stretch turn. Turn into the homestretch.

Sucker bet. One which gives hustler best chance to win.

Sulky. The two-wheeled cart used in stardardbred races.

Superfectas. Exotic wager in which you must pick, in exact order, the first four finishers in a race.

Sure thing. The dream of every gambler—a bet he cannot lose.

System player. Gambler who does not play hunches, only uses method established by himself or other authority. Usually based on a mathematical formula.

Systems. Methods of handicapping and betting. A "system bettor" adheres to a formula instead of relying on chance.

Take. Track's share of the mutuel pool.

Taking odds. Accept the short end of the odds.

Ten-cent line. A bookie's baseball or sports line that has a differential of ½ point between his lay and take odds.

Thoroughbred. A horse bred from the best blood through a long line. Any horse eligible to registry in English or American stud books.

Tip. Information on supposed winner as in horse racing, sporting events, and so forth.

Top weight. The horse that is carrying the heaviest weight in the race.

Toss-up. Races or sports events in which oddsmakers and handicappers feel each participant has an equal chance.

Totalisator. The computer that records all money bet and transmits the odds to the tote board.

Tote board. The infield board visible to stands showing totals bet and odds on horses before betting on each race is over. Shows payoff price on first three horses and name of fourth.

Tout. A person who sells information, usually of dubious quality but allegedly "inside" secrets. Same as *tipster*.

Tout sheets. In horse racing, supposedly reliable information on which horses will win.

Triperfecta. Exotic bet in which you must pick, in order, the first three finishers in a race. Same as a *triple*.

Triple Crown. The three most prestigious races for three year olds: The Kentucky Derby, The Preakness Stakes, and the Belmont Stakes.

Trotter. A standardbred horse trained for harness racing. A trotter races with a diagonally-gaited motion.

Turf Races. Races run on a grass course.

Twenty-cent line. A bookie's baseball or sports line that has a differential of one point between his lay and take odds.

Two-horse parlay. A wager placed on two horses, each in a different race. The player wins if both horses finish as stipulated by his bet.

Underdog. The team or player picked by the majority of bettors and handicappers to lose a sporting event.

Vigorish. Commission charged by bookmaker for handling a bet. Same as *juice*.

Weekly rating. A system of evaluating sporting teams on a weekly basis to show the top teams.

Welch. Refusal to pay a lost bet.

Wheel. System of betting in Daily Double, Perfecta, Exacta, and Quinella (any multiple-betting situation) in which bettor combines one key horse with all other horses, hoping to cover every possible win.

Win. The position awarded a horse that finishes first in a race.

Winner's circle. Enclosure or area near the racetrack where horse and jockey are brought for photographs and awards.

Wire. The finish line at a racetrack.

Wire-to-wire. A horse that leads in a race from start to finish.

Index

About the Author

Kelso E. Sturgeon, Jr., was born in Wellington, Kansas, and attended high school and college in Wichita. He played football (offensive tackle) in both high school and college, and began his career as a sports writer on the *Wichita Beacon*. He has also worked as a newsman and sports editor for the Associated Press in Louisville, Lexington, and Atlanta.

He has been director of Public relations for Churchill Downs, Laurel Race Course, Pimlico Race Course, and Arlington Park.

In 1972 he went to work for *Sports Action* as writer-editor in Great Neck, New York, where he now lives.

Bestsellers from SIGNET

* Price slightly higher in Canada

Buy them at your local
bookstore or use coupon on
next page for ordering.

Recommended Reading from SIGNET

- [ ] **ONE FLEW OVER THE CUCKOO'S NEST** by Ken Kesey.
  (#E8867—$2.25)
- [ ] **THE GRADUATE** by Charles Webb. (#W8633—$1.50)
- [ ] **SALEM'S LOT** by Stephen King. (#E9827—$3.50)
- [ ] **THE STAND** by Stephen King. (#E9828—$3.95)
- [ ] **THE SHINING** by Stephen King. (#E9216—$2.95)
- [ ] **CARRIE** by Stephen King. (#E9544—$2.50)
- [ ] **THE DEAD ZONE** by Stephen King. (#E9338—$3.50)
- [ ] **NIGHT SHIFT** by Stephen King. (#E9746—$2.95)
- [ ] **SAVAGE RANSOM** by David Lippincott. (#E8749—$2.25)*
- [ ] **SALT MINE** by David Lippincott. (#E9158—$2.25)*
- [ ] **TWINS** by Bari Wood and Jack Geasland. (#E9094—$2.75)
- [ ] **THE KILLING GIFT** by Bari Wood. (#J7350—$1.95)
- [ ] **SPHINX** by Robin Cook. (#E9194—$2.95)
- [ ] **COMA** by Robin Cook. (#E9756—$2.75)

   * Price slightly higher in Canada
